# FORENSICS
## *THE SEARCH FOR CLUES*
by James V. Sutton

T&S Educational

8944 Beckett Road    West Chester, Ohio 45069    (513) 860-4949    FAX (513) 682-8181

Copyright © Kemtec 1997
ISBN# 1-877960-24-1

# FORENSICS-THE SEARCH FOR CLUES
## by JAMES V. SUTTON

INTRODUCTION ................................................................................................1
CHAPTER ONE-**THE CRIME LAB** ................................................................3
CHAPTER TWO-**THE CRIME SCENE** .........................................................9
CHAPTER THREE-**PROOF OF IDENTITY** ................................................19
CHAPTER FOUR-**FINGERPRINTING** ........................................................25
CHAPTER FIVE-**BODY FLUIDS** .................................................................35
CHAPTER SIX-**TRACE MATERIALS** .........................................................45
CHAPTER SEVEN-**TOOL MARKS** .............................................................51
CHAPTER EIGHT-**FIREARMS AND BALLISTICS** ....................................57
CHAPTER NINE-**ILLEGAL AND LEGAL DRUGS** ....................................67
CHAPTER TEN-**CHEMICALS** ....................................................................75
CHAPTER ELEVEN-**CASTING AND RESIDUAL PRINTS** ......................79
CHAPTER TWELVE-**PAINT AND GLASS** ................................................87
CHAPTER THIRTEEN-**DOCUMENT ANALYSIS** ......................................91
CHAPTER FOURTEEN-**ARSON AND EXPLOSIVE DEVICES** ...............95
CHAPTER FIFTEEN-**DETERMINING HUMAN IDENTITY** .....................101
CHAPTER SIXTEEN-**THE CRIME SCENE SCENARIO** .........................107


## CRIME SCENE SCENARIO-"ACCIDENT, SUICIDE, OR HOMICIDE?"

**TABLE OF CONTENTS**................................................................**PAGE**

**INTRODUCTION** ............................................................................................8
PART ONE-**FIRST AT THE SCENE**............................................................16
PART TWO-**THE CRIME SCENE** ...............................................................21
PART THREE-**LATENT FINGERPRINTS**..................................................33
PART FOUR-**BLOOD AND TESTIMONY** ..................................................41
PART FIVE-**GSR AND TRACE MATERIAL** ..............................................49
PART SIX-**TOOL MARKS & GIRL NEXT DOOR** .....................................53
PART SEVEN-**WEAPON & THE MORGUE** ..............................................64
PART EIGHT-**BILL'S TESTIMONY** ............................................................72
PART NINE-**STEVE'S TESTIMONY** ..........................................................77
PART TEN-**VICTIM'S GRANDMOTHER** ...................................................83
PART ELEVEN-**MATT'S TESTIMONY**.......................................................89
PART TWELVE-**BILL IS CROSSEXAMINED** ...........................................93
PART THIRTEEN-**ANDREA'S STORY** ......................................................98
PART FOURTEEN-**IDENTITY OF THE VICTIM** .....................................104
PART FIFTEEN-**LAURA'S STORY**...........................................................107

ILLUSTRATION LISTING     FORENSICS: THE SEARCH FOR CLUES

## CHAPTER ONE-THE CRIME LAB .................................................................... SOURCES
| | | |
|---|---|---|
| Figure 1-1 | PAPER BAGS FOR EVIDENCE | 5 |
| Figure 1-2 | HANDGUN AND KNIFE BOXES | 5 |
| Figure 1-3 | RIFLE BOX | 5 |
| Figure 1-4 | EVIDENCE AND CHAIN OF POSSESSION FORM | 5 |
| Figure 1-5 | PHOTO EVIDENCE NUMBERS AND ALPHABET | 5 |
| Figure 1-6 | PHOTO EVIDENCE COLOR GUIDE, AND DIRECTION INDICATORS | |
| Figure 1-7 | LABORATORY GLASSWARE | 1 |
| Figure 1-8 | LABORATORY TOOLS | 1 |
| Figure 1-9 | GRAM SCALE AND WATER BATH | 1 |
| Figure 1-10 | SPECTROPHOTOMETER | 1 |
| Figure 1-11 | LIGHT MICROSCOPE | 1 |
| Figure 1-12 | DISSECTING SCOPE | 1 |
| Figure 1-13 | CENTRIFUGE | 1 |
| Figure 1-14 | ELECTROPHORESIS EQUIPMENT | 1 |
| Figure 1-15 | DUCTLESS FUME ENCLOSURE | 5 |
| Figure 1-16 | ATOMIC ABSORPTION (AA) SPECTROPHOTOMETER | 2 |
| Figure 1-17 | X-RAY SPECTROPHOTOMETER (SEM/EDX) | 2 |
| Figure 1-18 | FORENSICS LABORATORY | 8 |

## CHAPTER TWO-THE CRIME SCENE
| | | |
|---|---|---|
| Figure 2-1 | POINT-TO-POINT (SECTOR/ZONE SEARCH) | 7 |
| Figure 2-2 | GRID SEARCH PATTERN | 7 |
| Figure 2-3 | STRIP SEARCH PATTERN | 7 |
| Figure 2-4 | SPIRAL OR CONCENTRIC SEARCH PATTERN | 7 |
| Figure 2-5 | WOUND CHART | 1 |
| Figure 2-6 | CRIME SCENE NOTES | 1 |
| Figure 2-7 | BASELINE COORDINATE SKETCH | 1 |
| Figure 2-8 | TRIANGULATION SKETCH | 1 |
| Figure 2-9 | CROSS PROJECTION SKETCH | 1 |

## CHAPTER THREE-PROOF OF IDENTITY
| | | |
|---|---|---|
| Figure 3-1 | PIECES MATCHED TO BROKEN BUTTON ON A SUSPECT'S COAT. | 2 |
| Figure 3-2 | MATCHING MICROSCOPIC LINES ON TWO BULLETS INDICATE THEY WERE FIRED FROM THE SAME GUN | 2 |
| Figure 3-3 | PIECE OF BILL TORN BY BULLET MATCHED TO THE ORIGINAL BILL | 2 |

## CHAPTER FOUR-FINGERPRINTING
| | | |
|---|---|---|
| Figure 4-1 | SWEAT PORES ON FINGERTIP | 3 |
| Figure 4-2 | FINGERPRINT CHARACTERISTICS | 4 |
| Figure 4-3 | DELTA, CORE, AND TYPE LINE IDENTIFICATION | 4 |
| Figure 4-4 | FINGERPRINT BRUSH AND DUSTING POWDER | 5 |
| Figure 4-5 | MAGNETIC POWDER APPLICATOR | 5 |
| Figure 4-6 | LATENT PRINT LIFTING TAPE | 5 |

## CHAPTER FOUR-FINGERPRINTING-CONTINUED
| | | |
|---|---|---|
| Figure 4-7 | LATENT PRINT BACKING CARD | 5 |
| Figure 4-8 | HARD EVIDENCE (CYANOACRYLATE) AND FUMING CHAMBER | 5 |
| Figure 4-9 | NINHYDRIN SPRAY AND CRYSTALS | 5 |
| Figure 4-10 | FINGERPRINT CATEGORIES | 4 |
| Figure 4-11 | LOOP RIDGE COUNTS | 9 |
| Figure 4-12 | DETERMINATION OF PLAIN WHORL AND CENTRAL POCKET LOOP PRINTS | 9 |

| Figure 4-13 | NCIC FINGERPRINT CLASSIFICATION SYSTEM | 9 |
| Figure 4-14 | HYPODERMIC INJECTION TO RECONSTITUTE THE FINGERPRINT | 5 |
| Figure 4-15 | FINGERPRINT CARD HOLDER | 5 |
| Figure 4-16 | FINGERPRINT CARDS | 5 |
| Figure 4-17 | ROLLING A FINGERPRINT ON INK | 5 |
| Figure 4-18 | SIMULTANEOUS INK PRESS | 5 |
| Figure 4-19 | FILTER PLATE WHEN VIEWING WITH LASER | 5 |
| Figure 4-20 | FORENSIC LASER LIGHT SOURCE | 5 |
| Figure 4-21 | DUSTING FOR LATENT PRINTS | 8 |
| Figure 4-22 | CAL-ID COMPUTERIZED FINGERPRINT TRIANGULATION | 10 |
| Figure 4-23 | CROSS SECTION OF FRICTION SKIN | 10 |
| Figure 4-24 | FRICTION RIDGE CHARACTERISTICS (CLOSE-UP VIEW) | 10 |
| Figure 4-25 | COMPARISON OF LATENT (L) AND INKED (R) FINGERPRINTS | 10 |

## CHAPTER FIVE-BODY FLUIDS

| Figure 5-1 | BLOOD LEFT AROUND FAUCET AND DRAIN | 1 |
| Figure 5-2 | P-TRAP BENEATH SINK MAY CONTAIN SAMPLE OF SUSPECT'S BLOOD | 1 |
| Figure 5-3 | BLOOD DROP AT 20 CM. | 1 |
| Figure 5-4 | BLOOD DROP AT 40 CM. | 1 |
| Figure 5-5 | BLOOD DROP AT 60 CM. | 1 |
| Figure 5-6 | BLOOD DROP AT 80 CM. | 1 |
| Figure 5-7 | BLOOD SPLATTER WITH CHARACTERISTIC BOWLING PIN SHAPE | 1 |
| Figure 5-8 | BLOOD SPLATTER WITH CHARACTERISTIC BOWLING PIN SHAPE | 2 |
| Figure 5-9 | PAPER CHROMATOGRAPHY USED TO COLLECT DRIED BLOOD SAMPLE FROM KITCHEN RANGE | 1 |
| Figure 5-10 | PAPER CHROMATOGRAPHY USED TO COLLECT DRIED BLOOD SAMPLE FROM CRACK IN LINOLEUM | 1 |
| Figure 5-11 | SEALED TEST TUBE CONTAINING CHROMATOGRAPHY PAPER WITH COLLECTED BLOOD SAMPLE | 1 |
| Figure 5-12 | MATERIALS NEEDED FOR BLOOD COLLECTION | 8 |
| Figure 5-13 | COLLECTING DRIED BLOOD SAMPLE WITH SCALPEL | 8 |
| Figure 5-14 | PLACING BLOOD SAMPLE ON GLASSINE | 8 |
| Figure 5-15 | USE OF HEMASTIX FOR PRESENCE OF BLOOD | 8 |
| Figure 5-16 | BLOOD REMOVAL WITH SCALPEL ON GLASSINE | 8 |
| Figure 5-17 | BLOOD ON GLASSINE TO BE FOLDED INTO A BINDLE | 8 |
| Figure 5-18 | BLOOD COLLECTED WITH A COTTON-TIPPED SWAB | 8 |

## CHAPTER SIX-TRACE MATERIALS

| Figure 6-1 | ANATOMY OF A HAIR | 4 |
| Figure 6-2 | SCALE PATTERN OF HUMAN AND ANIMAL HAIR | 4 |
| Figure 6-3 | MEDULLA PATTERN IN HAIR | 4 |
| Figure 6-4 | PIGMENT GRANULE PATTERNS OF HUMAN AND ANIMAL HAIR | 4 |
| Figure 6-5 | CORTICAL FUSI (AIR SPACES) CONTRIBUTE TO PRODUCE LIGHT COLORED HAIR | 4 |
| Figure 6-6 | HAIR ROOT APPEARANCE IN HUMAN AND ANIMAL HAIR | 4 |
| Figure 6-7 | CUTICLE AND MEDULLA OF HUMAN HAIR | 2 |
| Figure 6-8 | PHOTOMICROGRAPH OF CAT HAIR | 2 |
| Figure 6-9 | FRAGMENT OF CLOTH FOUND ON VEHICLE MATCHES VICTIM'S CLOTH COAT | 2 |
| Figure 6-10 | PHOTOMICROGRAPH OF COTTON FIBER | 2 |
| Figure 6-11 | PHOTOMICROGRAPH OF WOOL FIBER | 2 |
| Figure 6-12 | MATERIALS NEEDED FOR TRACE EVIDENCE | 8 |

| Figure 6-13 | REMOVING TRACE EVIDENCE FROM CLOTHING | .8 |
| Figure 6-14 | REMOVING TRACE EVIDENCE (CLOSE-UP VIEW) | .8 |
| Figure 6-15 | TRACE EVIDENCE TAPE IN SQUARE PLASTIC PETRI DISH | .8 |
| Figure 6-16 | LABELED TRACE EVIDENCE IN PETRI DISH | .8 |

## CHAPTER SEVEN-TOOL MARKS

| Figure 7-1 | MIKROSIL CASTING PUTTY | .5 |
| Figure 7-2 | CASTING PUTTY INSTRUCTIONS | .5 |
| Figure 7-3 | KNIFE SCORING AT VARIOUS ANGLES | .2 |
| Figure 7-4 | BROKEN TIP MATCHED TO SUSPECT'S KNIFE | .2 |

## CHAPTER EIGHT-FIREARMS AND BALLISTICS

| Figure 8-1 | CROSS SECTION OF RIFLED BARREL | .2 |
| Figure 8-2 | CROSS SECTION OF RIFLED BARREL | .2 |
| Figure 8-3 | RIM FIRE .22 CALIBER CASING | .2 |
| Figure 8-4 | CENTER FIRE 32 CALIBER-3 SHOTS FIRED | .2 |
| Figure 8-5 | REVOLVER AND AUTOMATIC CARTRIDGE CASINGS | .2 |
| Figure 8-6 | DUST DEPOSITS IN RIFLE BARREL INDICATE THAT WEAPON WAS NOT FIRED RECENTLY | .2 |
| Figure 8-7 | TOP VIEW OF FIREARM SHOWING GAS PATTERN GENERATED DURING DISCHARGE | .2 |
| Figure 8-8 | TOP VIEW OF FIREARM SHOWING GSR DISPERSAL ON OUTER PORTION OF HAND | .2 |
| Figure 8-9 | GUNSHOT RESIDUE TEST DESCRIPTION | .5 |
| Figure 8-10 | GUNSHOT RESIDUE TEST KITS | .5 |
| Figure 8-11 | GSR TEST RESULTS SHOWING X-RAY SPECTRUM | .2 |
| Figure 8-12 | GSR AA AND SEM/EDX SAMPLING TECHNIQUE | .2 |
| Figure 8-13 | AA/GSR TEST FORM | .2 |
| Figure 8-14 | SEM/GSR TEST FORM | .2 |
| Figure 8-15 | COLEMAN VACU-PRINT™ LONG (RIFLE) CHAMBER | .5 |
| Figure 8-16 | BULLET CATCHER | .5 |
| Figure 8-17 | UNFIRED BULLET (LEFT) AND FIRED BULLED (RIGHT) | .2 |

## CHAPTER EIGHT-FIREARMS AND BALLISTICS-CONTINUED

| Figure 8-18 | BULLET STRIATIONS IN GROOVE IMPRESSIONS IN MATCHING BULLETS FIRED FROM SAME WEAPON | .2 |
| Figure 8-19 | SMITH AND WESSON MODEL 13, .357 MAGNUM FIXED-SIGHTED 6-SHOT REVOLVER | .6 |

## CHAPTER NINE-ILLEGAL AND LEGAL DRUGS

| Figure 9-1 | COCAINE HIDDEN IN COMMON HOUSEHOLD ITEM | .2 |
| Figure 9-2 | ETHER EXPLOSION DESTROYS THIS PCP CLANDESTINE LAB | .2 |
| Figure 9-3 | CHEMICALS FOUND AT A PCP LAB | .2 |
| Figure 9-4 | COCAINE IDENTIFICATION SWAB | .5 |
| Figure 9-5 | TUBE-STYLE DRUG TEST KIT INSTRUCTIONS | .5 |
| Figure 9-6 | POUCH-STYLE DRUG TEST KIT INSTRUCTIONS | .5 |

## CHAPTER TEN-CHEMCIALS-NO PICTURES

## CHAPTER ELEVEN-CASTING AND RESIDUAL PRINTS

| Figure 11-1 | GAIT PATTERNS | .2 |
| Figure 11-2 | SHOE DUSTPRINT RECOVERED INDOORS FROM A HARD SURFACE | .5 |
| Figure 11-3 | ELECTROSTATIC DUST PRINT LIFTER | .5 |
| Figure 11-4 | TEST IMPRESSION FROM SUSPECTS' SHOE IS MATCHED WITH CRIME SCENE SHOEPRINT | .2 |
| Figure 11-5 | TEST IMPRESSION MADE OF SUSPECTS' SHOE IN IMPRESSION FOAM | .5 |

| | | |
|---|---|---|
| Figure 11-6 | FABRIC IMPRESSION IN SOIL (A), CASTING MADE | 2 |
| | FROM IMPRESSION (B), AND TROUSERS OF SUSPECT (C) | |
| Figure 11-7 | CAST OF BITE MARK IN CHEESE (TOP) COMPARED | 2 |
| | TO DENTAL CAST IMPRESSION OF SUSPECTS' TEETH | |
| Figure 11-8 | TIRE AND FOOTPRINT CASTING FRAMES | 5 |
| Figure 11-9 | DENTAL STONE CASTING POWDER | 5 |
| Figure 11-10 | OBLIQUE LIGHTING FROM NORTH ON SHOEPRINT | 8 |
| Figure 11-11 | OBLIQUE LIGHTING ON NORTH FACE OF SHOEPRINT | 8 |
| Figure 11-12 | OBLIQUE LIGHTING FROM WEST ON SHOEPRINT | 8 |
| Figure 11-13 | OBLIQUE LIGHTING ON WEST FACE OF SHOEPRINT | 8 |

CHAPTER TWELVE-PAINT AND GLASS

| | | |
|---|---|---|
| Figure 12-1 | CONCHOIDAL GLASS FRACTURES | 2 |
| Figure 12-2 | RADIAL AND CONCENTRIC GLASS FRACTURES | 2 |
| Figure 12-3 | CONCENTRIC CONCHOIDAL FRACTURE (A) | 2 |
| | RADIAL CONCHOIDAL FRACTURE (B) | |
| Figure 12-4 | BULLET HOLE PRODUCING CRATER IN GLASS- | 2 |
| | ARROW INDICATES DIRECTION OF FORCE | |
| Figure 12-5 | GLASS BREAKAGE WITH HEAVY OBJECT. DIRECTION | 2 |
| | OF FORCE CARRIES MOST FRAGMENTS. SOME TINY | |
| | FRAGMENTS MAY FLY IN OPPOSITE DIRECTION. | |

CHAPTER THIRTEEN-DOCUMENT ANALYSIS

| | | |
|---|---|---|
| Figure 13-1 | EXAMPLE OF INDENTED WRITING | 2 |
| Figure 13-2 | HANDWRITING SOURCE TABLE | 1 |
| Figure 13-3 | PAPER CHROMATOGRAPHY REVEALING BLUE AND | 1 |
| | YELLOW PIGMENTS FROM A GREEN INK SAMPLE | |

CHAPTER FOURTEEN-ARSON AND EXPLOSIVE DEVICES

| | | |
|---|---|---|
| Figure 14-1 | SAFETY AND MILITARY TIME FUSE | 2 |
| Figure 14-2 | DYNAMITE, DETONATING CORD, AND BOOSTERS | 2 |
| Figure 14-3 | SCENE OF EXPLOSION (X) AND BUFFER ZONE (Y) | 2 |

CHAPTER FIFTEEN-DETERMINING HUMAN IDENTITY

| | | |
|---|---|---|
| Figure 15-1 | VICTIM EVIDENCE COLLECTION KIT (FEMALES) | 5 |
| Figure 15-2 | VICTIM EVIDENCE COLLECTION KIT (MALES) | 5 |
| Figure 15-3 | DENTAL CAST OF LOWER JAW-ARROWS POINT | 2 |
| | TO DECAYED TEETH | |

CHAPTER SIXTEEN-THE CRIME SCENE SCENARIO
Figure 16-1
Figure 16-2

SOURCES FOR ILLUSTRATIONS

1. Sutton, James. Classroom Photography and Sketches Taken At Poly High School, 1997.

2. Fisher, Barry., et. al. *Techniques of Crime Scene Investigation.* New York: Elsevier Science Publishing Co., Inc.,1987.

3. Dox, Ida G., et. al., Eds. *The Harper Collins Illustrated Medical Dictionary.* New York: Harper Perennial, Harper Collins Books, p.385, 1993.

4. Forensics Laboratory Manuals: Forensics Science, Chemistry and Crime Solving Kits. West Chester, Ohio. Kemtec Educational Corporation, 1980 to present.

5. Forensics Products Catalog. Salem, Oregon: Lightning Powder Company, Inc., 1996.

6. Marshall, Evan. "A Lawman Looks At Stopping Power." *Guns And Ammo Handgun Manual.*p. 51, 1985.

7. Administration of Justice Materials from Riverside City College, Riverside, California.

8. Williams, Peter. Photography by the Senior Forensics Technician at Riverside County Sheriff's Department, Riverside, California, February,1997.

9. Fingerprint Instructional Materials from the United States Marshall's Office, Los Angeles, California, no date.

10. Yankee, R.L. *CAL - ID and Presentation of Fingerprint Evidence at Trial* . Riverside, California: Riverside County Sheriff's Department, January, 1988.

# FORENSICS-SEARCHING FOR CLUES

## INTRODUCTION

Have you ever wondered how detectives solve a crime mystery? Most of us enjoy a good mystery on television or in a book. Yet very few of us have a good understanding of the basic tools detectives use to solve murder mysteries. Some of these tools involve blood type, DNA fingerprints, fingerprints, trace material analysis, tool marks, firearms and ballistics, illegal drug, poison, and chemical identification. We have all seen the detective who just happens to notice a chipped piece of wood or a mysterious white powder near a window in the room under investigation. It is with clues like the chipped piece of wood and the mysterious white powder that the detective begins to weave a crime scene picture.

The mystery of the criminal drama, preserved in time like a photograph in evidence at a crime scene, has fascinated the public for over a century in modern mystery writing. Charles Dickens coined the term 'detective officer' in his book *Bleak House*. A few years later a mediocre medical doctor, by the name of Arthur Conan Doyle, resorted to fictional writing as a means of livelihood. He had studied medicine and was interested in chemistry. Combining his scientific knowledge with a real-life character (a physician who used the art of deduction to solve difficult problems) Conan Doyle created Sherlock Holmes, a fictional detective character. This fictional crime hero became famous because of an uncanny ability to use science and the science of deduction while searching the scene of a crime.

Holmes was often pictured in his lab with a test tube filled with a sample of blood, poison, or soil found at a crime scene. Besides his reliance on the sciences, Holmes spent every waking moment using the scientific method and the art of deduction to solve crime mysteries. After a thorough crime scene search, Holmes would, in his own mind, make generalizations about the crime based on his initial observations. Then, by organizing known facts into a logical sequence, he would begin to make specific conclusions. Many times he would return to the crime scene to conduct specific experiments to verify or negate his hypotheses. Observation, hypothesis, experimentation, data gathering, analysis, and conclusion (all vital components of the scientific method) were addressed in one form or another by Holmes.

Deduction is the ability to make specific conclusions based on a general premise. Induction is also a very important thought process where the investigator has made a very specific observation which is then expanded to a general conclusion. Both deductive and inductive reasoning provide the logic necessary to utilize the scientific method in order to solve crime mysteries. It is believed that the use of science (together with deductive and inductive reasoning) to solve crimes began around the time of Conan Doyles' writings in the late nineteenth century. Although this fictional writing style has been copied again and again by more modern authors, the idea of a detective who utilizes the sciences as an aid in crime detection has become a reality in our world.

It is estimated that there are over 400 crime laboratories and about 40,000 forensic scientists in the United States today. Many of these laboratories were established by the various local police, county sheriff, or U.S. Marshals office as new forensic techniques were developed and as the demand for this expertise grew. There are also a number of private laboratories which provide various forensic lab services. Some of these facilities have the most sophisticated equipment and expertise which help forensic scientists to identify fingerprints, analyze blood and body fluids, evaluate chemicals and metals, determine the source of glass particles, fibers, hair, and a myriad of physical evidence collected from the crime scene.

Even with all the advances in forensic science, violent crime has not been eliminated. Los Angeles County just after 1947 had very few unsolved murders in a year. Now an unsolved murder occurs in Los Angeles County almost on a daily basis. There is an increasing demand for people trained in forensic science to aid the justice system in their search for criminals. The proper handling, marking, and analyzing of physical evidence taken from the crime scene has proven invaluable to prosecutors who must verify that a crime has been committed, identify and convict those who committed the crime and exonerate those who are innocent.

This manual is written to provide a view of the professionals and their techniques who solve crime on a daily basis. A composite of a myriad of techniques, procedures and protocols has been gathered into this document which are used by police, sheriff, fire departments, and other government agencies. It will, hopefully, provide the student of forensics a beginning knowledge with which to solve crime scene mysteries.

Forensics, when applied to criminal matters, is the application of the sciences (earth sciences, biology, chemistry, and physics) to the study of crime. Another term used today in the place of forensics is criminalistics. Criminalistics can been defined as a professional and scientific discipline which involves the recognition, identification, individualization, and analysis of physical evidence by application of the natural sciences in criminal matters. Criminology, not to be confused with criminalistics, is the scientific study of crime (in particular, the criminal and the penal system) as a social event. The crime scene investigator, when searching for motive, begins to shift from criminalistics to criminology. However, it is not the purpose of this text to include criminology and the psychology underlying criminal behavior, but to view the crime scene from an objective and scientific frame of reference.

# -CHAPTER ONE-
# THE CRIME LABORATORY

## INTRODUCTION

Not all police departments have a complete crime laboratory. Most local police departments have good crime scene forensic capabilities: they dust objects for fingerprints, collect blood, urine, hair, soil samples, fibers, and weapons found at the scene. However, many rely on private crime laboratories which are better equipped, for detailed analyses of samples taken from the scene of a crime. These private agencies specialize in analysis of evidence and can provide high levels of accuracy in the analysis of their results  Police and sheriff departments have a very strong network established with various government agencies as well as private companies who provide specific forensic services such as blood analysis and DNA fingerprinting. The FBI (Federal Bureau of Investigation) is the world's most complete facility for the analysis of fingerprinting. The AFT (Alcohol, Firearms, and Tobacco) agency has specific expertise in firearms, ammunition, and ballistics. Others are trained to analyze illegal drugs and other chemicals. Even with all this interdependent capability, the basic goal of the crime laboratory is to reduce uncertainty in the investigation by producing evidence which will stand the intense scrutiny of the court system.

Most local police departments provide training in crime scene work and have special departments dedicated solely to that purpose. The legal and scientific standards are very strict regarding the collection and processing of physical evidence from the crime scene. Mistakes from improper handling of evidence can negate its value in court, and force a jury to release a suspect, who may be guilty of the crime with which he or she is charged. This problem is not limited to local police departments. It can and has occurred with professional agencies and companies.Because the proper handling of evidence supports or refutes allegations, a homicide investigative bureau has been established in every police station in the U.S.

## FIRST AT THE CRIME SCENE

Often, uniformed police officers are the first people to arrive at the crime scene. When a homicide has been determined, homicide officers are called in with specialized equipment to begin a thorough analysis. The uniformed officer(s) have been instructed not to touch anything at the scene: their main duty is to interview witnesses, prevent anyone but homicide personnel from entering the scene, and detain anyone found at the scene. The uniformed officer must make a rough sketch of the scene (to record the position of all obvious evidence including the body or bodies), note the time of day, weather conditions, type and color of the victim's clothing, and anything out of the ordinary. When crime scene investigation officers and evidence technicians arrive at the crime scene a plan of action is decided by the senior officer or technician. Photography is utilized throughout the search and referenced to the crime scene sketches.

Police are thoroughly trained in the crime scene search where sketches are made and samples are properly collected and marked for laboratory analysis. Blood is collected from the victim and (if possible) from the clothing the victim is wearing, and from their immediate environment. There is always the search for the weapon used in the act of violence and, of course, the entire area is literally combed for fingerprints.

Any identifying marks are recorded and photographed for future reference. There are many detectives who have spent a number of years of 'on-the-job-training' where they have learned just what to look for in a crime scene search. With this experience comes an ability to spot the unusual or 'out-of-place' item which the untrained person would normally overlook.

There is a negative aspect to this type of work. There is usually a victim. The victim may be injured or even dead when the detective arrives at the scene. The crime scene can include the aftermath of a violent act where a person's life has been taken. The victim may have been dead a long period of time creating a nauseous odor. There is always the danger of the spread of disease at the crime scene. Aseptic procedures must be followed at all times. Latex gloves, masks, and goggles are worn to protect those searching the crime scene. The picture we have of the detective leaning over the victim, touching his bare finger to the blood or the white powder on the victim's sleeve is pure 'Hollywood'. No respectable detective would be that careless. Even the dental hygienist who cleans patients' teeth takes more precaution than that! Needless to say, the crime scene can be a potentially dangerous area where aseptic technique is mandatory.

The crime laboratory involves more than one site and often more than one company. The initial crime scene is where the field lab work of recording and gathering samples for later investigation and analysis occurs. The local police departments, then, become the center for collecting and storing evidence as well as the gathering of laboratory analysis from outside crime laboratories where evidence has been sent. Accurate records are kept by the local police department of each evidence movement during this analysis phase of crime detection. Evidence items are stored in paper sacks and boxes and labeled with an evidence form and a chain of possession chart (Figures 1-1 to 1-4). A record must be kept of the evidence chain of possession to guarantee the genuine evidence items in a court of law.

CRIME SCENE EQUIPMENT AND PHOTOGRAPHY

The local police department usually employs or provides professional photographers who produce an in-depth photo analysis of every single piece of evidence. The photographer typically will use a numbering system of 1 to 100 for actual items collected for evidence and a lettering system of A to Z and AA to ZZ in order to reference each

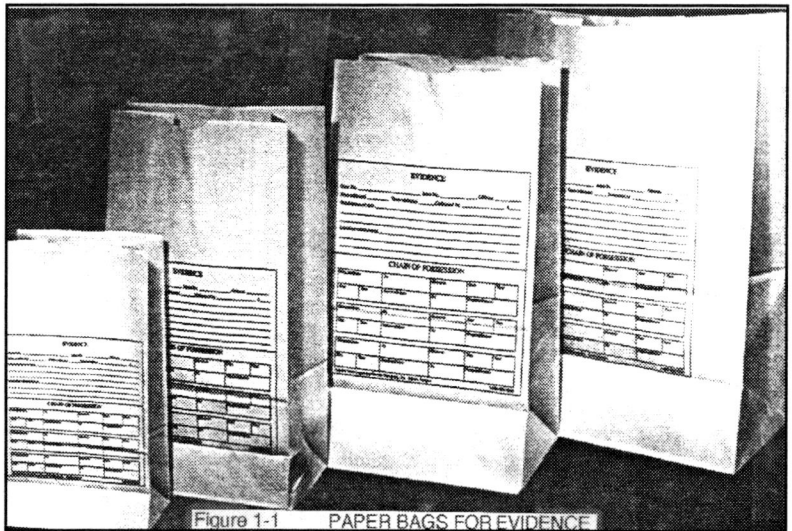

Figure 1-1     PAPER BAGS FOR EVIDENCE

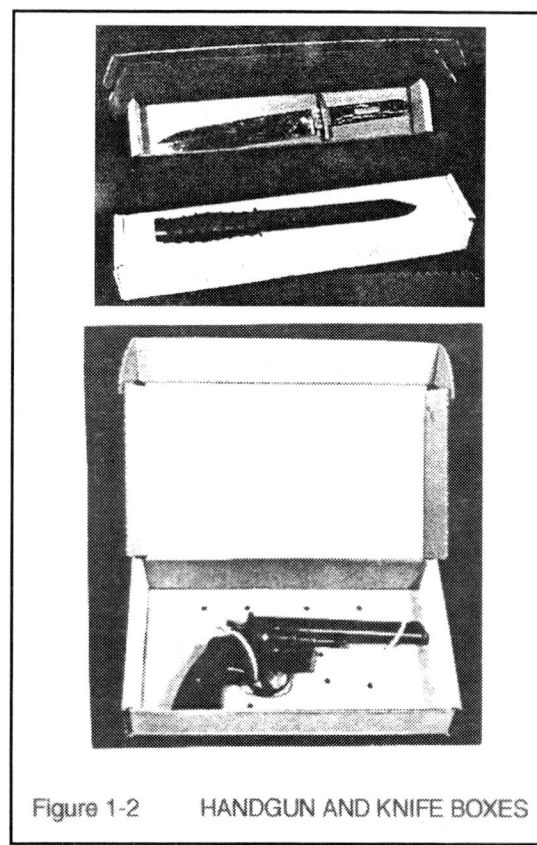

Figure 1-2     HANDGUN AND KNIFE BOXES

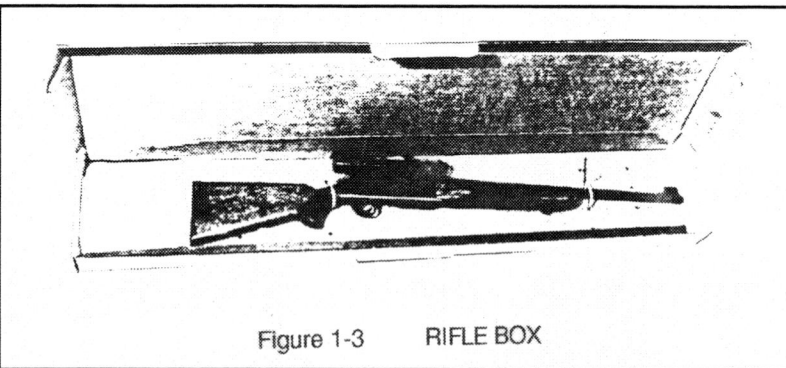

Figure 1-3     RIFLE BOX

*Paper will not trap moisture to cause metal evidence to rust or biological evidence to spoil.*

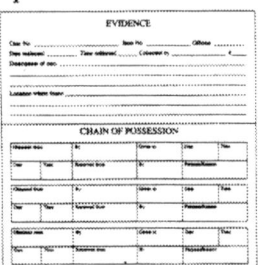

*Example of evidence form on each bag.*

Figure 1-4
EVIDENCE AND CHAIN OF POSSESSION FORM

Photo Evidence Numbers

Photo Evidence Alphabet
Figure 1-5

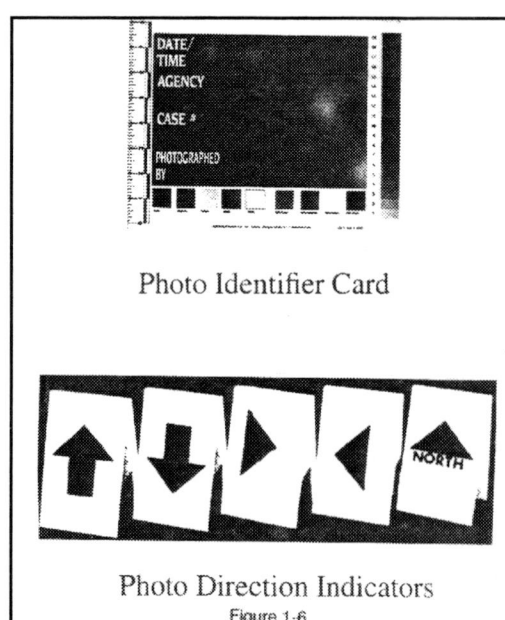

Photo Identifier Card

Photo Direction Indicators
Figure 1-6

4

photograph (Figure 1-5). Included in each photograph is a color bar (to produce accurate color reprints), a ruler (to produce enlargements which are actual life size), a North direction pointer (to provide a frame of reference at the crime scene), and the evidence item # or letter (Figure 1-6). These photographs provide vital location information to investigators. They make possible the ability to study the proximity of one piece of evidence to another. Also, evidence sent to a specialized crime lab without adequate comparison material can be relocated at a crime scene (even years after the event) by using photographs taken during the evidence collection process. The use of photography has also made possible the preservation of the actual sample of evidence. Instead of the sample being handled by countless individuals (police, lawyers, court officials, judges, and jurors), reproducible photographs can be substituted.

Specialized crime laboratories employ highly trained people who utilize specific standards and operating procedure as they perform their work. They are able, within a certain factor of error, to produce repeatable results of their analyses. This provides an accuracy and quality level which has become highly respected by the courts. Most crime labs include basic glassware (beakers, graduated cylinders, test tubes, funnels), specialized tools (burners, ring stands, tongs, probes, forceps, rulers, scalpels), scales, water baths, spectrophotometers, light microscopes and dissecting scopes, centrifuges, ductless vent hoods, and in some cases, electrophoresis equipment Figures 1-7 to 1-15). Some lab analysis requires highly specific and expensive equipment to analyze certain evidence items. GSR (gunshot residue), for instance, is analyzed using spectrophotometry equipment (Figures 1-17 and 1-18) which require highly trained technicians. GSR is discussed in more detail in Chapter 8- Firearms and Ballistics.

## CRIME SCENE RECONSTRUCTION

The crime scene investigator, or forensic scientist, is a highly skilled technician who is capable of recognizing, identifying, collecting, marking, preserving, and storing pertinent evidence to be later analyzed in a crime laboratory. These investigators spend the majority of their time involved in assault and homicide criminal investigations. Beside their expertise in fingerprint, trace material, and blood preservation they

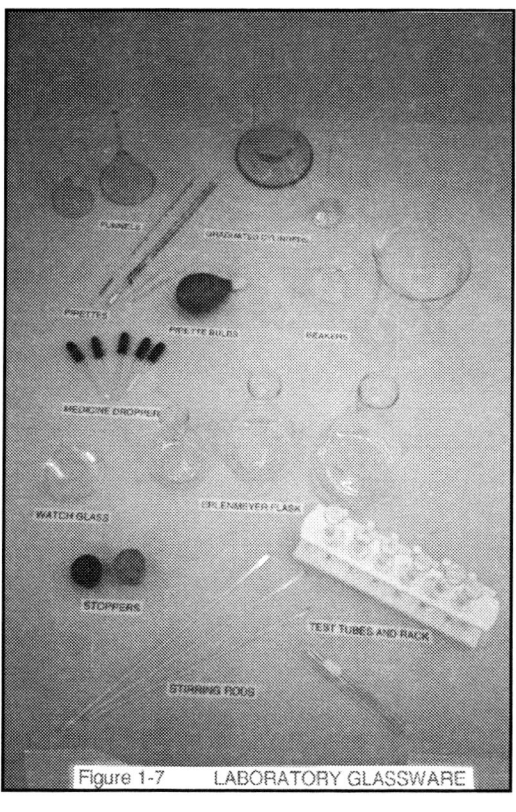

Figure 1-7    LABORATORY GLASSWARE

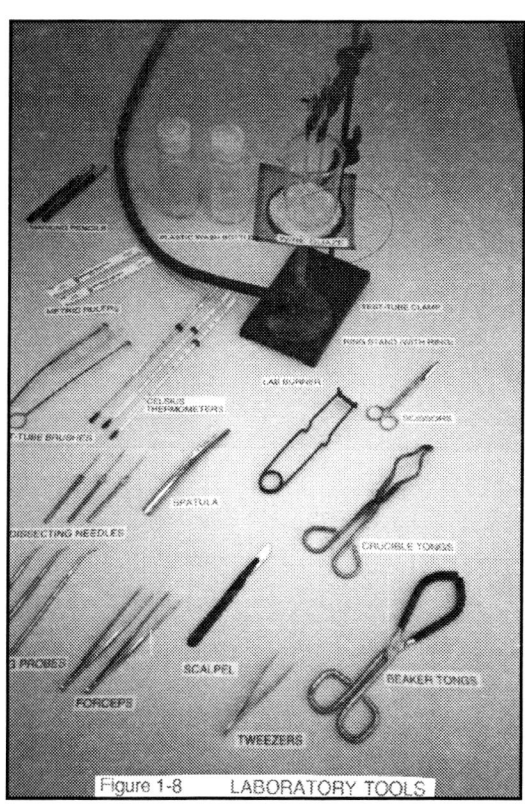

Figure 1-8    LABORATORY TOOLS

specialize in crime scene reconstruction. This technique involves establishing a beginning scenario with an orderly progression of events based on the initial facts. The crime scene investigator, after gathering samples of evidence from the crime scene, will return to the crime lab (Figures 1-18 and 1-19) and conduct various laboratory tests on the evidence, complete official reports on the lab tests performed, and be available to testify in court as an expert witness. Figure 1-18 is a photograph of an actual forensics laboratory. Notice the laser equipment on the left counter, the fume hood at the far right corner, fingerprint area on the right counter, and the wrapped evidence on the table in the center of the room. Figure 1-19 shows the same laboratory from a different angle. Notice the shower equipment, emergency lighting, and other posted safety signs. The white line through the left side of the picture is a structural support post. Other evidence, which their lab is not equipped to analyze, is sent to outside labs. As the crime scene investigator gathers results from the various labs, the crime scene scenario is modified from the initial scenario to match the new evidence. Witness, victim, and suspect testimony's are analyzed and possible motives are considered in the attempt to piece together the actual events leading up to, during, and directly after the crime. The items of evidence are like pieces of a large jig-saw puzzle which, when placed in the correct order, will provide an accurate account of the actions of each

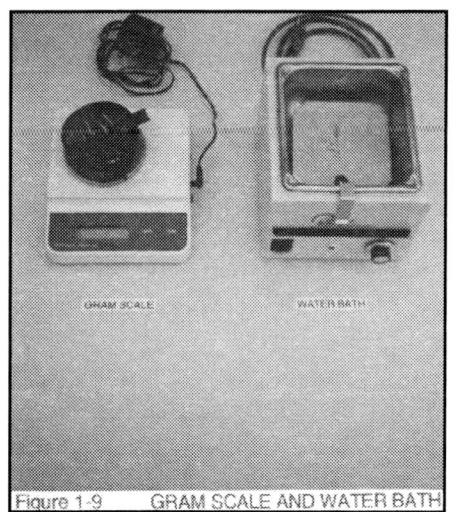
Figure 1-9  GRAM SCALE AND WATER BATH

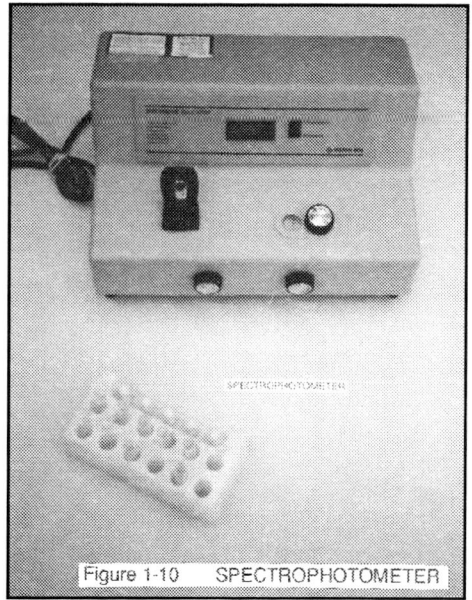
Figure 1-10  SPECTROPHOTOMETER

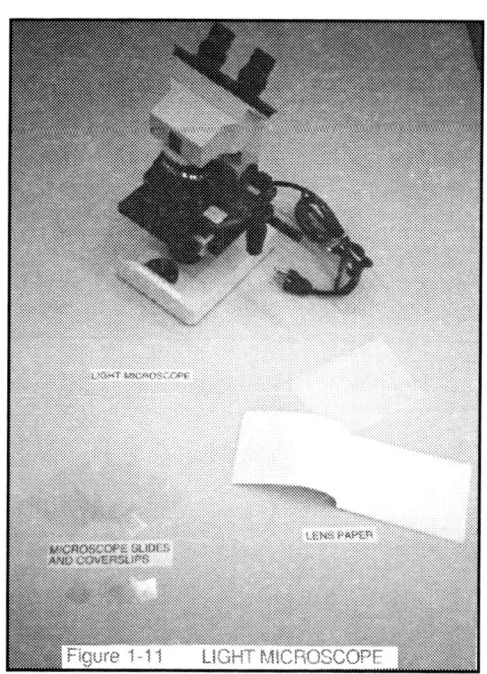
Figure 1-11  LIGHT MICROSCOPE

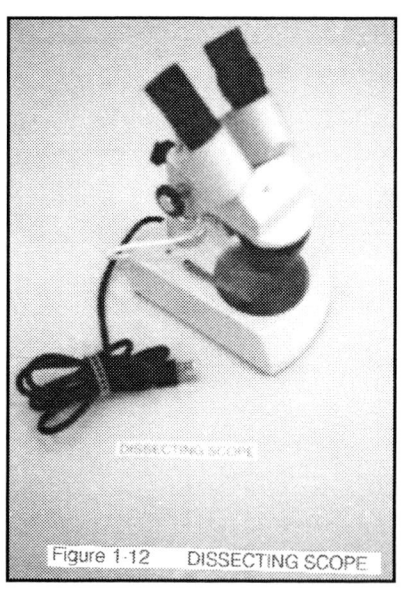
Figure 1-12  DISSECTING SCOPE

Figure 1-13  CENTRIFUGE

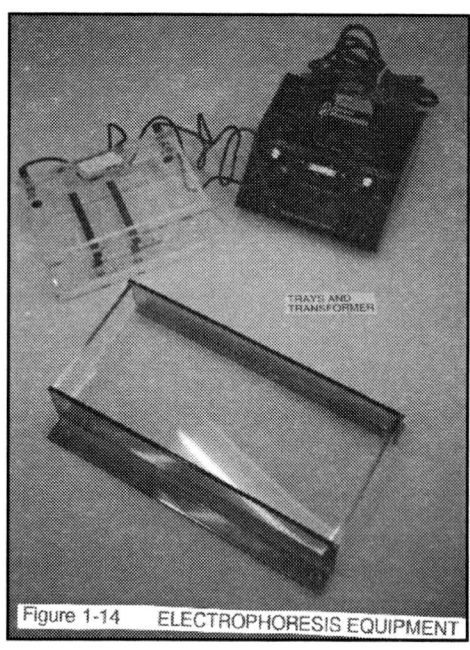
Figure 1-14  ELECTROPHORESIS EQUIPMENT

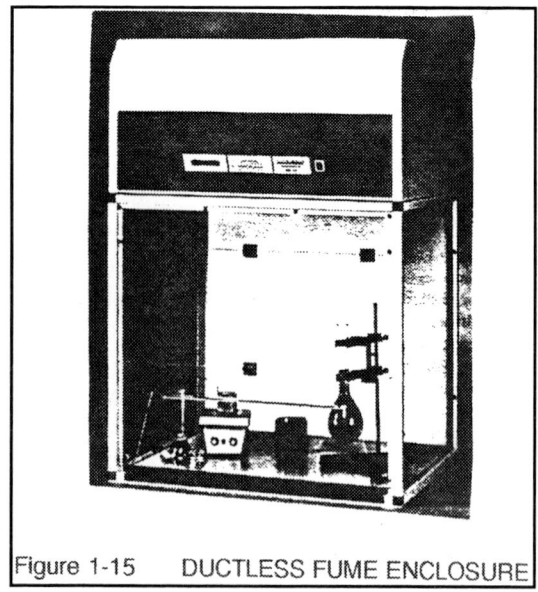
Figure 1-15  DUCTLESS FUME ENCLOSURE

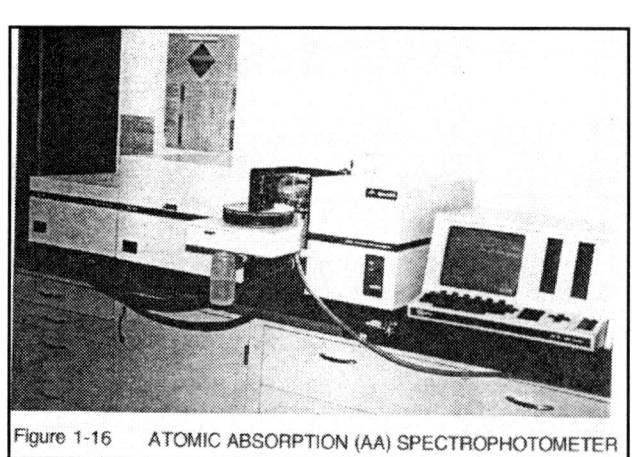
Figure 1-16  ATOMIC ABSORPTION (AA) SPECTROPHOTOMETER

individual involved in the crime scene. Crime scene reconstruction, then, is the primary purpose of every investigator

RELATED PROFESSIONAL PERSONNEL

There are other professional personnel who may become involved in the crime lab investigation. The medical examiner/coroner is called in to every homicide to determine the time and cause of death, to identify the deceased, and to remove the body from the scene of death. If the movement of the body would destroy valuable evidence, the crime scene investigator may delay calling the medical examiner until the evidence can be successfully preserved. Hospital emergency room personnel (doctors, nurses, admitting personnel, EMT and rescue personnel) may be able to provide the crime scene investigator with valuable evidence. This is especially true in rape and assault cases where specific physical evidence is collected. The district attorney, in many crime scene investigations, will work with the crime lab team by obtaining search warrants involving an alleged suspect's business, home, or vehicular property. Forensic odontologists (who aid in the identification of a victim by means of dental identification), forensic anthropologists (who provide identification of skeletal remains based on prior medical records and x-

Figure 1-17    X-RAY SPECTROPHOTOMETER (SEM/EDX)

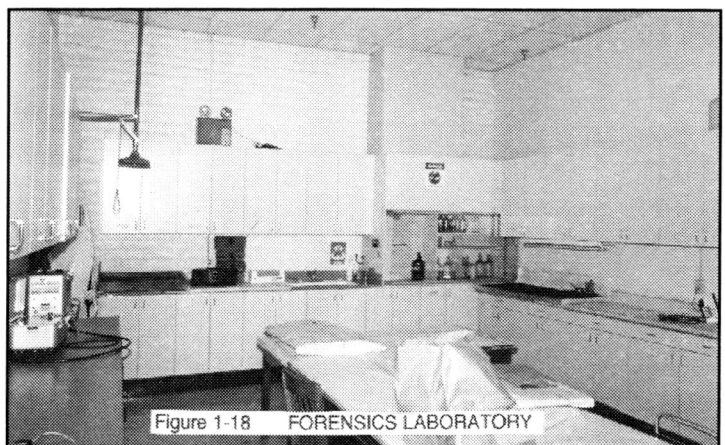
Figure 1-18    FORENSICS LABORATORY

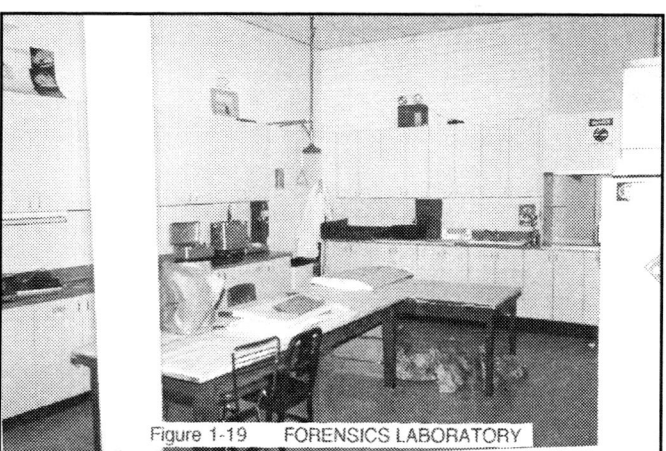
Figure 1-19    FORENSICS LABORATORY

rays), and forensic psychologists (a newer field where criminal profiles are under intense study to classify murderers) are areas of expertise which may also help assist the crime scene investigator in the crime lab analysis.

The 'team' concept where a local police department can mobilize a highly specialized 'crew' of professional crime scene investigators can provide an amazingly powerful tool in crime scene investigation. It is with this strong reliance on professional agencies and companies which provide highly specific analysis of submitted evidence that the local police department can efficiently and quickly solve crime mysteries. This interdependence of crime laboratories provides a broad spectrum crime lab capability to even the smallest police departments. The evidence gathered from the local crime lab and the outside crime labs and other associated professionals can then be expertly presented in a court of law to accurately reconstruct the crime scene, provide an organized order of events with evidence which will convict the guilty and, if necessary, exonerate the innocent.

# CRIME SCENE SCENARIO-"ACCIDENT, SUICIDE, OR HOMICIDE?"

## -INTRODUCTION-

Each chapter contains a new installment of the **CRIME SCENE SCENARIO-"ACCIDENT, SUICIDE, OR HOMICIDE?"** The reader, while reading each chapter, should record evidence regarding the crime scene, victim, suspect #1, and suspect #2 in the **CRIME SCENE EVIDENCE LOG** supplied in the Appendix A at the end of Chapter 16-THE CRIME SCENE SCENARIO. The **CRIME SCENE CHRONOLOG** (in the Appendix B) provides an organizer to record facts and events in a chronological manner. Also, record any testimony on the **CRIME SCENE WITNESS LOG** (in the Appendix C). Finally, record your conclusions and supporting evidence on the **CRIME SCENE OPINION** sheet (also located in the Appendix D at the end of Chapter 16).

Evidence described in each chapter is also collected from an imaginary crime scene and analyzed by fictional characters in the **CRIME SCENE SCENARIO**. All the characters and incidents in the **CRIME SCENE SCENARIO** are the pure invention of the author. They are not related to or based on any persons, living or dead, bearing the same or similar names, or to any actual events, past or present. The purpose of the **CRIME SCENE SCENARIO** is to reinforce and augment material presented in each chapter of the text. Happy Sleuthing!

SUGGESTED READINGS-

Fisher, David. *Hard Evidence: How Detectives Inside the FBI's SciCrime Lab Have Helped Solve America's Toughest Cases*. New York: Simon and Schuster, 1995.

Hall, Jay Cameron. *Inside the Crime Lab*. Englewood Cliffs, New Jersey:Prentice-Hall, 1974.

Saferstein, R., Editor. *Forensic Science Handbook*. Englewood Cliffs, New Jersey:Prentice-Hall, 1982.

Waters, John F. *Crime Labs: the Science of Forensic Medicine*. New York: Franklin Watts, 1979.

# -CHAPTER TWO-
# THE CRIME SCENE

## THOSE WHO ARRIVE FIRST

Law enforcement personnel arrive at crime scenes under various circumstances. Usually a uniformed police officer will arrive at the crime scene first. If a serious crime is suspected (rape, murder or armed robbery) the crime scene unit and homicide investigator will also be dispatched. After the crime scene investigator arrives, the uniformed officer will help to control the scene by keeping unauthorized people away and help with questioning and transportation of witnesses.

## THE SEARCH WARRANT

If the person in control of the location (owner or renter) is either unwilling or unable to sign a consent-to-search form, a search warrant will be necessary. While television and the movie makers would have you think otherwise, only law enforcement officers (not private eyes) are capable of obtaining search warrants. The local district attorney generally works with the crime scene investigator when a search warrant or a court order to seize specific evidence is required. There is a need to show probable cause based on fact, not on hunches or guesses in order to obtain a search warrant. An affidavit is prepared (in duplicate) which describes the area to be searched, the articles to be searched for, and why those items are expected to be at that location. A search warrant is then prepared in triplicate and taken to a judge for his signature.

It is very important to word the warrant in a way that will include _all_ items for evidence. There have been cases where evidence secured at a crime scene which was not listed on the search warrant was not admissible in court. The investigator, then, must anticipate beyond what is plainly visible and include all known evidence as well as all suspected evidence in the event that more items are discovered during the search. For instance, if a suspect was involved in a burglary was a known drug offender, the investigator should include illegal drugs and drug paraphernalia as well as specific items taken during the burglary. The burglary would serve as motive and probable cause for the use and/or sale of illegal drugs.

## RULES WHICH APPLY AT THE CRIME SCENE

Accuracy and attention to detail is essential at the crime scene. There is one overarching rule with which many investigators agree: DON'T TOUCH ANYTHING!!!! One exception to this rule occurs when someone needs medical attention. Otherwise, no exceptions. Other rules include writing everything down to the smallest detail, describing the entire crime scene, and isolating any witnesses (especially from one another as they might be influenced to change their statement of what they actually observed), photograph everything including the overall scene and any surrounding areas which may later prove useful in reconstructing the crime scene for a jury.

## PROTECTION OF THE CRIME SCENE

The crime scene scenario, depicted at the beginning of this chapter, is only a fictional glimpse of what a law enforcement officer or crime scene investigator might encounter. The number one priority is the protection of the crime scene. The crime scene can provide vital evidence in the final disposition of a crime. The mishandling of crime scene evidence can result in loss or contamination of important clues which might have otherwise been used to help solve the crime. It is the responsibility of the first official who arrives at the scene to secure the area for search and prevent the unnecessary movement of evidence.

The initial actions to be taken at the crime scene are:

1. Give aid to any injured persons discovered at the scene of the crime. This is a priority even at the expense of disturbing potential evidence.
2. The crime scene needs to be secured and protected. Prevent others from walking around, moving items, disturbing the body of the deceased, touching any surfaces, or removing any items from the scene. On-lookers are capable of offering assistance which may destroy evidence.

3. Take all close-up photos of the body and other important evidence items. This is especially important if you suspect that the body has been moved. The lividity factor (to be explained later in chapter 3) can provide vital clues as to position of the deceased at the time of death.
4. Make detailed sketches of the scene and record the location of the body and every piece of evidence. Record time of arrival, weather conditions, and persons present at the time of arrival.
5. Have the body removed to the morgue if this process doesn't disturb other evidence. An officer should accompany the body to take any additional photos and take possession of clothing and other personal articles found on the body. The medical examiner/coroner is responsible for this task in many areas.
6. Take fingerprints, including elimination fingerprints (see chapter 4).
7. Collect all other evidence from the crime scene.
8. Obtain assistance, if necessary, detain and interview witnesses, and arrest suspects.
9. Seal-off the crime scene from all unofficial persons.

## LEGAL AND SCIENTIFIC CRITERIA AT THE CRIME SCENE

The close scrutiny of a crime scene is not an easy task. The scene of violence and death leaves a lasting impression on the investigator. A thorough search can provide the otherwise missing information which can help convict the guilty and help to free the innocent. There are legal as well as scientific requirements of the crime investigator. The investigator must be able to:

1. Personally identify each piece of evidence.
2. Describe the exact location of each piece of evidence when it was collected.
3. Prove that the evidence has been in proper custody since its collection.
4. Account for any changes which may have occurred in the evidence between its collection from the crime scene to its introduction in a court.

The scientific requirements are simple—every precaution must be made to preserve evidence and avoid contamination by using clean or sterile containers. Proper handling, which prevents spilling or any kind of alteration of the evidence, is also necessary to satisfy the scientific requirements at the crime scene.

## PRELIMINARY CRIME SCENE SEARCH

Those who arrive first at the scene of a crime have the best opportunity to see and record the scene. The first view—by the uniformed officer—can provide an extremely accurate picture. Officer(s) must make written observations, sketches, and take photographs of every important object at the scene before a more thorough search is conducted. Those areas which hold the most potential for evidence should be marked to prevent evidence contamination. An area which has the least evidence potential should be selected as a collection site where items or trash from the search can be deposited and stored.

It is very easy to form initial ideas or hypotheses about the crime which has been committed. The initial hypothesis, based upon the preliminary search should include a set of logical assumptions concerning how the crime was committed and should include a general sequence of events which occurred during the crime. The investigator should be flexible in this early working hypothesis. As the crime scene search continues, new evidence may contradict earlier assumptions. Accurate notes and photographs need to be taken to record each stage of the search process.

## SEARCHING THE CRIME SCENE

There are several methods to conduct the search. The point-to-point method (sometimes called a sector/zone/room-to-room search) is used to follow a possible pathway utilized during a crime. The point of entry provides the beginning point as the investigators move from area to area (in a room) or from room to room as they believe the scenario progressed (Figure 2-1). The area grid method is used to study a large crime scene when only two people are available. It is the best method for outdoor scenes which are not too large. The strip search is very similar (using more searchers). In the grid method the two searchers work at right angles to each other so that each grid is covered twice. The strip search involves searchers walking next to one another in strips and returning searching a new strip until the entire area is covered (Figures 2-2 and 2-3). The concentric or spiral search method is utilized to study a potential evidence area that is very densely packed with objects. It is used indoors and outside as well. The search begins at the center of the scene (or in some cases were the victim's body is found) and expands in ever increasing circles as the search spirals in an outward direction (Figure 2-4). The decision of which method to use is up to the investigator and is mostly determined by the special circumstances found at the crime scene.

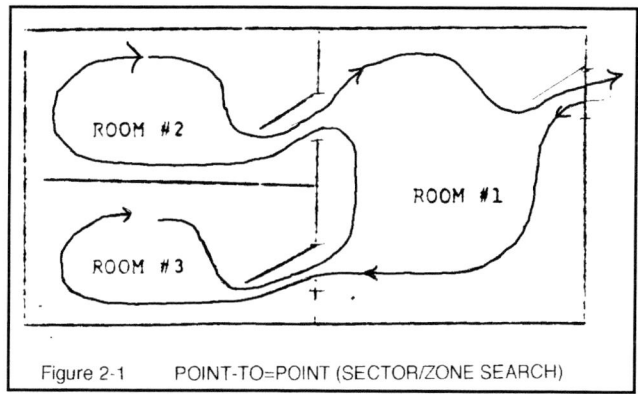

Figure 2-1    POINT-TO=POINT (SECTOR/ZONE SEARCH)

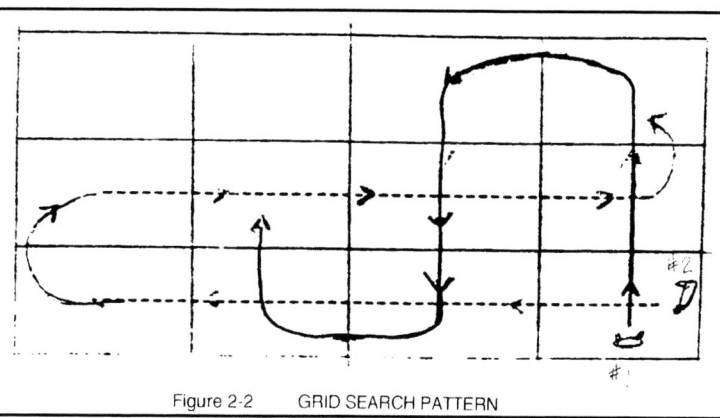

Figure 2-2    GRID SEARCH PATTERN

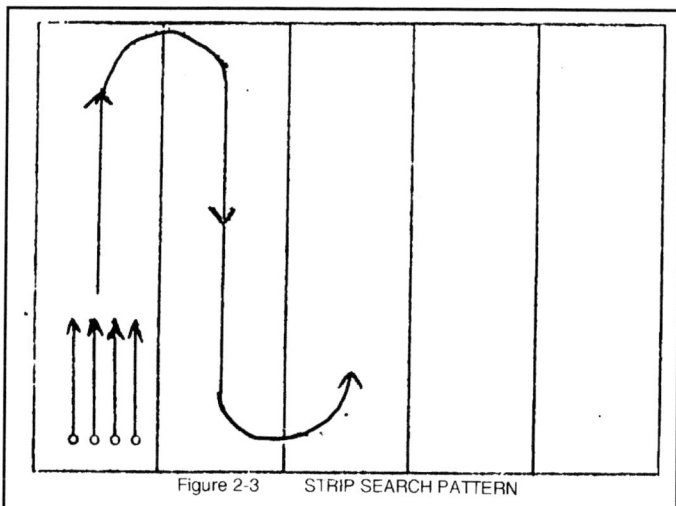

Figure 2-3    STRIP SEARCH PATTERN

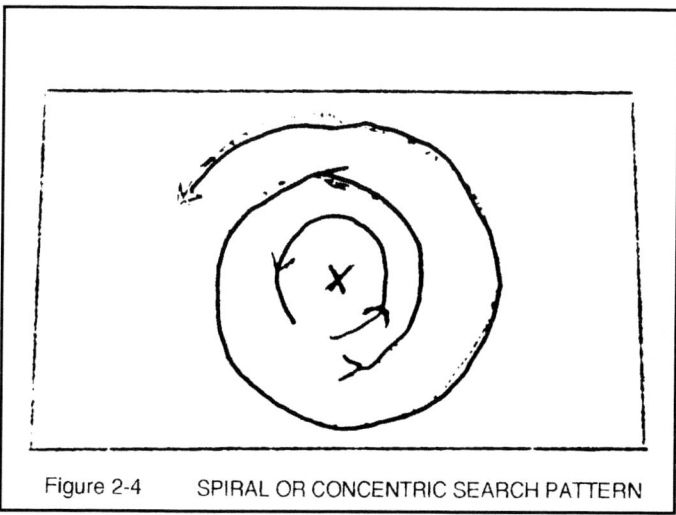

Figure 2-4    SPIRAL OR CONCENTRIC SEARCH PATTERN

## FINE POINTS OF THE SEARCH FORMAT

The following is a general summary of the crime scene search format:

1. First priority must be given to any evidence that is in danger of contamination or deteriorization.
2. Cast imprints and fingerprints should be lifted from objects and photographed before they are removed from the scene.
3. When a deceased person is involved, the evidence items lying between the point of entry and the body are first processed. The deceased person is then searched before the body is removed. A pathway is then provided for the medical examiner/coroner to remove the body.
4. Trace evidence should be searched for and collected before any dusting for fingerprints is done.
5. Surface areas to be swept or vacuumed should be segmented and residue or sweepings from each segment should be packaged separately and recorded.
6. Elimination fingerprints and physical evidence standards are collected after all the above tasks have been completed.

## SAMPLES OF BODY FLUIDS

Blood is probably the most common body fluid to be collected at the crime scene. Fresh blood, which is still liquid, should be collected with a clean medicine dropper and placed in a glass vial which contains a saline (salt) solution buffered to a pH which will protect the blood. Fabric, which is soaked in blood, should be removed and dried away from the sun or direct heat. Objects, which have dried blood on them, should be sent directly to the crime lab. If the object is too large to be sent to the crime lab, then the dried blood should be scraped from the surface of the object with a scalpel into a clean container and sent to the lab. Scrapings from areas surrounding the blood should also be sent into the lab to be used in control tests.

Items which have seminal, urinary, or other stains are also sent to the crime lab. As in the case of blood, if the object is too large to be handled, a small sample is taken from the object. The utmost care should be taken to avoid the possibility of contamination of the body fluid to be studied. The investigator should also take every precaution to prevent personal contact with any body fluids from the crime scene.

## TOOL MARKS

All marks found at the site can provide potential evidence. Marks found in metal are of a high quality. These marks, due to the hardness of the metal, will retain their shape. These marks can provide evidence which can link the tool or object which made the mark. Photographs should be taken of all potential tool marks.

## TRACE SUBSTANCES

Any trace items should be immediately removed, placed in a sealed package, and properly marked. Objects too large to be taken to the lab should be examined for blood, hair, fibers, and other materials which could be lost in the process of dusting for fingerprints. Any items to be taken to the lab should be dusted for fingerprints and covered with tape since any friction on a surface will destroy fingerprint traces. Sweepings and debris from vacuuming from the vicinity of the body are packaged and labeled and sent to the lab for trace material study. These should be recorded by location and kept individually packaged for crime lab analysis.

## STANDARDS TO BE USED AS A COMPARISON

Standards refer to material or objects which can provide a base of comparison. Scrapings from objects may influence tests on body fluids, especially blood. Objects which were broken or chipped during the act of the crime can be very valuable as standards. Paint chips, glass slivers, small pieces of metal, and fibers can serve as standards which can help link a suspect with the scene of the crime.

Standards also include elimination finger prints and palm prints from all persons having access to the crime scene. Shoe and tire tracks of all known persons and vehicles also serve as standards to narrow down the search. Collection of standards should be completed prior to leaving the crime scene. The investigator might find the crime scene cleaned of all broken objects should a return visit become necessary. It is better to collect too many samples at the initial visit than to risk a return visit to a crime scene where missed evidence has been removed or repaired.

## FIRES AND EXPLOSIONS

Most police departments have a special arson investigator as do most insurance companies. The suspected arson scene is handled much the same as the basic crime scene since the fire could possibly be a cover for another crime such as homicide (murder), burglary, or fraud (destruction of records or physical property so the owner could collect money from an insurance company).

The first concern in a fire investigation is to determine the origin of the fire. If there is more than one origin, it is possible that the fire was intentionally set. Investigators search for timers or other devices which might delay ignition and containers which might have supplied the arsonist with fuel. Specially trained dogs can locate flammable chemicals in parts per billion! More on this later. Investigators will also study the blast patterns where walls have been blown outward to determine if a gas (upper wall separation at the roof-line) or vapor (lower wall blown out first), or if a solid explosive was used (shattering effect produced at the center of the blast). This will be covered in more detail in Chapter 14-Arson and Explosive Devices.

# VEHICLE SEARCH

A systematic plan should be carried out in the search of a vehicle. If a hit and run crime is suspected, the undercarriage and outside of the vehicle should be closely scrutinized. In cases of homicide and burglary, the entire vehicle needs to be thoroughly searched.

The exterior should be searched first with particular attention given to the grill area and the hood. In some cases the vehicle is placed on a lift and thoroughly inspected from underneath. The investigator should look for broken or damaged areas, cloth imprints in dust or road grime on the vehicle's finish, hair fibers attached to any part of the vehicle, and parts missing from the car. A thorough record should be made including photographs, sketches, and samples of materials collected. A search should be made for fingerprints on the top of the car, the hood, the trunk, the doors and the door handles. Each fingerprint is developed, lifted, and marked as it is discovered.

After the exterior is thoroughly searched, the interior is photographed and sketched. The interior is divided into five areas: right front, left front, right rear, left rear, and the rear deck above the back seat. The investigator should sweep or vacuum the floor before entering the vehicle. The sweepings should be labeled and recorded. Care should be taken not to wipe off any fingerprints.

# SEARCHING THE VICTIM AT THE SCENE

There are three aspects of searching the victim: at the crime scene, at the hospital, or at the morgue. The search of an injured victim at the crime scene will be very limited with observations of clothing, general condition, and the extent of the wounds or injuries. A detailed sketch and photograph of the deceased victim must be made before the body is moved. Close-up detail of all wounds or injuries and positions of all evidence objects in relationship to the body should be sketched (including measurements) and photographed.

After this is completed, a detailed search of the body and clothing for hair, fiber, paint, glass chips, or other trace materials. The search should begin at the top of the head and progress down one side including the arm and the leg to the sole of the foot. The process should then be repeated down the opposite side. Hairs and fibers are often spotted by viewing the silhouette of the body against the light. Elimination fingerprints should be taken later and fingernails should not be scraped in the field. These tasks can be performed with more accuracy in the morgue. The medical examiner (M.E.) or coroner is responsible for the body and all related evidence until his examinations are completed. An officer may accompany the medical examiner and record information during the autopsy and gather the deceased clothing and other personal items at the morgue.

# SEARCHING THE VICTIM AT THE HOSPITAL

The investigator who visits the victim at the hospital should collect all items which would provide evidence including the victim's clothing if physical contact was made between the victim and the perpetrator of the crime. Fingernail scrapings and elimination fingerprints should also be collected. A sample of the victim's blood should be obtained for typing by the crime lab. The nature and the exact location of the victim's wounds should be obtained from the physician in charge of the victim. If the victim is alive and able to be interviewed, this should be accomplished as soon as possible.

# SEARCHING THE VICTIM AT THE MORGUE

Before a body is removed from the scene of the crime it is placed in a body bag to prevent the loss or contamination of any evidence. Once the body has arrived at the morgue, a pathologist (who is a medical doctor) will perform the autopsy. The investigator should also be present to record cause and time of death and the depth and nature of the wounds.

Before undressing the deceased victim, the clothing and hands should be examined for trace materials. Because the lighting is better, items missed in the field will show up in the morgue. The body is undressed. All items of clothing are allowed to air dry (especially if blood soaked) and wrapped individually to be taken to the crime lab for analysis. A wound chart (Figure 2-5) is made of all wounds and injuries. Close-up photographs are made at this time. If rape is suspected, vaginal smears are obtained by the pathologist to be analyzed by a medical laboratory. Head and pubic hair samples are collected. Most crime scene investigators supply a rape kit which is used by the examining physician. It must be immediately refrigerated and sent to the lab as soon as possible. Inked elimination finger and palm prints are taken at the hospital or morgue. The victim's hands are swabbed for firearm residue before prints are taken. Any recovered slugs (bullets) are marked and sent to the crime lab.

## SEARCHING THE SUSPECT

All clothing items, including the suspect's shoes, are recorded and sent to the crime lab. Samples of the suspect's blood, hair, fingernail scrapings, and any firearm residue are taken and sent to the crime lab. A full set of the suspect's fingerprints and palm prints are taken. If prints or impressions of bare feet were discovered at the crime scene, a set of inked footprints of the suspect are taken. If necessary, the suspect's vehicle, residence, and place of work is searched when search warrants have been secured. The suspect should be searched away from the crime scene so that the evidence found on the suspect or suspect's clothing will not be disqualified in court. It could be argued that incriminating evidence (fiber, hair, blood, or other trace evidence) could have been placed on the suspect during the search at the crime scene.

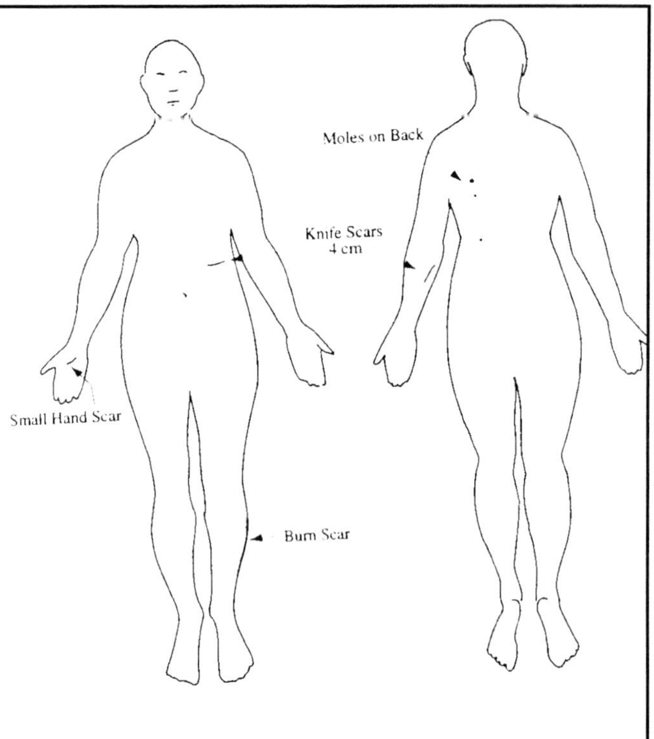

Figure 2-5   WOUND CHART

## RECORDING THE CRIME SCENE: NOTE TAKING

Three methods (note taking, scene sketching, and photography) are used to record the crime scene. The first is the use of note taking. The investigator's notes are the written account of the crime scene and the recording of items to be used as evidence in a court of law. These notes should include an accurate picture of the details of the crime scene (Figure 2-6).

CRIME SCENE NOTES TAKEN 1-8-97 AT 12:08 PM. AT 398 MYERS RD
RECORDED BY DETECTIVE DODGE, BADGE 462

| ITEM # | DESCRIPTION | LOCATION |
|---|---|---|
| 1. | Head of male victim | 37" from baseline established from right front door jamb to left read window jamb, 6'-0" from left rear window jamb. |
| 2. | Feet of male victim | 45" from baseline, 10'-3" from front door jamb. |
| 3. | Several spots of blood | 35" from base line, 13'-5" from right front door jamb. |
| 4. | Shoeprint in soil | Along exterior rear wall of garage, 47" from right window jamb of rear garage window. |
| 5. | Fingerprints on window | Prints on left side of sill, prints on lower left window pane. |
| 6. | Fabric on top of fence | Along backyard fence, 6'-0" high, 27'-3" from east border of property |
| 7. | Blood splatter pattern 7 spots with footprints | "V" shaped pattern originating at feet of victim, extending outward toward front door 72", reaching a distance of 54" at the widest point. |

Figure 2-6   CRIME SCENE NOTES

To be included in the investigator's notes are:

1. Dates, times, and locations.
2. A detailed description of the victim and clothing.
3. The victim's wounds and injuries.
4. A description of the crime scene.
5. The type of camera and film used in photographing the crime scene.
6. A description (on sketch, in writing, by number or letter, and in photograph) of every item of evidence found at the crime scene.
7. The failure to locate certain items.

## RECORDING THE CRIME SCENE: SKETCH MAKING

There are several methods of making sketches of a crime scene. These are the coordinate, triangulation, and cross-projection methods. These three methods (illustrated in Figures 2-7, 2-8, and 2-9) use the **CRIME SCENE SCENARIO** described at the end of this chapter. The measurements should be taken with a tape measure and not estimated. The sketch should include:

1. The full name and rank of the investigator.
2. The crime classification, time, date and case number.
3. The full name of anyone assisting in taking measurements.
4. Address of the crime scene, its position in a building and landmarks.
5. The scale of the drawing.
6. The major items of physical evidence and other critical features of the crime scene. All items should be located with accurate measurements.

Rough sketches are usually made at the crime scene and smooth sketches are completed at a later time. This smooth or finished sketch does not have to be prepared by the investigator who drew the rough sketch. When accurate detail is essential to a case, the crime scene investigator may have a draftsman or architect provide the drawing. However, the investigator must be able to verify the accuracy of the smooth or finished sketch.

## THE COORDINATE METHOD OF SKETCH MAKING

This methods uses the principle of measuring the distance of an object from two fixed points in rectangular or baseline coordinate sketching, and from one fixed point in radial-polar coordinate sketching. One form utilizes the baseline which is drawn. between two fixed points. It may also be a wall or the mathematical center of the room. Measurements to an object are then taken at right angles to this established baseline. The area is marked with a number which is listed in a legend at the bottom of the sketch with a full description. The sketch is made as if an aerial view of the room from the ceiling looking towards the floor (most closely resembling an architect's blueprint).

## THE TRIANGULATION METHOD OF SKETCH MAKING

The method is particularly useful in outdoor crime scene areas but may be used indoors as well. Measurements are taken from identifiable fixed objects such as trees, fences, signposts, and corners of buildings. Each item or the victim's body should be located from at least two fixed points. A scale should be included and a legend to describe items found at the scene.

## CROSS-PROJECTION METHOD OF SKETCH MAKING

This method is extremely useful when items of evidence are in or on the wall surfaces in an enclosed area. The walls, windows, and doors are drawn as though the walls had been folded flat on the ground. Measurements are then taken from a given point on the floor to the location on the wall.

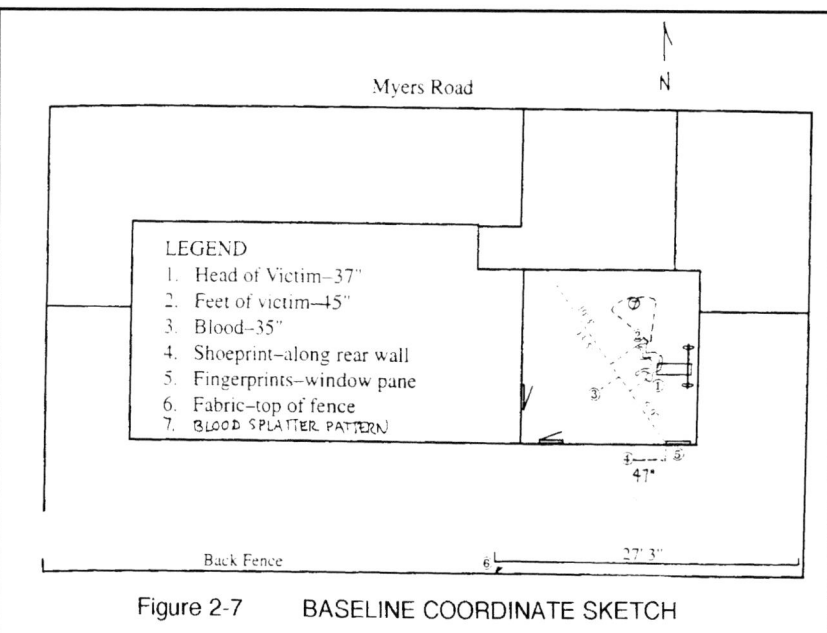

Figure 2-7    BASELINE COORDINATE SKETCH

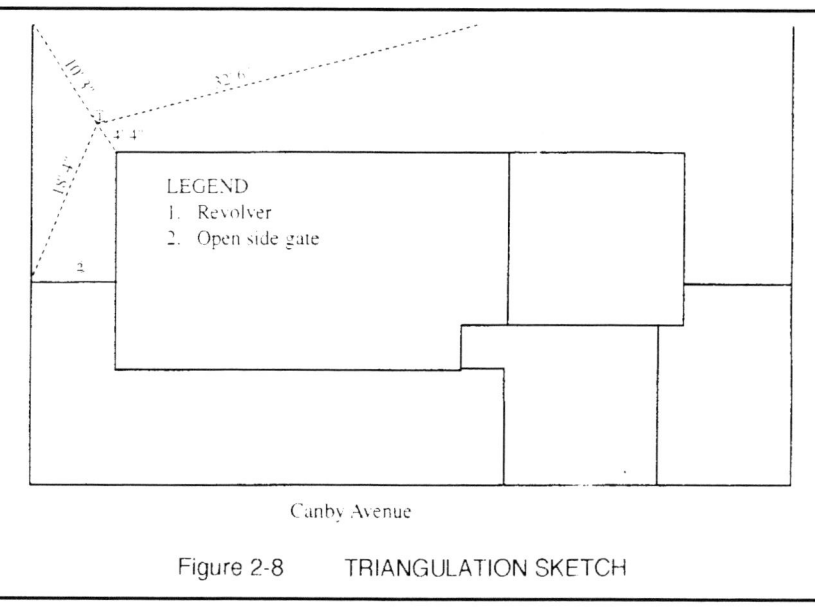

Figure 2-8    TRIANGULATION SKETCH

## USE OF PHOTOGRAPHY AT THE CRIME SCENE

Photography can be a very useful tool for the crime scene investigator. There are certain conditions which apply. Photographs can be used as evidence in court if the investigator can testify that the photographs submitted as evidence accurately depict the area observed during the search. Possession of the negatives will suffice as proof to refute allegations that pictures have been altered. No workers should be included in the pictures of the crime scene. Each picture must be accompanied by an accurate written record of the item or items in question. Custody of crime investigation photographs must be carefully maintained.

Either 35 mm or four-by-five cameras are used with very high speed color film. Accurate scales should be included in evidence pictures to provide a standard for enlargement of the negatives to actual size finish photos. These actual size photos can be used to compare actual physical evidence ( such as shoes, tires, and tools) recovered from a suspect.

Photographs serve to refresh the memories of investigators and witnesses, show the relationship of evidence articles at the crime scene, take the place of the actual evidence, and provide the real-life drama of the crime scene to the jury.

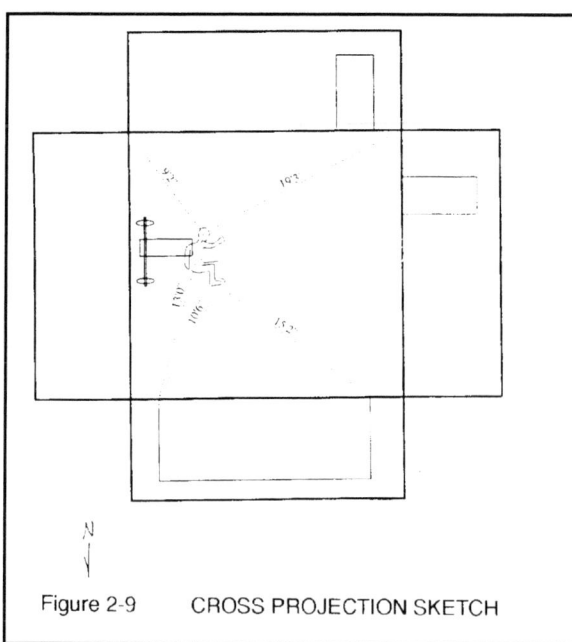

Figure 2-9   CROSS PROJECTION SKETCH

## THE CRIME SCENE: A FINAL NOTE

Crime, especially violent crime, does not always occur in ideal settings under ideal conditions. There are times in outdoor crime scenes when it begins to rain or snow. Crime scene investigators and technicians continue their search regardless of the environmental conditions. Indoor crime scenes can also produce unsavory working conditions. The odors and suffering from assault and loss of life can cause a large amount of stress on forensic professionals. There are some individuals who are unable to work under such stressful conditions. The successful technicians are able to focus on their primary tasks with the knowledge that their work may possibly lead to the arrest and conviction of the criminal/s involved. There is also a high level of satisfaction when an individual, unjustly accused of a crime, is set free based on the forensic evidence gathered at the crime scene. Crime scene investigation requires a vast array of knowledge and technique and is a costly enterprise. Most crime scene investigators and technicians agree that the cost is well worth the effort to solve crime.

## A CRIME SCENE SCENARIO-"ACCIDENT, SUICIDE, OR HOMICIDE?"
### -PART ONE: FIRST AT THE SCENE-

Detectives Wilson Dodge and Kelley Summer had just finished interviewing a witness involved in a current assault case. They were in transit to the County Hall of Records when the following message blasted out of their radio at 11:32 am.:

"Any available unit respond to a possible homicide at 9453 Myers Road." Detective Dodge looked at his partner, Kelley Summer, who was driving their unmarked car. Summer was avoiding eye contact with her partner. "Come on, Kelley, we're only five blocks away," Dodge insisted.

Summer, still hesitating, reached for the microphone. "Unit 62 is on route to 9453 Myers Road . . . our ETA is five minutes." "Look, Dodge, don't expect me to get excited about every call that comes from dispatch."

Detective Dodge knew just what his partner was getting at. They had been working on several difficult homicide cases and the newest assault case was troubling both of them. They had put in a lot of extra hours. "Maybe this is just a prank call?"

"With our recent record," replied Summer, "don't count on it!"

Their car arrived at 9453 Myers Road at 11:37 am. They drove up the small driveway. People were starting to gather from the neighborhood. There were several people standing in front of the open garage door. Dodge got out of the car and told the on-lookers to stand back. Dodge and Summer noticed a body slumped next to a weight bench on one side of the garage on the cement floor. There was plenty of blood next to the body and in a number of places on the garage floor. The body didn't move. Dodge had to remind the onlookers to wait out on the driveway a second time. Summer pulled out her cellular phone to call for the crime lab people. They carefully walked over to the body while pulling on latex gloves. Summer reached her hand out and felt for a carotid pulse on the victim's neck. No pulse. The victim's body was still very warm and the blood on the t-shirt hadn't dried. There was no apparent weapon in sight. There appeared to be a bullet entry wound on the left side of the victim's chest region. There was no exit wound. There were no bullet casings in sight.

They quickly surveyed the garage, being careful not to disturb anything. Dodge quickly made a mental sketch of the garage. There was blood on the weight bench, the floor surrounding the bench, and scattered drops of blood facing the front of the garage. There appear to be footprints in the blood by the back door and toward the front garage door. The door leading into the house was locked from the inside. There was no response to his knock at the door. Detective Summer asked a responsible looking on-looker to keep others from entering the garage.

Dodge directed his search to an open passage door leading out of the garage into the back yard. He noticed shoeprints in the soft dirt just outside the garage door. They were quite distinct and were made a short time ago. The shoeprints were less distinct across the dry lawn. Dodge followed these, being careful not to damage them, to the back fence. There was a torn piece of denim cloth hanging from the top of the fence where the shoeprints ended. Upon closer examination, he notice that the torn cloth was damp. Dodge looked at the blue sky overhead and noticed there were no clouds in the sky. It hadn't rained for nearly two weeks. He looked over the fence and noticed a shiny object in the dirt lying beneath a shrub. The object had the general shape of a handgun.

Dodge retreated back into the garage where Summers was already making a rough sketch of the room. He pulled out his cellular phone. This time he called for police units to respond. Summer asked "What did you find?"

"Footprints and a gun. . .looks like someone's on the loose." They both knew that the whole neighborhood would have to be sealed off in order to conduct a more thorough search of the area, unhindered by neighbors. They knew that time was of the essence. A suspect had just fled the scene. Evidence must be collected and recorded in its undisturbed state. Interviews must be conducted before memories began to fade. There was a lot to do and they were keenly aware that everything must be done by a strict protocol for their work to stand up in court. Crime lab technicians arrived in a specially equipped van and immediately sealed off the crime scene area with yellow crime scene tape. Dodge and Summers began to interview the on-lookers, standing in the driveway, who were potential witnesses. They would also have to go door-to-door to interview neighbors who might have heard or seen the suspect.

Detectives Dodge and Summer had been partners for nearly three years and had become the departments' top investigators. Dodge took out a quarter and flipped it high in the air. He caught it and placed it on his other hand. "Call it, Summer!" demanded Dodge.

"Heads, of course!" replied Summer. Dodge slowly lifted his hand which covered the quarter. The side view portrait of George Washington was plainly visible. Dodge put on a sad face and looked dejected.

"Cheer up" insisted Summer, "I'll work the scene this time." Kelley had won the toss the last three times and would usually choose to conduct interviews with on-lookers and neighbors. Dodge's face assumed a rare smile as he walked toward the on-lookers and began the interview process. Summer walked to their car and returned with a notebook, camera, and tape measure. Their work was just beginning.

SELECTED READINGS-

*Basic Police Photography.* 2nd. Edition. Eastman Kodak Co., 1968.

Collinson, J.G. "The Role of the Investigating Officer." *Journal of Forensic Science* 10(4): 199, 1970.

Buckhout, R. "Eyewitness Testimony." *Scientific American* 231(6): 2, 1974.

Goddard, K.W. *Crime Scene Investigation.* Reston, Virginia: Reston Publishing Co.,1977.

Kirk, P.L. *Crime Investigation,* 2nd Edition. Thornton, J.I., Editor. New York: John Wiley and Sons, 1974.

National Institute Of Justice. *Crime Scene Search and Physical Evidence Handbook.* Washington, D.C.: U.S. Department of Justice, 1973.

Taft, Donald R. *Criminology.* 4th Edition. New York: Macmillan Publishing Co., 1964.

Wingate, Anne. *Scene of the Crime, A Writer's Guide to Crime-Scene Investigations.* Cincinnati, Ohio: Writer's Digest Books, 1992.

# -CHAPTER THREE-
# PROOF OF IDENTITY

## IDENTITY AT THE CRIME SCENE

Most of us have never given a single thought wondering what our name is. When we see someone new whose name we don't know we simply ask that person. Maybe, if we are embarrassed, we ask another person who might know the name of this unknown person. This is not always possible when determining the identity of victims and suspects involved at a crime scene. Therefore, one purpose of physical evidence is to identify the victim and suspect, and to establish the identity of the suspect with evidence items used in conducting the crime. Identity of persons or evidence at the crime scene is of prime importance in criminal investigations. There are occasions when the victim has no identification. There was no identification found on the body slumped next to the weight bench in the garage. Was the revolver found under a neighbor's backyard shrub the one that fired the bullet found in the body of the murder victim? If so, who fired it? Identity, then, becomes important not only to identify the victim, but the identity of the revolver and identifying marks on the revolver are important clues which could link it to a specific suspect.

Many times physical evidence must be used to make a positive identification of an object or person. Fingerprints, blood typing through serum testing and DNA analysis, handwriting, hair and fiber analysis, and medical and dental records are among the types of physical evidence to establish identity of an individual. Each of these will be covered in more detail in future chapters. Family and friends also provide a positive source of identification. There are times, however, when a bereaved spouse or parent, in their zeal to end the agony of a victim search, will make a positive identification on a badly decomposed or mutilated body. Crime scene investigators must rely on factual evidence to make a positive identification. The quality and usefulness of physical evidence, however, become dependent upon the following important identity concepts: mathematical probability, categories, comparisons, individuality, rarity, and exchange.

## IDENTITY: MATHEMATICAL PROBABILITY

Most events and their outcomes can be logically estimated using mathematics. The estimate is, of course, related to known conditions, past performance, and experience in the outcome of similar events. A coin, when tossed in the air, will either land on its head or its tail. There is a 50% chance of landing with its head up and a 50% chance of landing with its tail up in a single toss. Each subsequent coin toss has the same probability: 50% to 50%, or expressed in statistical terms, 1:1.

Probability, when applied to fingerprints, becomes a very useful tool in forensics to identify a victim or suspect. When considering the type of pattern, ridge count of the loops, tracings of the whorls, and the relationship of the ridge details of the pattern, the likelihood of two prints being the same is estimated to be as high as $1:10^{60}$ (a number which, expressed in traditional form, would be a 10 followed by 60 zeros). Since the world's population is about $10^8$ people, it is easy to see that no two people have the same fingerprints. Mathematical probability supports the concept that fingerprints provide an excellent method to establish positive identity.

Blood type is another example where mathematical probability can help to provide identity. There are four major types of human blood: A, B, AB, and O. Any human bloodstain can be identified as one and only one of the four types of blood. Blood grouping is determined by the genetic makeup of the person. The table below

| BLOOD TYPE | % OF OCCURRENCE IN POP. | PROBABILITY IN POP. |
|---|---|---|
| O | 40 | 8:20 |
| A | 40 | 8:20 |
| B | 15 | 3:20 |
| AB | 5 | 1:20 |

illustrates the probabilities of the various blood types in our population. For example type O blood is eight times more common than type AB. If type O blood sample were found, far fewer people would be eliminated than if an AB sample were found. A and AB is therefore a higher quality evidence than a sample of O blood. Blood type cannot provide the certainty of identity that fingerprints can provide. If blood type A is found at the scene of the crime, it may be concluded with certainty that the blood found at the scene of the crime was not that of any suspect with a blood type other than type A.

The are same forms of evidence which do not lend to statistical probability. Tool marks do not show enough consistency to lead to a probability estimate. However, even though statistical data would be lacking, it is possible to relate the particular observation of an event (a metal tool prying against a wooden window frame) by showing similarity in marks on the tool which are made in the wood when the event occurred.

Statistically, it can be shown that most burglars are men. Although most burglars are men, this information for a given event is not probable by statistics. This type of crime can require exceptional physical strength and mechanical skills. So, while the statistical probabilities do not rule out a particular burglary being committed by a woman, they provide a strong lead as to the gender of the offender.

Finally, many criminals operate in a particular manner known as the modus operandi (method of procedure). Crimes which are committed in a certain and consistent style can be related to a statistical probability. However, the relationship between the modus operandi and certain individuals can only provide clues for the investigator because the events and the individuals cannot be predicted with mathematical consistency.

## IDENTITY BY CATEGORY

All evidence can be ranked as to particular category. Category is referred to as class characteristics by some investigators. Shoe prints can be linked to the type of the shoe (tennis shoe, hard leather sole street shoe, boot, etc.) and possibly the brand of the shoe (many shoes bear the manufacturer's name and logo). The shoe print might also be categorized as small, medium, large or possibly a particular size. The shoe print might be classified as a man's or woman's shoe. There is a computer software program available which can provide the manufacturer and model of a wide variety of popular footwear. A copy of a shoe casting, taken from a crime scene, is placed on a computer scanner. Data from the scanner is analyzed and matched to known sole tread patterns and markings of shoe manufacturers. Useful only as a lead clue in a criminal investigation, items which have been ranked or classified into a particular category (such as a particular brand and size of shoe) can later provide a positive identification of a particular suspect.

Figure 3-1   PIECES MATCHED TO BROKEN BUTTON ON A SUSPECT'S COAT.

## IDENTITY BY COMPARISON

Probably the most important use of comparison is the actual match of a piece of evidence with another piece of evidence. Pieces of a button recovered from a crime scene were matched to a broken button on a suspect's coat (Figure 3-1). A slug (spent bullet) taken from a victim can be positively matched with the actual handgun or rifle from which it was fired if both are available to the investigator (Figure 3-2). A more detailed view of firearms and ballistics can be found in Chapter 8.

Figure 3-2   MATCHING MICROSCOPIC LINES ON TWO BULLETS INDICATE THEY WERE FIRED FROM THE SAME GUN.

It can be seen, then, that the investigator is looking for a rip, tear, shard, or other type of breakage that would yield a possible match with an object used to cause the damage. A victim, murdered by a single bullet through the chest, was robbed of a wallet taken from the chest pocket. The suspect, apprehended later that same day, was found with a large amount of currency. Although a handgun was never retrieved, one of the pieces of currency was torn along one side with a small piece missing. Attached to the bullet that was removed from the victim was the matching piece of currency (Figure 3-3). This provided identity by comparison and, along with other substantial evidence, gained a court conviction.

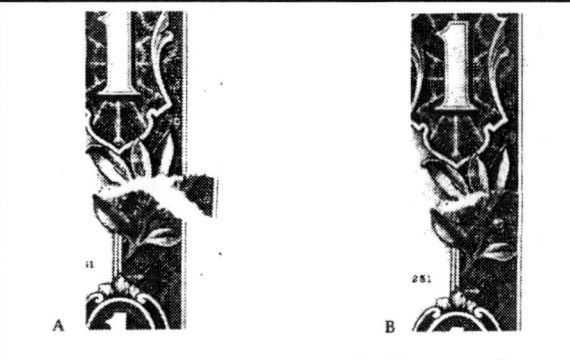

Figure 3-3   PIECE OF BILL TORN BY BULLET MATCHED TO THE ORIGINAL BILL.

IDENTITY BY INDIVIDUALITY

The process of identification of any object or person is basically one of establishing the fact that it belongs to a large group or class. To establish identity, then, depends on establishing that the object or person is the only one of its kind in that group. It is not possible to establish identity with blood type, semen, and hair since these can only place identity in larger categories.

Firearms and tools, however, usually do have a high degree of individuality. Tools can leave traceable and repeatable markings. The rifling of a pistol or rifle also can impart highly individualistic markings that can establish identity.

IDENTITY BY RARITY

Location of certain objects in relationship to the crime scene can provide a valuable source of identity. A woman's hair burette found near her body will provide less value than a man's cuff-link found near the same body. The cuff-link would certainly fit the criteria of rarity because of its unusual location. The crime scene setting (bathroom, alley, or wherever) and circumstance linked with unusual items found at the same scene can provide identity. Identity by rarity is a function of the experience of the crime scene investigator. They are trained to look for the unusual or out-of-place items at a crime scene.

IDENTITY BY EXCHANGE

Exchange occurs when two objects come into contact with one another and some amount of material from one object is transferred to the other object. This is a common occurrence when fabrics come into contact with rough surfaces. When a suspect comes into contact with the victim and various objects at the crime scene, there is often left behind trace amounts clothing, living tissue, or other material. The suspect also picks up trace amounts of the things that were touched. Trace materials are defined as minute or microscopic bits of materials that are not immediately apparent. Even the most gentle physical contact can result in a transfer of trace materials.

**CRIME SCENE SCENARIO-"ACCIDENT, SUICIDE, OR HOMICIDE?"**
-PART TWO: THE CRIME SCENE-

In the crime scene scenario described at the beginning of chapter two, detectives Dodge and Summer discovered a body in a residential garage with various evidence that contributed to the hypothesis that an suspect had fled the scene of the crime by fleeing across the backyard and over a wooden fence. A damp, torn piece of cloth was visible at the top of the wooden fence. On the other side of the fence (in a neighbor's back yard) was a shiny object lying under a shrub at the right-hand corner of the house.

After back-up help was summoned, a house-to-house search was initiated at 11:42 am to apprehend the suspect. After the forensics technicians arrived on the scene at 11:52 am, the shiny object (a Smith and Wesson .357 magnum, 6-shot revolver) was retrieved from under the neighbor's backyard shrub. One spent cartridge casing was found in the cylinder and the revolver's serial number had been filed off with a metal file. A good set of latent fingerprints was found on the barrel of the revolver and a partial latent print on the cartridge casing. The torn piece of damp cloth was collected in a sealed plastic vial and sent to the medical lab for analysis. The victim's blood was collected in a test tube containing an anti-coagulant. Blood was discovered on the garage floor between the victim and the rear door of the garage and in a "V" shaped pattern originating at the feet of the victim and expanding outward toward the front garage door. Blood was also discovered under the fingernails of the left hand of the victim. All collected blood samples were marked, sealed, and sent to the medical lab for analysis. Latent fingerprints were found on the rear garage door and on the rear garage window and window sill. The revolver was labeled and placed in a sealed plastic bag and sent to the crime lab for analysis. Additional evidence was photographed, labeled, packaged, and sent to the crime lab.

A request was conducted through the phone company and the names and work phone numbers were obtained for the residents of the house. They were informed of the homicide in their garage and asked to return home to identify the victim. A Mr. Morganson arrived at 12:05 pm and was unable to identify the victim. Shortly afterwards, Mrs. Morganson arrived and was greatly relieved that the victim was not her son. She was unable to identify the victim by name, since she had only seen him a few times in the neighborhood. According to the Morganson's, their son was in school. A quick check by detective Summer revealed that their son, Bill

Morganson, had not been in school that day. A search of the residence provided no additional information. Bill Morganson was missing and was assumed to have fled out the back door of the garage. Summer, at 12:10 pm, radioed an APB to all units and provided the description of Bill Morganson given by the parents.

A young man (Caucasian, about 5'-10", medium length dark brown hair, wearing blue jeans which were torn on the back of the right leg, white tennis shoes, and a brown silk shirt) was apprehended at 1:15 pm about five blocks from the crime scene about sixty-five minutes after the search was initiated. He was standing by an abandoned commercial building talking to a young male who fled the area and is still at large. Mr. Rodriguez, a witness at the crime scene, had given a detailed description of three teenagers which was provided to the police network. When patrol officers Bodine and Lancaster noticed two youths who matched two of the descriptions given by a witness, they stopped to detain them. One youth, who did not attempt to run, denied any connection with the crime scene. He said his name was Eric Bendor and presented an out-of-state drivers license. He refused to reveal the identify of the young male who had run away. Officer Lancaster told Eric Bendor that he was being arrested as a suspect in connection with a homicide. Office Bodine recited the Miranda provision which informs individuals of their right to remain silent and their right to seek legal aid. Bendor chose to remain silent. He was taken to police headquarters. After a search warrant was obtained, he was told to remove his clothing (over clean white paper) and given detention clothing. Each piece of clothing was carefully folded and placed in individual paper bags which had been labeled. About 15 hair samples (scalp, chest, underarm, groin, and leg) were pulled from each area and stored in individually marked containers. A blood sample was also collected by a blood lab technician. Fingernails were clipped and scrapings from them saved in marked plastic vials. His hands and clothing were sampled for gunpowder residue. After his physical markings were recorded, he was taken to a holding cell.

All of this was done in order to be able to connect this individual with the crime scene, or, to eliminate him as a possible suspect. Notice that the police had probable cause (based on a description supplied by a witness) to suspect this individual of the crime. All affidavits and search warrants were completed before the search was conducted. Had this procedure not been conducted, an attorney would be able to clear this suspect, even if he was guilty, because there would have been a violation of the 4th Amendment of the United States Constitution's Bill of Rights, which states: "The right of the people to be secure in their persons, houses, papers, and effects, against unreasonable searches and seizures, shall not be violated, and no Warrants shall issue, but upon probable cause, supported by Oath or affirmation, and particularly describing the place to be searched, and the persons or things to be seized."

The following is a list prepared by detectives Dodge and Summer of the evidence found at the scene of the crime: (refer to Figures 2-6 to 2-9 for sketches)

1. Shoeprints found in the soft soil behind the garage.
2. Fibers found on the wooden window ledge at the rear of the garage and on the victim's shirt.
3. Blood drops and smeared blood found on the floor of the garage near the back door. Indication of a partial shoeprint in smeared blood.
4. Blood found on and near the weight bench and on the victim.
5. Blood drops and splatters in a "V" shaped pattern originating near the weight bench and expanding outward toward the front garage door. Indication of partial shoeprints in several areas.
6. Fingerprints found on the weight bench, rear garage door, exterior surface of the rear garage window, and rear garage window sill.
7. Hair collected from the victim's clothing.
8. Fibers found on victim's jeans and t-shirt and weight bench.
9. Torn piece of damp denim fabric found on top of backyard fence. Sent to blood lab for analysis of possible body fluids and blood.
10. One .357 Smith and Wesson, 6-shot revolver, recently fired, one empty cartridge casing in cylinder in firing position, serial number filed off.
11. Blue paint on end of barrel of revolver.
12. Latent fingerprints found on barrel of revolver.
13. Round tool mark found by doorknob of rear garage door.
14. White powder scattered on garage floor (note: washer and dryer are located on house side of garage wall between garage-to-house door and front of garage).

The following is a list of the evidence which was found on or in possession of the suspect, Eric Bendor:

1. Hair samples collected from the suspect's clothing.
2. Blood samples taken from the suspect's shirt.
3. Fibers collected from the suspect's shirt and jeans.
4. Shoe casts taken from the suspect's shoes.
5. Gunpowder residue found on the inside of the suspect's shirt.
6. Torn blue jeans with missing piece of cloth on back of right leg.
7. Blood samples taken from vicinity of tear in jeans.
8. Scratches on back of suspect's right leg.
9. Dried blood recovered from tread of tennis shoe.
10. Scratches on back of suspect's right leg.
11. Sample of dried blood taken from suspect's tennis shoes.
12. A sample of the suspect's blood was taken for analysis.
13. Fingerprint and palm prints were taken of the suspect.

As can be seen by this **CRIME SCENE SCENARIO**, there are many possibilities for the exchange of trace materials which can provide an important identity link between the suspect and the scene of the crime. These will be discussed in future chapters in more detail. The following chapters are designed to elaborate the crime scene technique used to collect and analyze items of evidence discovered at the crime scene.

SUGGESTED READINGS-

Joyce, Christopher, and Eric Stover. *Witnesses from the Grave: The Stories Bones Tell.* Boston: Little, Brown, and Co., 1991

Wilson, Keith. *Cause of Death: A Writer's Guide to Death, Murder and Forensic Medicine.* Cincinnati: Writer's Digest Books, 1992

# -CHAPTER FOUR-
# FINGERPRINTING

## HISTORY OF FINGERPRINTING

Fingerprints were imprinted as a seal for business contracts in eighth-century China. This practice of fingerprint impression was required on all government documents in fourteenth-century Persia. In 1686, a professor of anatomy by the name of Malpighi, described elevated ridges on the palmar surfaces which ended as loops and spirals at the ends of the fingers. Another professor of anatomy, John Purkinje, published a paper in 1823 which included the diversity of skin ridge patterns. He categorized these patterns into nine categories. It wasn't until 1858 that Sir William Herschel (a British administrator in Bengal, India) required contracts to be sealed with fingerprints as well as signatures that the modern world began to accept fingerprinting as a means of identification. The famous Scotland Yard in England accepted this form of evidence as early as 1859. Criminals were marked with tattoos or the loss of a finger before the use of fingerprinting became more common.

About 1879, a Frenchman named Alphonse Bertillon pioneered an identification method of identifying people by measuring different parts of their bodies (fourteen different measurements were taken). It was estimated that the chances of two people possessing the exact same Bertillon measurements was about 300,000,000 to 1.

Sir Edward Richard Henry, Inspector-General of Police in Bengal, India, designed a simplified fingerprint classification system in 1901. He based his classification system on the previous work of Vucetich (this system still used in many Spanish speaking countries today). In 1902 and 1903 the State of New York established a systematic use of fingerprinting for the New York Civil Service Commission (to prevent applicants from using others from taking their tests) and the New York State Prison system began to use fingerprinting to identify criminals.

After an incident involving two men, both named Will West, at the Fort Leavenworth Prison in 1903, the United States switched officially to fingerprinting over the Bertillon method of identification. The three methods for determining identity (photographs, names, and Bertillon measurements) were shown to be fallible with these two nearly identical men. In 1904 the U.S. State Penitentiary at Leavenworth, Kansas, and the St. Louis, Missouri, Police Department, working with a sergeant from Scotland Yard, established fingerprint bureaus. A year later, the U.S. Army established a fingerprint bureau with the other branches of the service following their example during the next several years.

Today, many fingerprints are checked through the AFIS (Automated Fingerprint Identification System) which is a computer-based system utilized by the FBI as well as state and local law enforcement agencies. Computers linked with scanners can accomplish in minutes what used to take months of backbreaking and agonizing work.

One of the hardest points to convince crime investigators was the individuality of fingerprints. The possibility of finding two individuals with the exact same fingerprints is one out of ten to the sixtieth power. Fingerprints have become the most common form of physical evidence where identity is established between the perpetrator of a crime and the crime scene.

There are three criteria which make fingerprints a unique tool to the crime scene investigator. First, a fingerprint is an individual characteristic. As far as this writer can find, no two persons possess identical ridge characteristics. Second, it is impossible to alter a person's fingerprint patterns. Even scarring or purposeful destruction to the skin of the pads of the fingers and thumbs cannot permanently eradicate the fingerprint ridge patterns. Third, since fingerprints display characteristic ridge patterns, they can be organized into distinct groups or categories which helps to streamline fingerprint identification.

## FINGERPRINTING DEFINED

There are three categories of fingerprints: **direct**, **latent**, and **plastic**. A **direct** or **visible** (sometimes called an inked) fingerprint is an impression of the ridge detail of the underside of the fingers (palms of hands, toes and soles of the feet are also included) on a receptive surface. This type of print occurs when a substance (dust, ink, pigments, soot, oils, fine powders, flour, etc.) adheres on the friction ridges. When the friction ridges come into contact with a clean surface, a fingerprint is left behind. Fingerprints made with blood and grease are sometimes indistinct and can be very difficult to identify. A **latent** print is an impression caused by perspiration through the sweat pores (exuding grease, sweat, and dirt) on the ridges of the skin which is deposited to a surface (Figure 4-1). The secretion is about 99% water and only 1% organic and inorganic components. However, the 1% is enough material to leave behind a fingerprint. Most latent prints are invisible to the naked eye and require special oblique lighting to locate. The laser light system, when viewed through special colored filters (to protect the eyes) vividly enhances the detail of latent fingerprints. There are some latent prints which are visible, but which require special techniques to develop and preserve. Finally, there are **plastic** fingerprints which are formed when a finger presses against a soft, pliable material (such as putty, chocolate, wax, soap, oil films, tar, clay, fresh paint, adhesive tapes, and resin) and leaves a negative friction ridge pattern impression.

The fingerprint is based upon the ridge structure and specific characteristics known as minutiae which include ridges, ridge endings, islands, enclosures, short ridges, type lines, bifurcations, deltas, and cores (Figures 4-2 and 4-3). The location of these ridges and minutiae make each fingerprint unique. There can be as many as 150 or more different ridge characteristics on a single fingerprint. Most fingerprint experts need only 10 or 12 of these individual characteristics to identify a set of fingerprints. To prove the identity of an individual in a court of law, a point-by-point comparison must be graphically shown for at least 12 different sites in the comparison between the unknown fingerprint and the person's actual fingerprint. There are three basic fingerprint configurations: the arch, the loop, and the whorl. There are variations of these three basic designs and each one will be discussed in detail and illustrated later in this chapter.

Figure 4-1    SWEAT PORES ON FINGERTIP

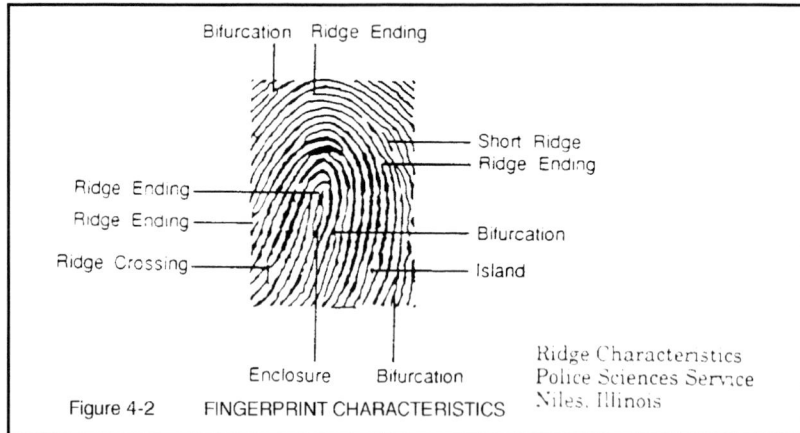

Figure 4-2    FINGERPRINT CHARACTERISTICS

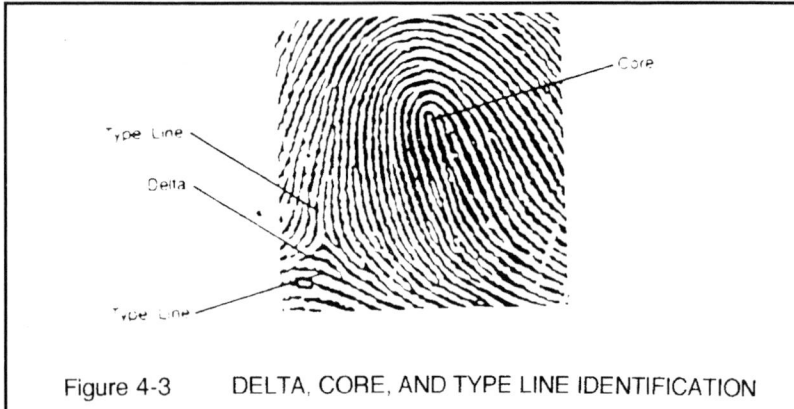

Figure 4-3    DELTA, CORE, AND TYPE LINE IDENTIFICATION

## LIMITATIONS OF FINGERPRINTS

There are certain facts which cannot be revealed by fingerprints. The age or sex of the person is not able to be gained from a fingerprint. Fingerprints do not reveal the age of the fingerprint itself. Only when associated with facts (for instance, the room was dusted six days ago) can a time factor be related to a fingerprint. Also, the race or occupation of the individual cannot, with any accuracy, be obtained through fingerprint analysis.

## CONDITIONS WHICH AFFECT FINGERPRINTS

There are a number of conditions which affect the quality of latent fingerprints. The type of surface, the manner in which the print was transferred, the nature and quantity of the perspiration or oil which covered the ridge surfaces, and weather conditions can all have a dramatic effect on the fingerprint.

Some surfaces are better than others for readable fingerprints. The surface must be clean and smooth for the fingerprint ridge detail to be clearly seen. Surfaces which are rough and porous, such as coarse cloth and unfinished wood, usually do not provide good fingerprints. If the person moved their hand slowly which touching an object, it is possible that the ridge pattern could be laid over the real ridge pattern, which would produce a blurred fingerprint. When too much perspiration is present there is a tendency for the print to be overdeveloped (which is very similar to the condition which would exist when too much dusting powder is applied by the investigator to prepare a latent print for lifting). In general, the more oil deposited with perspiration, the longer the fingerprint will last.

## FORENSICS RESPONSIBILITY FOR FINGERPRINTS

The crime scene investigator should include in the search for fingerprints areas which are not normally thought about. These would include the underside of counter top edges and toilet seat covers, drawers, dishes and utensils, filing cabinets, backs of chairs, rearview mirrors, and the hoods and trunk lids of vehicles. Sometimes objects which are handled on a regular basis (like a doorknob or a telephone receiver) do not provide the best lifts of fingerprints.

The crime scene investigator should not assume that the offender wore gloves at the scene of the crime. Gloves are difficult to work in and there are many occasions when an offender will remove one glove to perform a more intricate operation and leave behind a good fingerprint. Also of importance in the search for latent fingerprints is the consultation with someone who is somewhat familiar with the crime scene. This person or persons might be able to notice if anything is out of its usual place or if anything new has been brought into the crime scene. These identified objects may provide the investigator with latent fingerprints which might have otherwise been overlooked. It is also a good idea to provide a lift of any serial number or other physical identity marking on an object which could provide a positive link with the latent fingerprint taken from it during the crime scene search.

## DEVELOPING FINGERPRINTS

Fingerprints created when the criminal touched blood, grease, paint, ink, dirt, or some other material will generally not need further developing. These fingerprints, called visible prints, should be photographed and covered with tape. The entire surface will then be removed and taken to the crime lab for analysis. Fingerprints created by ridge impressions on a soft material such as putty, wax, and soap are called plastic prints and are handled by a similar method to visible prints. Latent fingerprints are developed with methods based on the type of material they are discovered on. The techniques vary depending whether the latent print in on a nonabsorbent, hard surface or an absorbent, porous material.

## DEVELOPING PRINTS ON NONABSORBENT, HARD, SMOOTH SURFACES

Fingerprints created on hard, smooth, and nonabsorbent surfaces and objects exist in the form of a delicate liquid or semisolid deposit of oil and water. These fingerprints are called latent prints and are not always easily seen. This deposit expands upward from the surface and makes an ideal adhesive base for fingerprint powder. A small amount of fingerprint powder is applied with a brush (carefully rolled between the palms of the hands to remove all existing dust and foreign particles) to the area to be examined (Figures 4-4 and 4-6A). The brush should just touch the powder and the entire area should be covered using light, even strokes until some ridge detail begins to show. As the pattern of the ridges becomes visible the brush strokes should be directed to follow the contour lines. It should be noted here that there are magnetic brushes available which simply hold the magnetic dusting powders in the form of a brush (Figure 4-5). The only material which touches the fingerprint is the dusting powder which means fewer damaged prints. After all the details of the print have been developed, the excess powder should be removed by

Figure 4-4

FINGERPRINT BRUSH AND DUSTING POWDER

gently brushing or blowing it away. The powder should be allowed to adhere to the wet, tacky area of the latent print but not to the surface on which the print is deposited.

The print can be lifted by holding the folded or loose end of the lifting tape (Figure 4-6) with the thumb and the forefinger of one hand and the roll of tape in the other hand, pulling out enough tape to cover the area to

Figure 4-5 MAGNETIC POWDER APPLICATOR

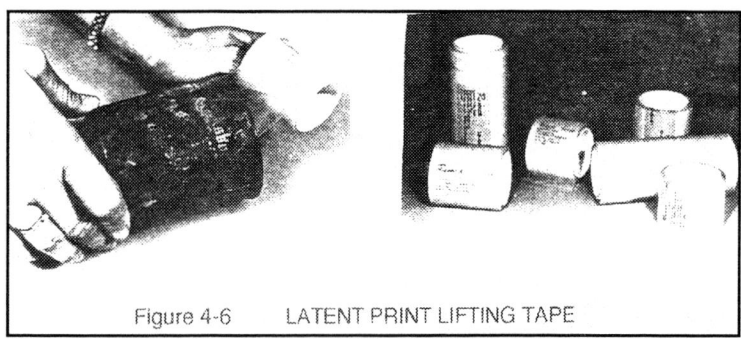

Figure 4-6 LATENT PRINT LIFTING TAPE

be lifted, securing the loose end of the tape beside the print to be lifted and holding it there with the forefinger. Then the thumb should slide along the top of the tape forcing it gently down over the print. The roll, which is in the other hand, should not be released during this operation. The print is now protected. The powder used to develop the print is trapped between the tape and the surface of the object. Using care, the tape should be smoothed down over the print to force out all the air bubbles.

Once the tape has been secured, one of two procedures may be followed. If the surface would be destroyed by removing the tape, the tape may be left on and the entire object submitted to the crime lab for analysis. If this is not practical, the print may be removed by pulling up on the roll end. When the tape is free of the surface, it is placed on a latent fingerprint card (Figure 4-7) in the same manner as the tape was placed over the latent print. When the lift is secured to the card, the tape should be severed from the roll and the loose end folded up. If the

**Figure 4-6A DUSTING FOR LATENT PRINTS**

developed latent print is larger than the width of the tape, it may be lifted by placing one strip beside another, allowing about 1/4 inch overlap with each additional strip of tape until the desired area is covered.

If wet items are selected for prints they should be allowed to air dry first. Prints with no identifiable ridge detail should be included with those which are identifiable since they might help the fingerprint technician to identify which finger the print came from.

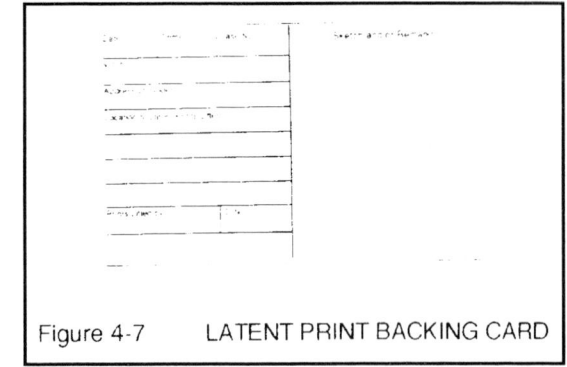

Figure 4-7 LATENT PRINT BACKING CARD

## DEVELOPING PRINTS ON POROUS, ABSORBENT, SMOOTH SURFACES

When fingerprints are present on pieces of paper, currency, cardboard or other absorbent material, no attempt should be made by the crime scene investigator to develop these latent prints with fingerprint powder. These items should be placed in a container with tweezers or handled carefully by the edges and marked "to be processed for latent prints." A fuming technique, using various chemicals, is used to develop prints on porous paper. Superglue (cyanoacrylate), ninhydrin, silver nitrate, and gentian violet are all chemicals used to fume objects or paper until the latent prints are developed and hardened (Figures 4-8 and 4-9). Once this 'hardening' process is completed, the print can be retrieved with a number of techniques including the use of fluorescent powders and either ultraviolet or various wavelengths of laser electromagnetic radiation. The latent prints can then be photographed and dusted with regular black fingerprint powder, lifted with tape, and preserved on a fingerprint card.

IDENTIFYING FINGERPRINTS: LOOPS, WHORLS, AND ARCHES

There are three basic categories for all fingerprints.

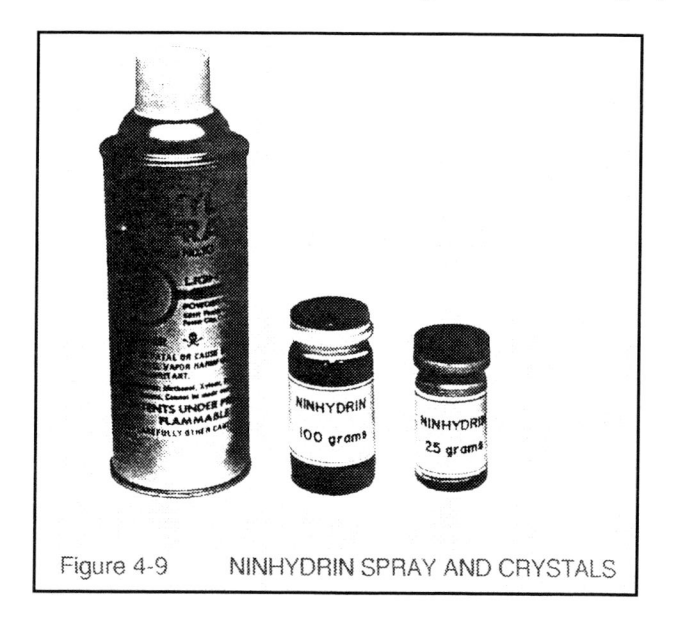

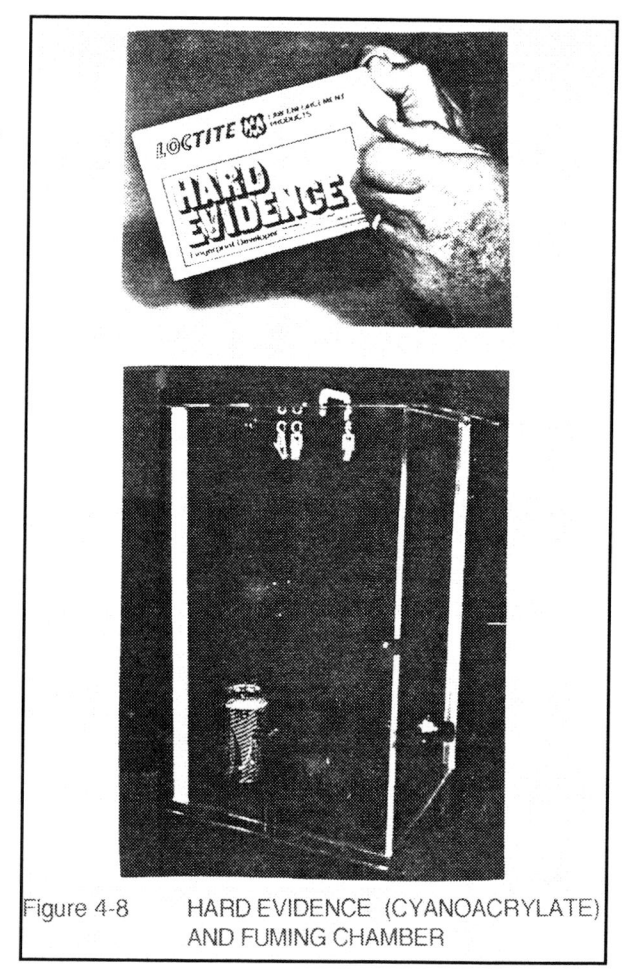

Figure 4-9  NINHYDRIN SPRAY AND CRYSTALS

Figure 4-8  HARD EVIDENCE (CYANOACRYLATE) AND FUMING CHAMBER

About 60% of the total population have **loops**, about 35% have **whorls**, and about 5% have **arches**. Each of these three basic categories have subcategories which are based upon differences which exist within each particular category.

The **arch** is subdivided into the plain arch and the tented arch. The **loop** is subdivided into the ulnar loop and the radial loop. The **whorl** is divided into four subcategories: the plain whorl, the central pocket whorl, the double loop whorl, and the accidental whorl (Figure 4-10).

THE ARCH

Of the two types of arches, the plain arch is the simplest. It is symbolize by the letters AA. It is formed by ridges entering from one side of the print and exiting on the opposite side. These ridges rise at the center forming a wavelike pattern. The tented arch (symbolized by TT) rises abruptly at the center. Arches do not have type lines, deltas, or cores. Type lines are two diverging ridges usually coming into and splitting around an obstruction, such as a loop. A delta is the ridge point nearest the type line divergence. The core is the approximate center of the pattern (Figure 4-3).

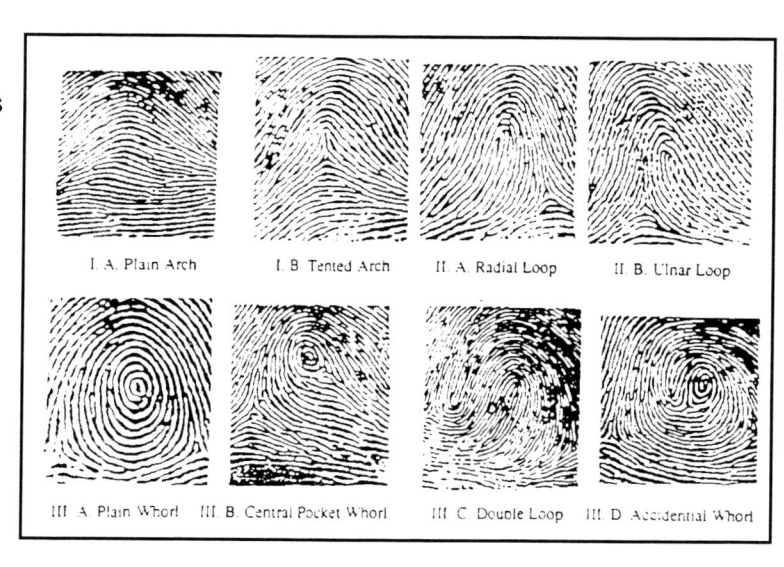

I. A. Plain Arch    I. B. Tented Arch    II. A. Radial Loop    II. B. Ulnar Loop

III. A. Plain Whorl    III. B. Central Pocket Whorl    III. C. Double Loop    III. D. Accidental Whorl

## THE LOOP

A loop must have one or more ridges entering from one side of the print, recurring, and exiting from the same side. If a loop opens toward the little finger, it is called an ulnar loop (symbolized with two numeric characters by the exact number of ridges counted from the delta to the center ridge of the loop). If the loop opens toward the thumb, it is called a radial loop (symbolized with two numeric characters by the exact ridge count plus 50) (Figure 4-11). The patterned area of any loop is surrounded by two type lines. All loops must have one delta.

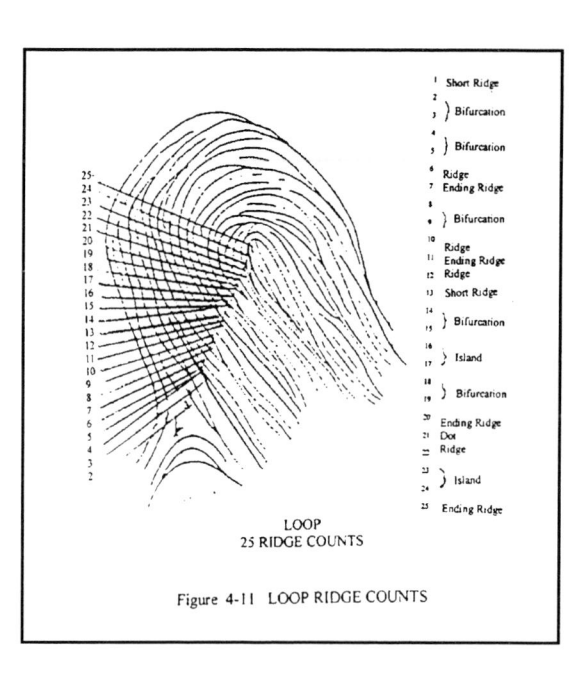

## THE WHORL

All whorl patterns must have type lines and a minimum of two deltas. A plain whorl and central pocket loop whorl have at least one ridge that makes a complete circuit. This ridge may be in the form of a spiral, an oval, or any variant of a circular form. The main difference between these two patterns can be shown if an imaginary line is drawn between the two deltas contained within the two patterns. If the line touches any one of the spiral ridges, the pattern is determined to be a plain whorl (symbolized by the letter P followed by I, M or O by tracing the imaginary line for inside, middle, or outside the whorl pattern) (Figure 4-12). If no ridge is touched, the pattern is a central pocket loop whorl (symbolized by the letter C followed by I, M, or O by tracing the imaginary line for inside, middle, or outside the whorl pattern. A double loop is made up of any two loops combined into one fingerprint (symbolized by the letter d followed by the letter I, M or O). Any print classified as accidental either contains two or more patterns (not including the plain arch) or the pattern is not covered by other categories (symbolized by the letter X followed by the letter I, M, or O). Missing fingers and amputations are indicated by the letters XX. Complete scars and mutilations are indicated by the letters SR. Refer to Figure 4-13 for the NCIC Fingerprint Classification System.

## MARKING FINGERPRINTS

When a latent fingerprint has been developed, lifted, and placed on a card, specific information must be supplied for proper identification. The date, title of the case or number, address of the crime scene, name of the crime investigator who made the lift, the exact place of the lift, and the type of object. A rough sketch of the object the print was taken from on the back of the card would prove helpful. Most crime scene investigators rely heavily on the use of photography of fingerprints with the objects they are located on.

## ELIMINATION FINGERPRINTS

Elimination prints of all persons who may have had access to the crime scene area should be made before lifted latent prints recovered from the crime scene are submitted to the crime lab for analysis. This makes it possible to excuse from the prints all persons who had legal access to the crime scene. All personnel

Figure 4-11 LOOP RIDGE COUNTS

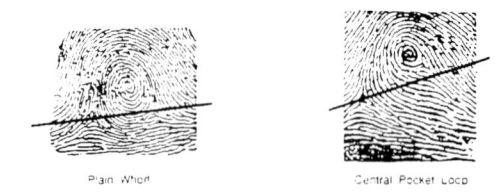

Figure 4-12 DETERMINATION OF PLAIN WHORL AND CENTRAL POCKET LOOP PRINTS

Figure 4-13 NCIC FINGERPRINT CLASSIFICATION SYSTEM

are fingerprinted at the crime scene (including the victim and any individuals who live there) and these elimination prints are sent with the evidence prints for standards of comparison.

When the victim's fingers are wrinkled or distorted, a special solution can be injected into the finger to accommodate the fingerprinting process (Figure 4-14).

Figure 4-14   HYPODERMIC INJECTION TO RECONSTITUTE THE FINGERPRINT

## PROCEDURE FOR COLLECTING ELIMINATION FINGERPRINTS

Equipped with a fingerprint ink pad, a card holder, and the appropriate fingerprint card (Figures 4-15 and 4-16), the crime scene investigator uses the following step-by-step procedure to obtain elimination fingerprints:

1. The subject signs the fingerprint card.
2. The crime scene investigator signs and dates the same card.
3. The subject washes his hands.
4. The investigator instructs the subject to relax arm and hand muscles.
5. The investigator holds the subject's hand, holds the four fingers back, and inks the thumb by rolling it toward the body. He immediately rolls the inked thumb in the designated space on the card and repeats the process for each of the fingers, rolling them away from the subject's body.(Figure 4-17).
6. Simultaneous impressions are made by using a straight downward pressure, with the the four fingers, extended and joined. (Figure 4-18). The process is repeated for the thumbs (with no rolling action).
7. To make palm prints (if palm prints were found at the crime scene), the entire palm and fingers are inked. The hand is then pressed straight down on a card. A different card should be used for each hand.

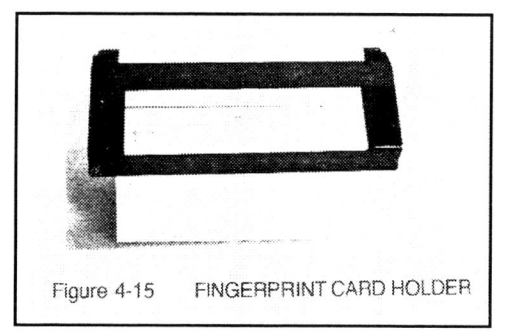

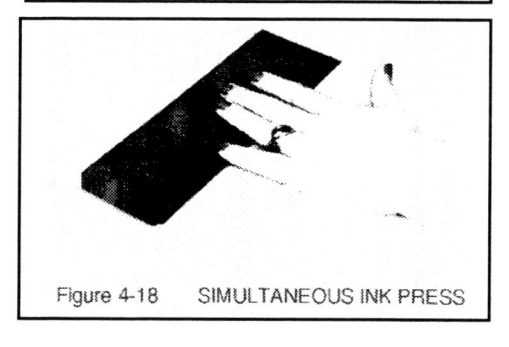

Figure 4-15   FINGERPRINT CARD HOLDER

Figure 4-17   ROLLING A FINGERPRINT ON INK

Figure 4-18   SIMULTANEOUS INK PRESS

Figure 4-16   FINGERPRINT CARDS

Special laser and eye filter equipment is used at the crime scene and in the crime laboratory to help locate latent fingerprints otherwise hidden from view (Figures 4-19 and 4-20). The elimination prints, gathered by the crime scene investigator from all individuals working the crime scene, can be used to eliminate latent prints on articles of evidence. This elimination process will tend to isolate the unknown fingerprints which are sent out for identification.

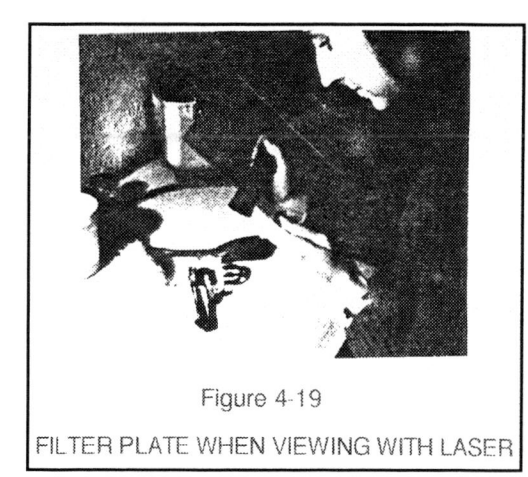

Figure 4-19 FILTER PLATE WHEN VIEWING WITH LASER

The Omniprint™ 1000 is a user-tuned-wavelength source of light for forensic examination and offers up to one watt of optical power. This unit is sturdy, easy-to-use, and the wavelength filters were chosen as the most useful for the examination of physical evidence and crime scenes. It is useful for developing latent prints, for searching for blood stains, body fluid stains, narcotics, and semen and for use in specialized photography.

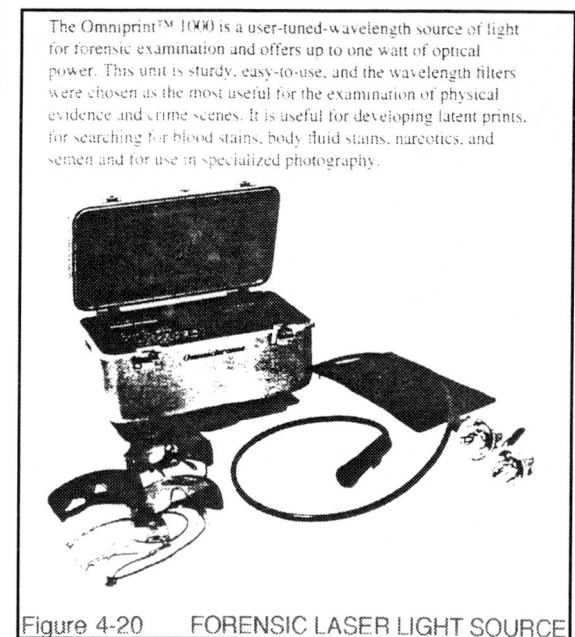

Figure 4-20 FORENSIC LASER LIGHT SOURCE

The law requires, in the case of a homicide, that prints of the victim, including palm prints, must be obtained. The law requires positive identification of all murder victims. These are also used as elimination prints.

## CAL-ID SYSTEM OF FINGERPRINT IDENTIFICATION

The letters CAL-ID are short for the California Identification System which is operated by the State of California Attorney General's Office. It is a computer based system which uses a mathematical formula system based on the concept of triangulation to store and retrieve fingerprints. Triangulation is established between ridge endings, dots, bifurcations, islands, enclosures, deltas, type lines, and cores (Figure 4-22) through the use of a computer scanner and specially prepared

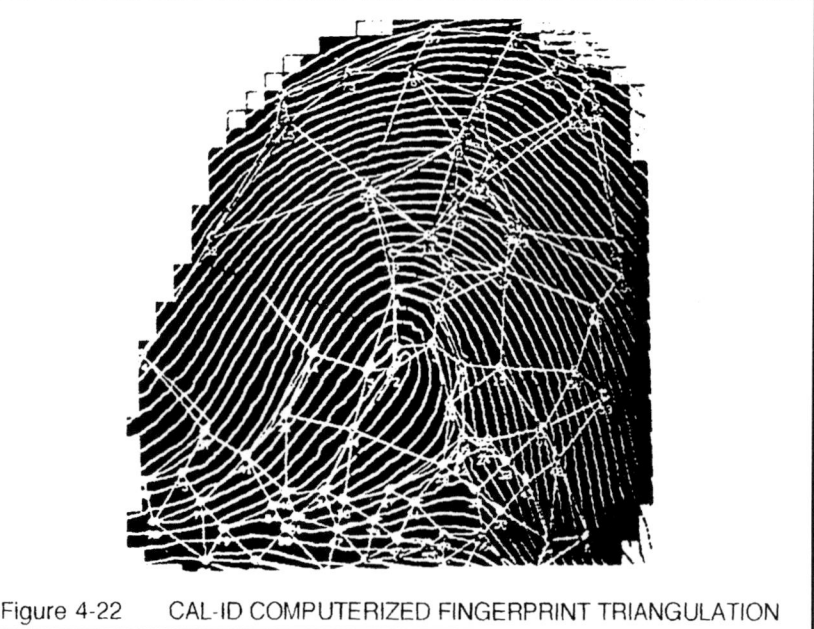

Figure 4-22 CAL-ID COMPUTERIZED FINGERPRINT TRIANGULATION

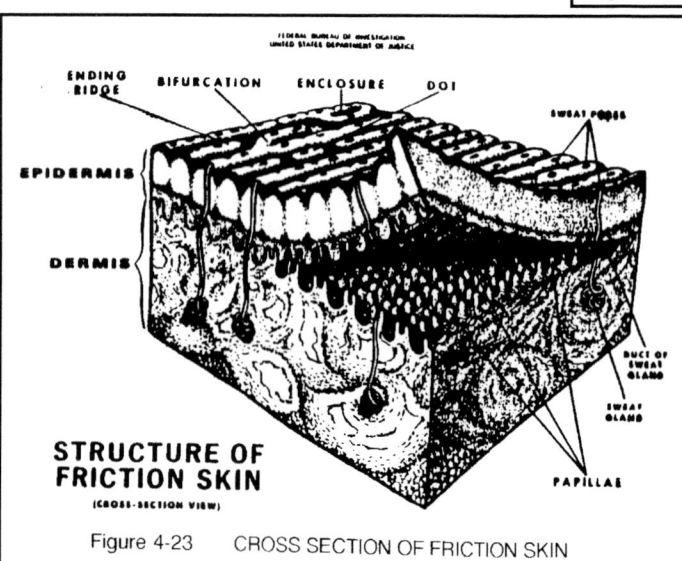

Figure 4-23 CROSS SECTION OF FRICTION SKIN

computer software. Figures 4-23 and 4-24 illustrate how friction ridge forms particular patterns that can be categorized. Usually, several sets of fingerprints are provided by a computer search. These computer generated fingerprints have to be compared to collected fingerprint samples by a fingerprint expert. The CAL-ID is the most comprehensive automated fingerprint system in the world. With the rising value and use of computer technology, the many various fingerprint agencies (FBI, the Armed Services, Interpol, Police, Sheriff, U.S. Marshal, Motor Vehicle, and other governmental departments) will soon be joined to provide a vast selection of fingerprint data. This becomes especially important to identify criminals who commit crimes in different geographical areas.

# REVIEW OF DIRECT (INKED), LATENT, AND PLASTIC FINGERPRINTS

It is interesting to note the similarities between the latent and inked fingerprint impressions (Figure 4-25). The friction ridges in both types of prints appear as raised material (fingerprint dust and ink, respectfully) above the surface of the valleys between the ridges. With the plastic fingerprint, however, the friction ridges appear as indentations or valleys and the valleys appear above the ridges. The analogy of the photograph and its negative can be applied to the plastic fingerprint. The plastic fingerprint is the negative to the latent and inked fingerprint.

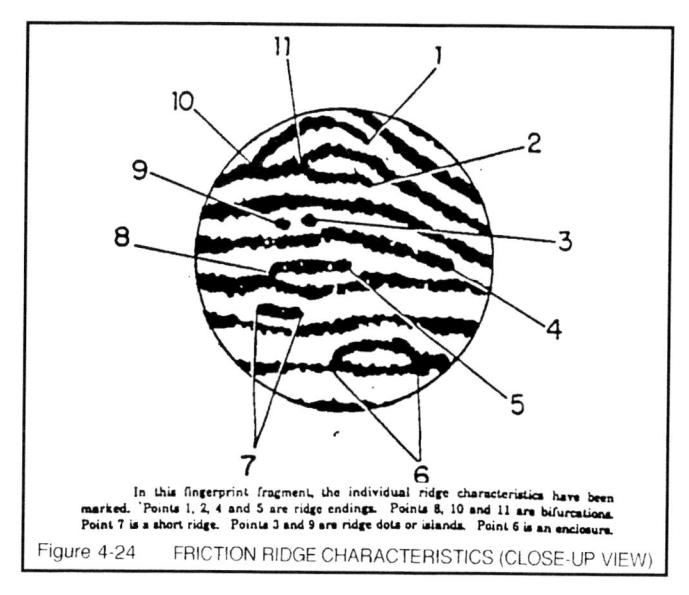

Figure 4-24    FRICTION RIDGE CHARACTERISTICS (CLOSE-UP VIEW)

In this fingerprint fragment, the individual ridge characteristics have been marked. Points 1, 2, 4 and 5 are ridge endings. Points 8, 10 and 11 are bifurcations. Point 7 is a short ridge. Points 3 and 9 are ridge dots or islands. Point 6 is an enclosure.

Figure 4-25    COMPARISON OF LATENT (L) AND INKED (R) FINGERPRINTS

## CRIME SCENE SCENARIO-"ACCIDENT, SUICIDE, OR HOMICIDE?"
### -PART THREE: LATENT FINGERPRINTS-

Various evidence has been gathered and described in Chapter 2 and 3 in the on-going **CRIME SCENE SCENARIO**. Latent fingerprints were discovered on the rear door to the garage, on the outside of the back window and window sill, on the barrel of the revolver, and on the single cartridge casing. The suspect had to touch the 6 foot fence to climb over it, but no prints were found on the porous cedar fence boards.

The revolver was labeled, placed in a plastic bag, sealed in an evidence box, and taken to the police crime lab where four different techniques were used to retrieve the latent prints on the barrel and the cartridge casing.

First, the gun and cartridge casing were fumed in a cyanoacrylic fuming chamber using peel-open Hard Evidence Pouches by Loctite (super glue also works well in this process) (Figure 4-8). The cyanoacrylic chemical reacts with the residues in the fingerprints to produce a hardened, whitish visible impression. Second, the 'hardened' fingerprints were dusted with a magnetic fluorescent powder using an improved magnetic powder applicator which uses a strong magnet to hold the powder on its tip. This allows the forensic technician to 'lightly' dust the 'hardened' latent fingerprint without disturbing the ridge patterns (Figure 4-5).

The third technique involved the use of an ultraviolet or laser light source and a 35 mm camera with a close-up lens to photograph the prints as they fluoresce the ridge pattern under the different wavelengths of light. The technician wears protective glasses to shield the eyes from harmful electromagnetic radiation (Figures 4-19 and 4-20). Once the third technique is completed, the 'hardened' prints were dusted with black fingerprint powder, and a 3M Poly Tape was used to lift the prints. The tape (which stretches and conforms to curved surfaces) with its 'lifted' prints was then placed on a standard white 3 inch by 5 inch Latent Print Backing Card (Figure 4-7). Copies were produced and sent to the various state and federal fingerprint agencies.

The suspect, Eric Bendor was fingerprinted at the police station and later identified by fingerprint analysis as Steve Sorensen, age 19. The computer generated search had returned four very close possibilities. These were physically compared to Eric Bendor's fingerprints which were taken at the police station. He had been arrested on three prior occasions for disorderly conduct and defacing public property with no convictions. His fingerprints matched those recovered from the back garage door, the window glass and the window sill. However, his prints did not match those 'lifted' from the barrel of the revolver. The revolver prints were submitted to the state and national fingerprint registry for identification. Another strange turn of events occurred when there was gun powder residue found only on the palms of Sorensen's hands. Gun powder residue was also found on the inside of his brown silk shirt.

SUGGESTED READINGS-

Allison, H.C. *Personal Identification.* Boston: Holbrook Press, 1973.

Burnes, K.R. and Maples, W.R. "Estimation of Age from Individual Adult Teeth." *Journal of Forensic Science* 21(2):343, 1976.

Cowger, J. *Friction Ridge Skin.* New York: Elsevier, 1983.

Dalrymple, B.E. "Case Analysis of Fingerprint Detection by Laser." *Journal of Forensic Science* 24(3):586, 1979.

Kobus, H.J., et. al. "Two Simple Staining Procedures Which Improve the Contrast and Ridge Detail of Fingerprints Developed with 'Super Glue' (Cyanoacrylate Ester)." *Forensic Sci.* 23:233-244, 1983.

Lampton, C. *DNA Fingerprinting.* New York: Franklin Watts, 1991.

Menzel, E.R., et. al. "Laser Detection of Latent Fingerprints: Treatment of Glue Containing Cyanoacrylate Ester." *Journal of Forensic Science* 28(2):307-317, 1983.

Menzel, E.R. and Fox, K.E. "Laser Detection of Latent Fingerprints: Preparation of Fluorescent Dusting Powders and the Feasibility of a Portable System." *Journal of Forensic Science* 25(1):150-153, 1980.

Reichardt, G.J., et. al. "A Conventional Method for Lifting Latent Fingerprints from Human Skin Surfaces." *Journal of Forensic Science* 23(1):135-141, 1978.

Richardson, L. and Kade, H. "Readable Fingerprints from Mummified or Putrefied Specimens." *Journal of Forensic Science* 17(2):325-328, 1972.

Trowell, F. "A Method for Fixing Latent Fingerprints Developed with Iodine." *Journal Forensic Science Society* 15(3):189-195, 1975.

# -CHAPTER FIVE-
# BODY FLUIDS

One of the negative aspects of crime investigation involves the study of body fluids. The crime scene often involves injury and death. Blood and other biological fluids are present at most crime scenes where violence has occurred. Blood, saliva, tears, perspiration, pus, semen, and human milk can all provide the investigator with important identity information. There are potential hazards when working with body fluids. Hepatitis and the HIV virus are two very good reasons for this concern. Surgical gloves need to be worn by any individuals who handle any body fluids whether these fluids are at the crime scene or at the laboratory.

The body fluids of the victim, as well as those of the suspect, can provide vital clues. The crime lab has not progressed to the point which would allow for a positive identification of an individual on the basis of body fluids alone. Even with the advancements in DNA fingerprinting, the courts and the general population are not yet convinced of its reliability. Fingerprinting, because of its universal use around the world, will remain the mainstay of positive identification, at least until there is a more general acceptance of DNA fingerprinting.

The collection of samples of body fluids and whether they will be useful to the forensic lab analyst depends on a number of factors. Blood and semen are the most common body fluids found at the crime scene. Body fluids which have not yet dried need to be collected as quickly as possible to provide purity and to prevent the degradation of the sample. Body fluids which have dried need to be removed from the object in question and sent to the crime lab.

There have been advancements in blood analysis which have made it possible to further subgroup the four basic blood groups (see chapter 3 for a table of blood type percentages in the human population). Blood type O occurs in 40 out of every 100 persons (about 40% of all people). With further subgroupings (the identification of additional blood proteins on red blood cells) a type O person can be given a probability factor of one in 10,000 persons which is one hundredth of one percent. This would increase the identity factor considerably.

## SECRETORS AND NONSECRETORS

A field that is becoming more important is forensic serology. Since blood is present at most violent crime scenes, it can be studied to understand a sequence of events at the crime scene. It can also be used to link a suspect with the crime scene or with a particular object found at the crime scene. The success of forensic serology largely depends on the methods and techniques used in the field to collect and preserve samples of blood and other fluids.

All people have either blood type A, B, AB, or O. The factors (certain proteins) which make it possible to distinguish blood type are present in every type of cell in the body. In some cases these factors are present in enough quantity in saliva, semen, tears, urine, and perspiration to allow the crime lab to determine the blood type of the individual. Blood type is the best and easiest method of establishing what is known as type classification. When blood is not available, however, there are other methods to learn the blood type of the victims and suspects.

Individuals whose body fluids can be blood typed are known as secretors. From 65% to 80% of the population are secretors. The remainder of the population are known as nonsecretors whose body fluids cannot be blood typed. It is important to note that both groups, secretors and nonsecretors, can be blood typed using their blood. Saliva, because of the high incidence of typing factors, is the easiest of the body fluids to blood type. Semen is also a fairly good source for blood type. Urine, tears, and perspiration are less suitable for blood type analysis because they contain lower concentrations of blood typing factors. Crime labs have been able to identify blood type groups from the saliva left on a glass or cigarette and even from the perspiration found in the fabric of a garment.

## LABORATORY POTENTIAL FOR BLOOD ANALYSIS

Because blood samples are collected in different forms, laboratories must be prepared to process the blood in different ways. Also, the circumstances of blood collection may vary (i.e., blood drawn from a bleeding wound and blood drawn from a victim who is not bleeding) and these special circumstances must be taken into account before the blood analysis is conducted. The blood lab needs to know what information is sought by the crime investigator in order to determine what type of test to conduct. The following is a table which helps the lab technician determine whether a wet or dry sample will furnish certain information:

| Blood information desired by investigator | Wet Samples | Dry Samples |
|---|---|---|
| 1. Ascertain that the sample is blood | X | X |
| 2. Determine if the blood is human or animal | X | X |
| 3. Determine the type and subgroups | X | X |
| 4. Determine the alcohol content of the blood | X | |
| 5. Determine if blood is venous, fetal, or menstrual | X | |
| 6. Determine if drugs are present in the blood | X | |
| 7. Determine possible ways blood was deposited | X | X |

## BLOOD AND BLOODSTAINS

Blood analysis is used as evidence in court in a variety of ways. Although blood type is not an indicator of a positive identification of an individual, it can be used as a positive exclusion of a person who is under suspicion for a crime. Blood may be collected in fluid form at the crime scene from a pool of blood. Blood may be collected from the victim whether alive or dead. Blood may even be collected in the form of dried blood found in fabric or on an object. The location of blood and bloodstains is sometimes very obvious. However, there are many places for a drop of blood to 'hide' which requires special techniques and at times special chemicals to locate.

## BLOOD SAMPLING PROCEDURES

Since blood begins to clot in about 3 to 4 minutes of exposure to the air. Blood turns from bright red to a brownish-red color when it is drying. Blood is a dark brown color when it is completely dry. If there is contamination, blood may appear to be blue, green or even black in color. Color, then, does not always provide a clear-cut identification for blood. The crime investigator must be trained to look for other physical characteristics of blood. Blood is absorbed by porous materials like fabric or soft, unfinished wood in a particular manner leaving a dull, dark brown appearance. Blood which has dried on a hard surface (like a wooden floor) will exhibit a glossy appearance if light is shined at a low angle (known as oblique lighting) along the surface of the floor.

Wounded suspects may wipe blood from their hands or wound with paper towels or may wash their hands in the bathroom sink. Blood search should include soap and soap dishes, sinks, and even the p-trap beneath the sinks. If blood has been wiped up or mopped, investigators must even search for cracks in the flooring where blood may have been trapped. (Figures 5-1 and 5-2).

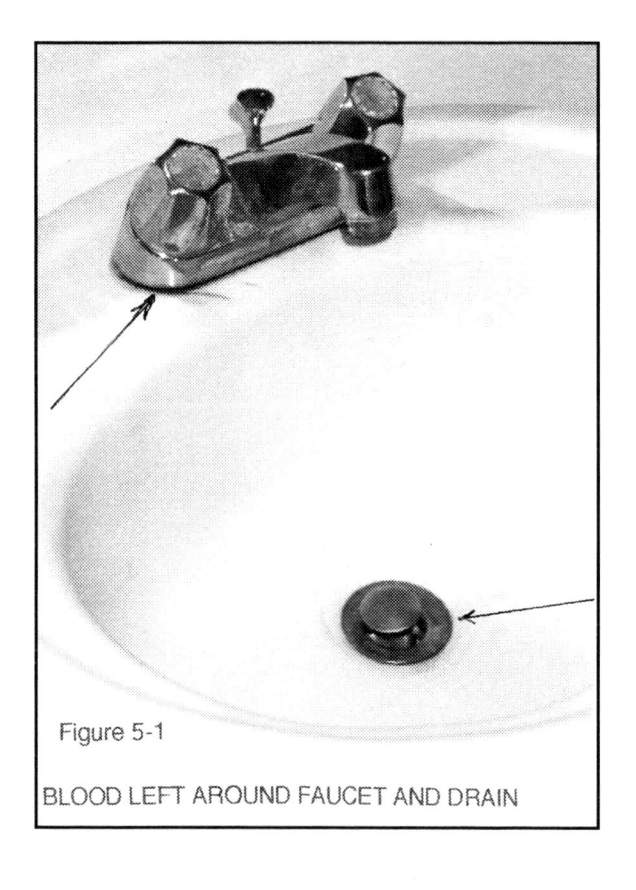

Figure 5-1

BLOOD LEFT AROUND FAUCET AND DRAIN

Figure 5-2

P-TRAP BENEATH SINK MAY CONTAIN SAMPLE OF SUSPECT'S BLOOD

# BLOODSTAIN AND CRIME SCENE RECONSTRUCTION

The shape and appearance of bloodstains may provide vital information to help the crime scene investigator reconstruct the crime scene scenario. Spots of blood can be used to determine their direction and provide an estimate of their velocity, angle of impact, and, sometimes, the distance fallen from their source to their place of landing. If blood falls straight down for a short distance, the drops of blood are generally smaller and thicker than drops falling straight down from greater heights. The diameter of a blood spot provides very little evidence in actual distance fallen. Distance fallen is determined by the type of edge pattern left when the drop hits a surface. The edge pattern produced by a falling drop of blood is composed of even edge serrations at 20 cm, larger serrations called scallops at 40 cm, scallops with tiny spikes at 60 cm, and scallops with spikes and small outward splatters at 80 or more cm. (Figures 5-3 to 5-6). The type of surface struck by blood drops determines the type of edge pattern. Blood dropping from heights greater than 100 cm will produce pronounced splattering on surfaces which are not smooth. Blood dropping from 100 feet onto a smooth surface (such as glass) will produce a smooth edge pattern with no edge serrations or splattering. Blood drops may vary from a circular pattern to less symmetrical oval shapes (usually due to hitting a surface from an angle). Both will exhibit a symmetrical serrated or scalloped edge. The distance blood falls may help the investigator decide whether a victim was standing or seated when wounded. Depending upon the individual circumstances, the blood drop pattern may shed light on a homicide or a suicide.

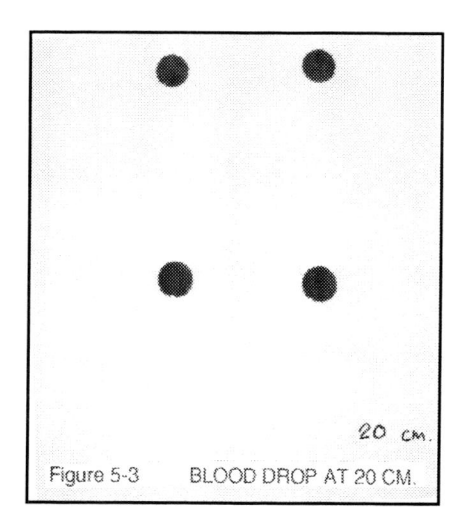

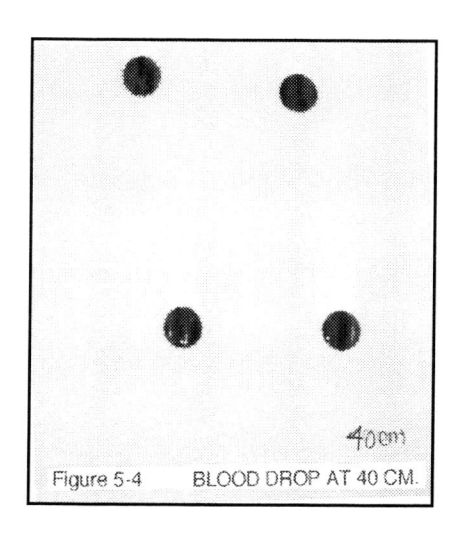

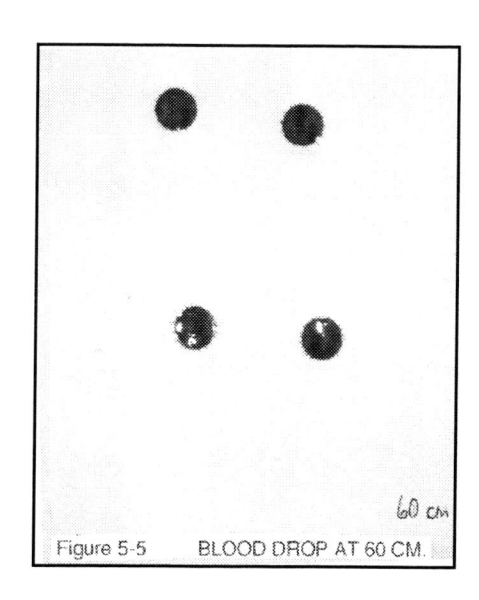

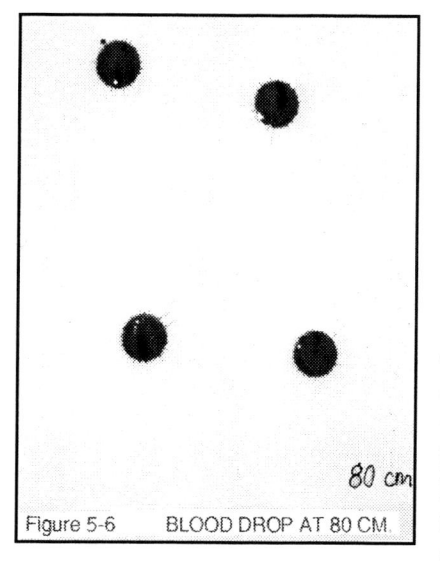

Figure 5-3    BLOOD DROP AT 20 CM.

Figure 5-4    BLOOD DROP AT 40 CM.

Figure 5-5    BLOOD DROP AT 60 CM.

Figure 5-6    BLOOD DROP AT 80 CM.

Blood which falls at an angle due to some force other than gravity alone, usually have a characteristic bowling pin shape. The smaller end of the pin indicates the direction of force. The greater the force, the more the shape appears like an exclamation point with the point or dot displaying the direction of the force. This kind of shape could be produced by the swinging action of a bloody instrument or hand. (Figures 5-7 and 5-8).

Very small blood stains (less than 1/8 inch in diameter) may be the result of an overcast or splatter resulting from an impact. Generally, the higher the velocity of the impact (such as a bullet would produce) the smaller the size of the drops (as small as 1/1000 inch in diameter).

The position and shape of bloodstains on the victim can be helpful in determining if the victim had been moved. Any blood flow not due to gravity may indicate that the body was moved after the wound was inflicted.

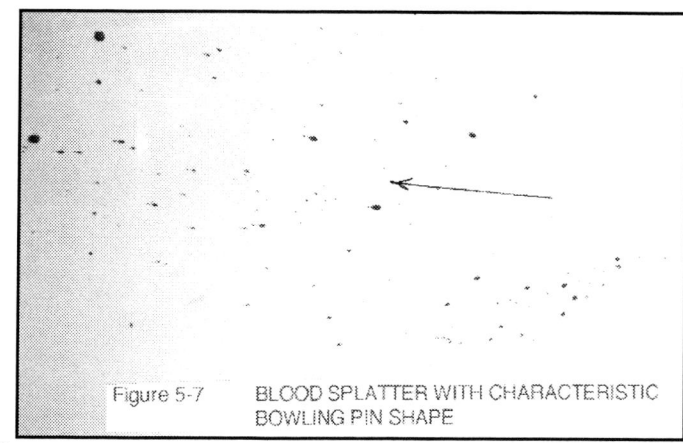

Figure 5-7    BLOOD SPLATTER WITH CHARACTERISTIC BOWLING PIN SHAPE

Also, blood found in areas which are not near the victim may be the assailant's blood. These might supply information as to the nature and location of the wound of the suspect. The amount of blood may also provide some information as the the extent of the assailant's wound. Back spatter of blood may result from a bullet wound. The range of back spatter is less than the spatter of blood which accompanies the movement of the bullet.

Lividity is a condition where the blood settles to the lowest portion of the body after blood stops circulating. This is due to the effect of gravity on the blood. There is a blue to reddish appearance on the skin in about one hour reaching a full color in about three or four hours after death. Bruising (with the characteristic black, blue, or yellow marks) can be confused with lividity. The discoloration will not occur if there is pressure applied on the body by an object or piece of clothing. If the body is moved during the three to four hour period of time, the original color pattern may be altered or disappear and new discoloration patterns may appear. If the body is moved after the three or four hour time period, the original color patterns will remain and weaker new patterns will appear. After 12 hours, there are usually no new livid stains formed. Also, if there was a large blood volume loss at death, the livid stains will usually be very weak.

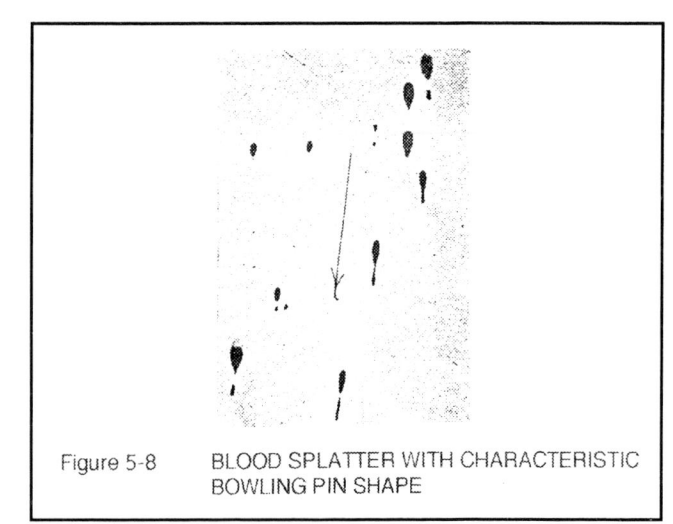

Figure 5-8   BLOOD SPLATTER WITH CHARACTERISTIC BOWLING PIN SHAPE

Besides lividity, the path of blood on a body can help to determine position at the time of death and if the body has been moved after the time of death. Analysis of bloodstain pattern, lividity discoloration, and the location and direction the blood travels can all be used to help reconstruct the events at the crime scene.

## METHODS OF COLLECTING WET AND DRY SAMPLE OF BLOOD

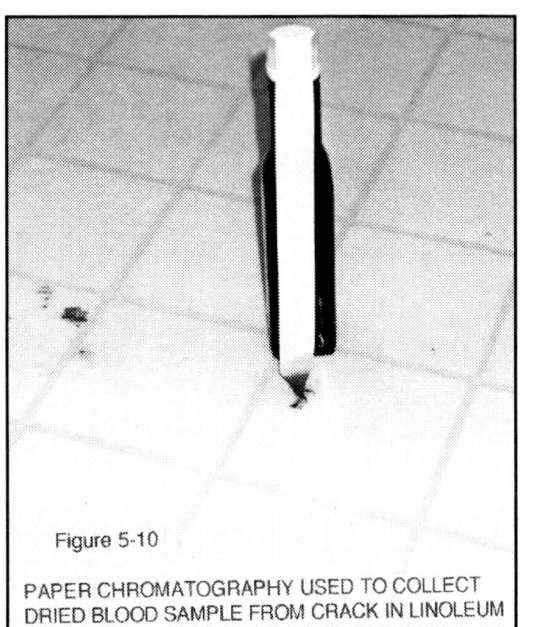

All articles found at the crime scene, including guns, knives, spent bullets, or other objects possibly used to inflict a wound, may possibly have traces of blood on them. These items must be handled very carefully to prevent contamination as well as to preserve any fingerprints.

Figure 5-9   PAPER CHROMATOGRAPHY USED TO COLLECT DRIED BLOOD SAMPLE FROM KITCHEN RANGE

A clean razor blade is used to remove dried blood from an object. The razor blade and dried blood sample are placed in a clean piece of paper and placed in a marked envelope. Some technicians use a scalpel for this procedure and have eliminated including the blade because of the danger to other lab technicians. A sample of the unstained surface material near the recovered bloodstain should be removed and placed in a separate container to be used as a comparison standard. This will help the laboratory to prove that the results of the tests performed were brought about by the blood and not by the material on which it was deposited.

Figure 5-10   PAPER CHROMATOGRAPHY USED TO COLLECT DRIED BLOOD SAMPLE FROM CRACK IN LINOLEUM

Small dry stains which cannot be scraped off may be removed by wiping the surface with a small piece of moist, clean filter paper. The filter paper is then placed in a test tube, sealed, and sent immediately to the laboratory. Blood in cracks and on hard absorbent surfaces can be collected by using wet filter paper which is allowed to lay on the stained area. A strip of filter paper which is attached to an upright can or bottle with a piece of tape at the top is allowed to lay over the stain area. A small amount of distilled water added to the stain area will migrate up the filter paper carrying the blood with it in the process. The filter strip is removed from the upright object and placed into a marked test tube. (Figures 5-9 to 5-11). The location of all bloodstains is carefully recorded in the crime scene sketch report and on the evidence container.

Figures 5-12 through 5-18 illustrate the blood collection process at the crime scene. Figure 5-13 shows a crime scene forensic expert collecting a dried blood sample from the carpet using a scalpel to cut the sample and a portion of the carpet. The technician then places the collected blood sample on a glassine sheet (7.5 cm by 7.5 cm) which is folded and placed in a coin envelope or other suitable envelope (Figure 5-14).

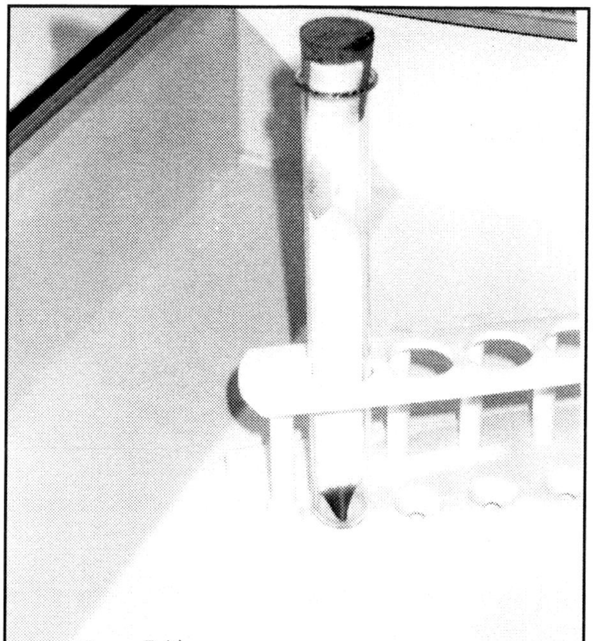

Figure 5-11
SEALED TEST TUBE CONTAINING CHROMATOGRAPHY PAPER WITH COLLECTED BLOOD SAMPLE

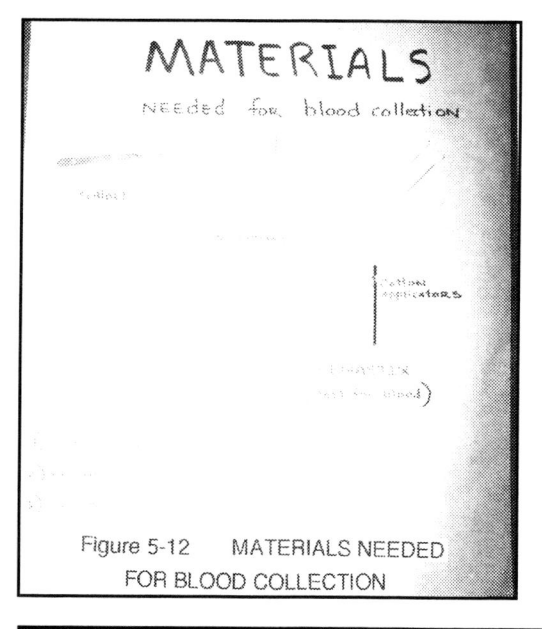

Figure 5-12   MATERIALS NEEDED FOR BLOOD COLLECTION

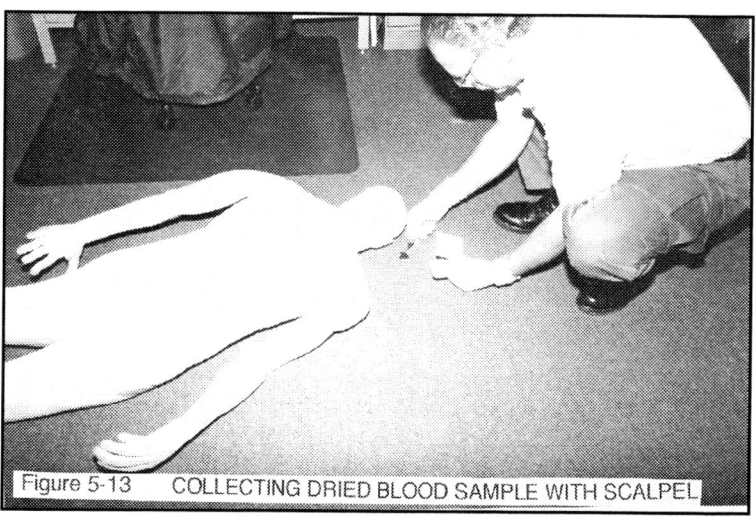

Figure 5-13   COLLECTING DRIED BLOOD SAMPLE WITH SCALPEL

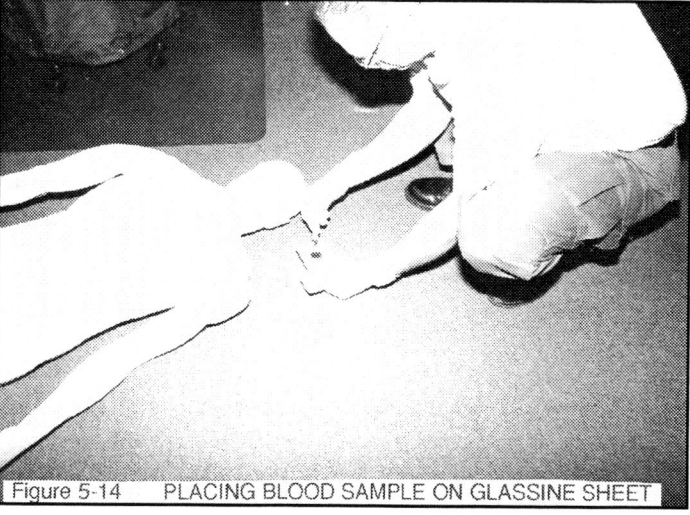

Figure 5-14   PLACING BLOOD SAMPLE ON GLASSINE SHEET

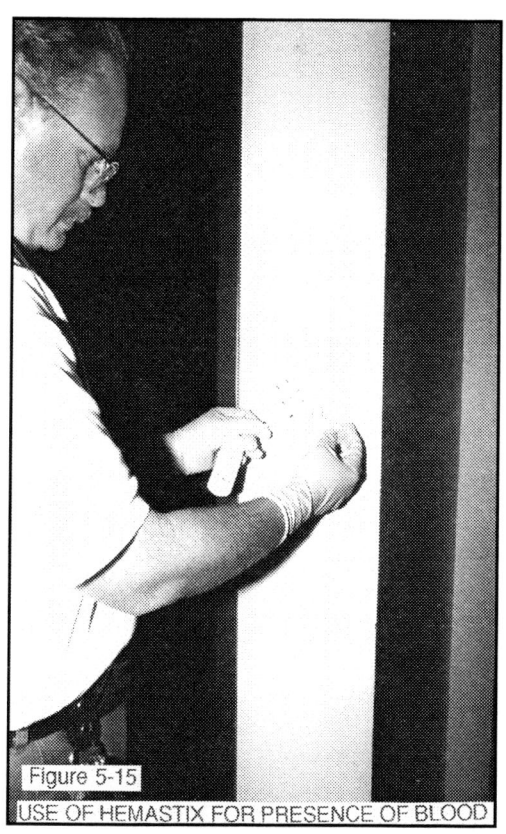

Figure 5-15   USE OF HEMASTIX FOR PRESENCE OF BLOOD

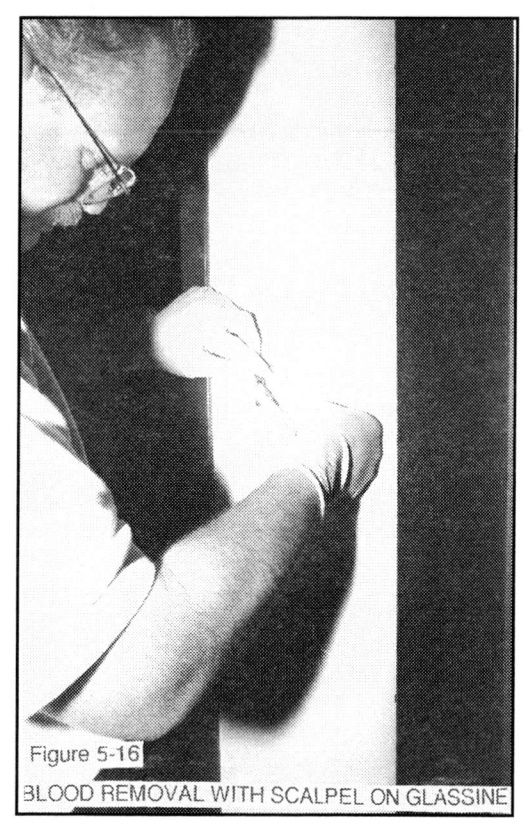

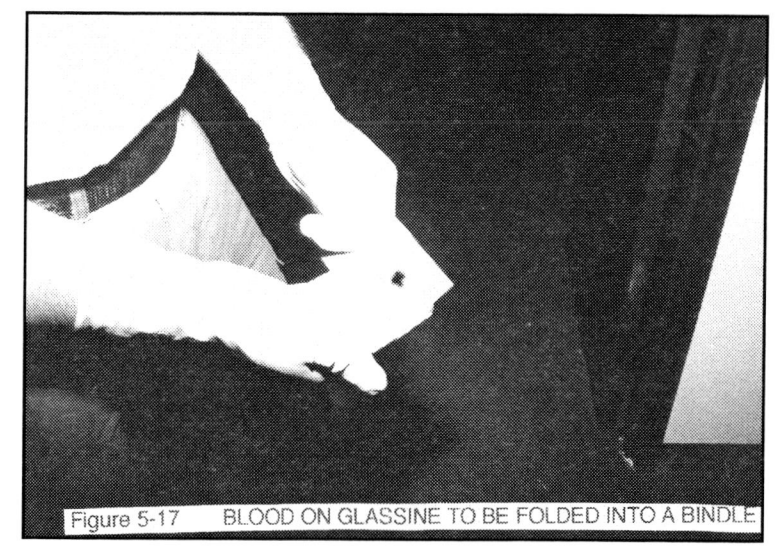

Figure 5-16
BLOOD REMOVAL WITH SCALPEL ON GLASSINE

Figure 5-17  BLOOD ON GLASSINE TO BE FOLDED INTO A BINDLE

Figure 5-15 illustrates how to determine if suspicious marks are blood. The technician is applying a drop of distilled water to a suspicious mark while placing a Hemastix to the moistened mark. The Hemastix turns a dark bluish-green when blood is present. The determination of the kind of blood (human or animal) and the blood type will have to be made in a blood laboratory after the sample is collected. Two collection methods are shown (Figures 5-16 to 5-18). The first method shows a technician using a scalpel to physically remove the blood with a portion of the wall surface which is then placed on a glassine sheet, folded in a specific pattern called a bindle, and stored in a coin envelope for analysis. The second method shows a technician using a cotton swab and a drop of distilled water to moisten the blood mark.

The collected blood on the cotton swab is folded in a glassine sheet and also place in an envelope for analysis. Samples of the surface from which the blood was collected are also taken and used as a control or comparison standard by the laboratory. The lab technician is then able to determine if the surface material had produced any effect upon the collected sample.

There are a number chemical tests to determine the location of suspected blood when there is the possibility that the suspect washed and cleaned the scene of the crime. Luminol, leuco malachite green, phenolphthalein, and orthotolidine are chemicals which help to screen surfaces for the presence of blood. Some of these chemicals require special handling to prevent harm to the technician. Each chemical reacts with blood in a characteristic manner (luminol will luminesce under certain lighting conditions and orthotolidine will turn a greenish-blue color when it reacts with blood).

Figure 5-18  BLOOD COLLECTED WITH A COTTON-TIPPED SWAB

Bloodstains found in soil need to be collected in a glass container, marked and recorded, and sent to the lab as soon as possible since bacteria in the soil will destroy the value of the evidence.

Wet blood samples are collected with a medicine dropper and placed in a glass test tube. An equal amount of a saline (salt) solution or a commercial anti-coagulant (such as EDTA or ethylenediamine tetracetic acid) is added to the blood sample before it is sealed. This procedure helps to preserve the blood. Blood taken from the deceased should be collected from the heart or major blood vessel. If the amount of wet blood is very small, a piece of the material or object is removed with the wet sample of blood and placed in a marked and sealed container. A sample of material with no blood is also removed to be used as a comparison standard by the laboratory. Another option for the crime scene investigator is to allow the blood to dry and use the dry blood removal method described above.

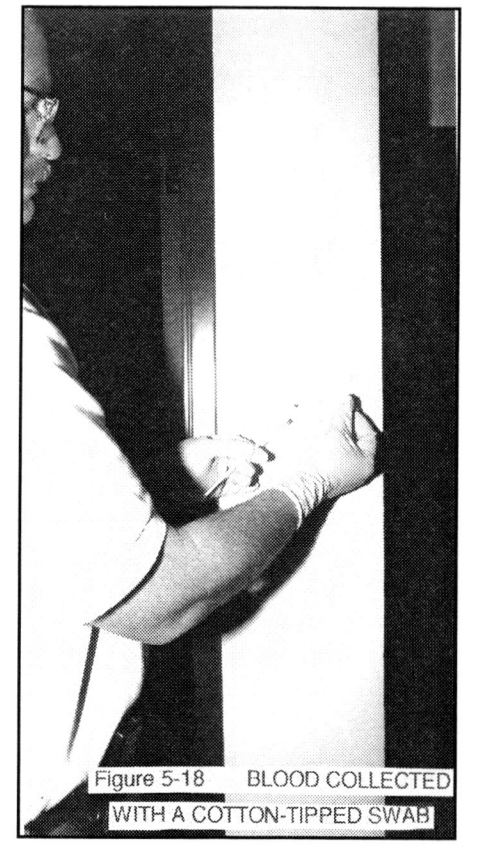

Clothing with wet stains must be wrapped so that the stains are not transferred to other areas of the garment. If transfer of blood occurs from mishandling of the victim's clothing, it will not be possible to determine the position of the body during the time the bleeding occurred. A clean piece of paper is used to prevent blood transfer from one item of clothing to another during transportation to the lab. Care should also be taken to prevent loss of hair, fiber, or other fluid contamination during transportation to the lab. Blood samples from both the victim and the suspects are important for the lab to gain the maximum evidence value from blood and bloodstains.

USE OF DNA FINGERPRINT ANALYSIS

DNA (deoxyribonucleic acid) is a chemical which forms genes. The human genetic pattern has about 100,000 genes which form the 23 pairs of chromosomes. The spiral structure of the DNA molecule is constructed from four interlocking chemical subunits known as bases. Each gene is composed of 10,000 to 150,000 of these interlocking base pairs. Ninety-nine percent of the 3 billion base pairs in human DNA are identical. DNA typing isolates the relatively few variable pairs. These regions contain short DNA sequences that are repeated in tandem a variable number of times from person to person. Although the repeat sequence (or stuttering) remains the same in all people, the number of repetitions varies. This stuttering might occur ten times in one person and 300 times in another. When these stuttering regions are isolated out of the DNA chain, the length of the fragments varies with the number of repetitions.

In one type of genetic analysis, DNA is extracted from saliva, blood, semen, hair roots, or bone. It is then snipped into fragments using restriction enzymes that act like molecular scissors. The enzymes recognize certain sequences in the base pattern and cut the DNA molecule at those specific points. The resulting mixture of fragments are then placed in wells located at one end of an agarose gel and an electric current is applied. The DNA, which is negatively charged, moves through the gel toward the positive electrode. The shorter fragments move through the gel more quickly than the longer fragments and end up closer to the positive electrode. Radioactive probes are then used to bind to any fragment containing a specific repeat sequence. The positions of these sequences are recorded as dark bands on x-ray film. Different probes can be used to identify different repeat sequences. If the positions of all the variable fragments of the sample match those from a suspect, a computer analysis calculates the probability of such a match occurring by chance.

The public and court resistance to the DNA fingerprint process coupled with the laboratory technique differences has prevented its full potential. Eventually, according to a number of prominent scientists, the DNA fingerprint will become accurate enough to duplicate the accuracy of the fingerprint.

SEMINAL STAINS

Seminal stains are usually associated with sex offenses (rape) but may also be present in other crime scenes. Wet seminal stains provide the lab technician with a better chance of analysis than the dry and fragile seminal stains. The same precautions and procedures apply for the collection of seminal stains as in blood sample collection. Both the victim and the suspect's garments should be carefully handled to prevent contamination and stain transfer to other portions of the clothing.

There is a newer technique which allows the crime scene investigator to utilize a lighting technique which causes an iridescence to manifest in the seminal stains. A Wood's lamp (which is a source of ultraviolet light) is used to locate seminal stains. This makes it much easier to locate and then collect samples for lab analysis.

**CRIME SCENE SCENARIO-"ACCIDENT, SUICIDE, OR HOMICIDE?"**
-PART FOUR: BLOOD AND TESTIMONY-

Detective Dodge conducted interviews with on-lookers and neighbors. The 911 call was placed by a Mr. Rodriguez, who lives at 9450 Myers Road, at 11:30 am on the day of the crime. Mr. Rodriguez' home is directly across the street from the crime scene residence. Mr. Rodriguez had seen three male teenagers in the open garage earlier in the morning. When he heard loud talking and laughing, he looked out his living room window. He had looked long enough to be able to give a general description of each youth. One youth was short and stocky with short blond hair. He was wearing a white t-shirt, shorts, and white tennis shoes. The second youth was about 5'- 8" and had black hair. He was wearing a green shirt, blue jeans, and white tennis shoes. The third youth was about 5'- 10" and had medium length brown hair. He was wearing a dark colored shirt, blue jeans, and white tennis shoes. At 11:28 am Mr. Rodriguez heard a single gun shot from across the street. He quickly walked to his living room window and noticed one of the youths running away from the open garage in a westerly direction down Myers road. Mr. Rodriguez immediately called 911 and reported a gun shot. The dispatcher relayed the information which was received by detectives Dodge and Summer who were only five minutes away from the reported location. The events of the initial contact with the crime scene are recorded in chapter two. Dodge continued his interview with Mr. Rodriguez.

Dodge asked, "Can you describe the youth who ran out of the garage and down the street?" This was the first indication that there might be two suspects to search for.

"The boy, who ran out of the garage, stopped in the middle of the driveway and looked up and down the street several times," replied Mr. Rodriguez. "He looked scared and had trouble making up his mind which way to run."

Dodge took a picture of Bill Morganson out of his notebook. "Is this the youth you saw running out of the garage?"

"Yeah, that's the boy," insisted Mr. Rodriguez. "Only, he was wearing a green shirt and blue jeans and his black hair was a little longer."

Detective Dodge returned to his car and radioed this new information to the dispatcher at 12:23 pm. He gave a detailed description of two possible suspects based on information given by the Morganson's and Mr. Rodriguez.

Dodge continued his door-to-door search. Since it was in the middle of the day there were very few people at home. Additional information gained from witnesses and on-lookers confirmed the account reported by Mr. Rodriguez. Another on-looker (a neighbor by the name of Mrs. Blake) lived at 9461 Myers Road, which was three houses away from the crime scene residence on the same side of the block. Mrs. Blake was able to give a good description of all three youths. She had seen and spoken with the Morganson youth on many occasions. Her description matched the school pictures supplied by the Morganson couple. Bill Morganson was about 5'- 8", Caucasian, short, styled black hair and brown eyes. She had only noticed a dark brown haired youth a few times as she was walking home from the local shopping center at the west end of Myers road. All she could add was that he was taller than Bill. She had also seen a third youth on several occasions with the Morganson youth at the crime scene residence. Although she did not know his name, she was able to provide an accurate physical description. He was Caucasian, shorter than Bill, had blond hair cut extremely short, always wore shorts, a t-shirt and tennis shoes. She thought they all went to the same high school.

The splattered blood near the weight bench was photographed. Initial analysis indicates the direction taken by the blood splatters was toward the front door of the garage. There were two partial shoeprints in blood near the back door and seven shoeprints in blood reaching from the weight bench to the front door of the garage. These visible shoeprints were photographed. Since they were imprinted in blood which had since dried, they were dusted with a fingerprint powder and lifted with a clear 3-M tape. The tapes, which contained the 'lifted' shoeprints, were placed on clean white paper. These samples would be returned to the crime lab and photographed.

Dodge returned to the crime scene at 1:17 pm and found his partner and officer Kenneth Grand, Senior Forensics Technician for the department, examining the victim's body.

"Where have you been?" asked Summer. "They just picked up a youth who matched one of your descriptions!"

"That's what I call service!" retorted Dodge. "One down, and one to go!"

"One to go?" questioned Summer.

"A neighbor by the name of Rodriguez saw three youths here this morning and reported seeing one of them run out the front of the garage just after the gun was fired."

"This is getting too complicated," Summer insisted, "I'll never get any time off!" She motioned for Dodge to take a close look at the wound site on the victim's chest.

"It's a bullet wound, all right," interrupted Officer Grand, "I estimate, from the amount of powder burn, that the barrel of the gun wasn't more than five feet from his chest."

"Could it have been an accident, or maybe a suicide?" asked Dodge.

"Don't know," replied Grand. "We had better treat this as a homicide until we have more evidence." "So far, we haven't found any note left by the deceased."

Summer looked up just as the County Coroner's vehicle drove up into the driveway. It was 1:21 pm. "Do we have everything we need?"

Grand replied, "I think so, maybe I'll take a few more photographs from a reverse angle before they take the victim to the morgue." The body was signed over to the Coroner at 1:36 pm, and taken to the County morgue for autopsy, identification, and notification of next of kin.

The blood lab began their analysis early in the afternoon. A fiber from the torn piece of denim recovered from the wooden fence in the back yard of the crime scene was inserted into an agarose gel prepared over a gel-electrophoresis plate. The plate was inserted into a electrophoresis box and a direct electric current of 70 volts was applied for approximately two hours. The electric current was used to separate the different proteins in a blood group. A standard was used as a comparison or control. The electric current caused the molecules of protein to migrate through the gel. The lighter proteins travel faster than the heavier proteins and therefore migrate further through the gel. After the current was turned off, the gel was stained with a biologically reactive chemical specific for protein. The gel was then photographed. Analysis and measurement of different bands of protein produced requires a great deal of training and experience. A standard 'wet' blood test was conducted as well. Results of both tests revealed the blood to be type AB negative.

Similar blood lab testing was conducted on the fibers surrounding the tear in Sorensen's jeans. Type AB negative blood was found on the fibers. The torn piece of denim matched the missing piece of denim in Sorensen's jeans. There were trace amounts of type O positive blood found on the barrel and handle grips of the revolver. Samples from the garage yielded type O positive blood.

The blood recovered from the victim was type O positive. Blood recovered from the clothing of the victim was also O positive. Steve Sorensen's blood was typed as AB negative. Blood spatters on Sorensen's brown silk shirt were O positive. Blood recovered from the crime scene on the weight bench and the floor just surrounding the weight bench was O positive. Blood found on the garage floor near the back door and leading out the front of the garage was also O positive. A return to the crime scene by forensic technicians yielded a small sample of dried blood (O positive) on the doorknob of the back door of the garage.

SUGGESTED READING-

Culliford, B.J. *The Examination of Typing of Bloodstains in the Crime Laboratory.* U.S. Government Printing Office, 1971.

Eckert, W.G. and Hames, S.H. *Interpretation of Bloodstain Evidence at Crime Scene.* New York: Elsevier, 1989.

Gaensslen, R.E. "Blood sweat and tears . . . and, saliva and semen—The Forensic Serologist Provides Expert Identification of body Fluids." *Law Enforcement Communications* 23-30, February, 1980.

Gaensslen, R.E. *Sourcebook in Forensic Serology, Immunology, and Biochemistry.* U.S. Department of Justice, National Institute of Justice, U.S. Government Printing Office, 1983.

Hunt, A.C., et. al. "The Identification of Human bloodstains." *Journal of Forensic Medicine* 7: 112-130, 1960.

MacDonell, H.L. *Bloodstain Pattern Interpretation.* Corning, New York: Laboratory of Forensic Science, 1982.

MacDonell, H.L. *Flight Characteristics and Stain Patterns of Human Blood.* U.S. Department of Justice, 1971.

Zweidinger, R.A., et. al. "Photography of Bloodstains Visualized by Luminol." *Journal of Forensic Science* 18(4):296-302, 1973.page 48

# -CHAPTER SIX-
# TRACE MATERIALS

Trace evidence can be defined as materials that are small enough to be easily overlooked by a crime scene investigator. Because they are so small, trace materials can be exchanged through contact or transferred in the air by air currents. The major advantage of gathering trace evidence occurs when specific trace materials can be matched up with the suspect thus linking that person to the crime scene. Evidence standards become highly important in the collection, marking, analysis, and storage of trace materials. The Locard Exchange Principle states that it is highly improbable to come in contact with an environment without changing it in some small way. There will always be something added or something removed from it. The search for trace evidence is based, at least in part, on this concept.

## TRACE MATERIALS FOUND ON CLOTHING

Since the clothing of the suspect has a high probability of accumulating trace materials, it should be collected and submitted for lab analysis as soon as possible. The suspect should stand on a clean piece of white paper while undressing to catch any trace materials which should fall off to the floor. Each piece of clothing should be carefully folded and placed in a clean paper bag which has been properly labeled. After the suspect has undressed, the white paper should be carefully folded and placed in a paper bag. Any moisture or wet areas on the clothing must be allowed to air dry first before being placed in a paper bag. Plastic bags should not be used since they would promote the growth of mold. The suspect should sign his/her name on each paper bag.

The suspect should only be brought to the scene of a crime after the scene and the suspect have been searched. The suspect might otherwise claim that the trace evidence used to connect him/her to the crime scene was actually transferred or deposited at the time he/she was brought on the scene and not during the commission of the crime.

Recovery of the victim's clothing can be difficult. Trace materials on the clothing of the victim are particularly susceptible to contamination or loss at a hospital. Clothing is cut apart and sometimes thrown into a heap by hospital personnel in their attempt to save life. If the clothing has been piled up together it may be collected in one paper bag and sent to the lab for analysis.

Fragments of cloth and impressions of cloth in paint are important trace evidence. Impressions of cloth captured in paint, wax or other soft material are many times just as valuable as the cloth itself. Cloth fragments are photographed first using a ruler as a scale. Many cloth impressions involve hit-and-run automobile accidents. When cloth fragments are discovered, their position should be recorded before the cloth fragment is removed. Color, pattern of weave, type of material (if possible), size and shape and exact location should be recorded. When carefully removed, care should be taken to not fold the cloth fragment.

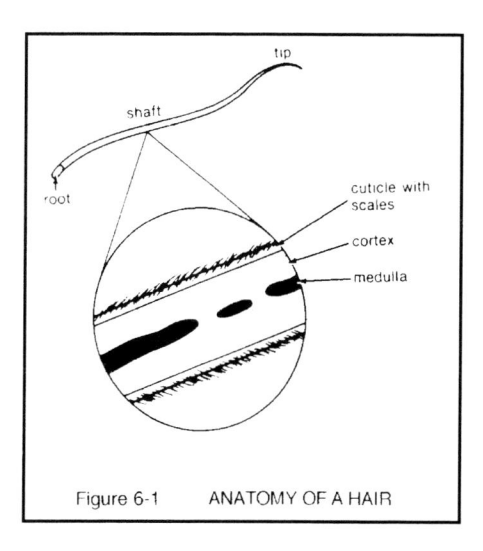

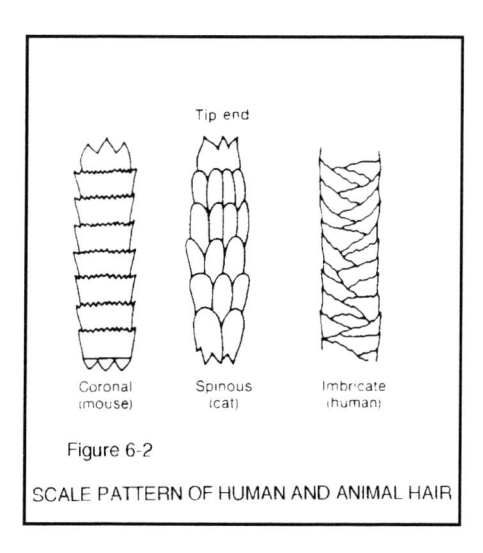

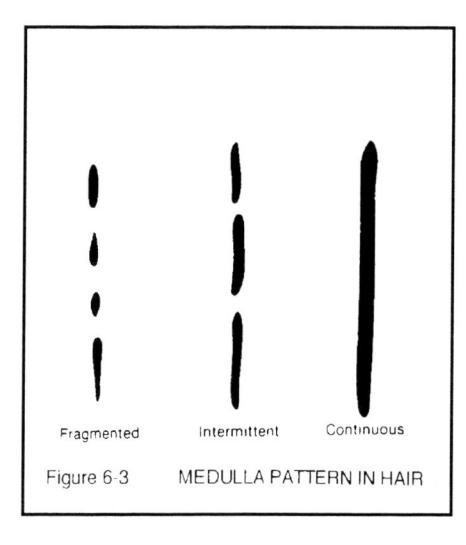

Figure 6-1  ANATOMY OF A HAIR

Figure 6-2  SCALE PATTERN OF HUMAN AND ANIMAL HAIR

Figure 6-3  MEDULLA PATTERN IN HAIR

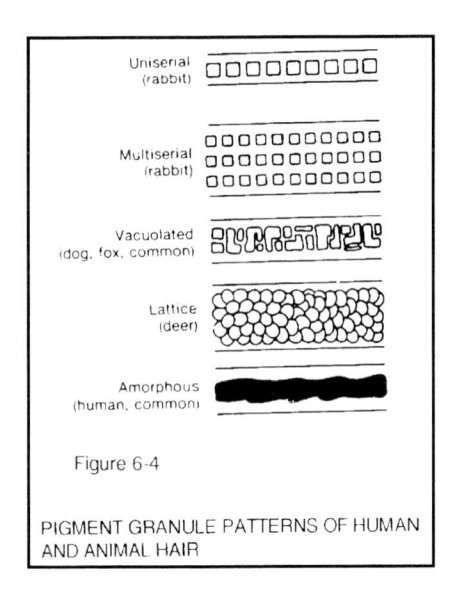

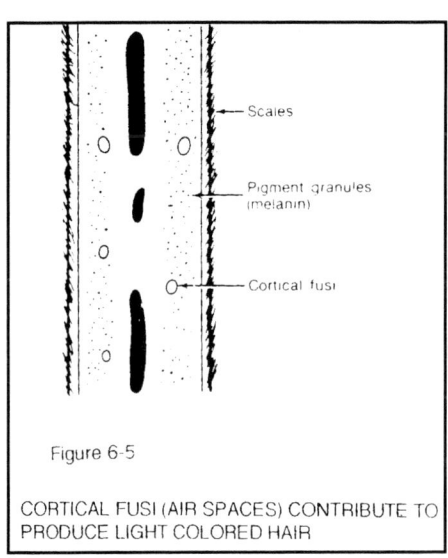

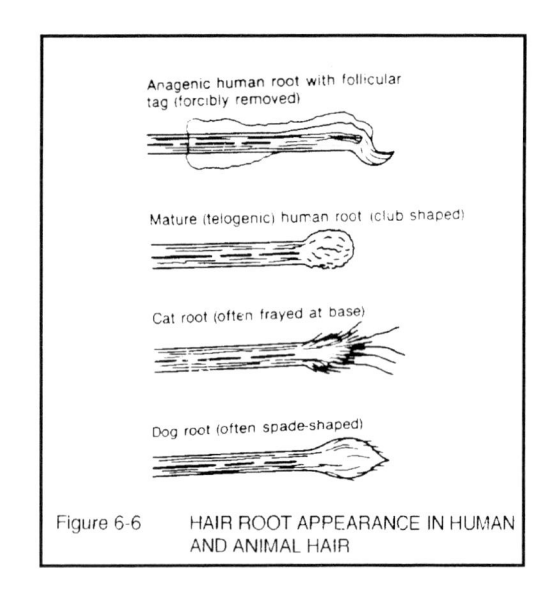

**Figure 6-4** PIGMENT GRANULE PATTERNS OF HUMAN AND ANIMAL HAIR

**Figure 6-5** CORTICAL FUSI (AIR SPACES) CONTRIBUTE TO PRODUCE LIGHT COLORED HAIR

**Figure 6-6** HAIR ROOT APPEARANCE IN HUMAN AND ANIMAL HAIR

## HAIR SAMPLES

Hair has a definite value in aiding the investigator in solving the crime. However, the evidence from hair is rarely conclusive. Only when hair is combined with other trace materials (blood and fibers) is its value enhanced.

The basic anatomy of a hair (Figures 6-1 to 6-6) consists of a **root** (proximal end), a central area called the **medulla** (which may or may not be present), the main shaft or **cortex** surrounding the medulla, the **cuticle** or scaly outer covering of the hair, and the **tip** (dorsal) end. Valuable trace evidence can collect on the surface of the hair. There is usually a very fine coat of oil on the surface of the hair.

Analysis of hair samples can inform the investigator if the hair is human or animal (Figures 6-7 and 6-8). The race of the individual, origination point on the body, whether the hair was forcibly removed or if it had been cut with a dull or sharp instrument, if the hair had been treated with a chemical dye or bleach, and whether the hair had been crushed or burned can all be determined by a lab analysis.

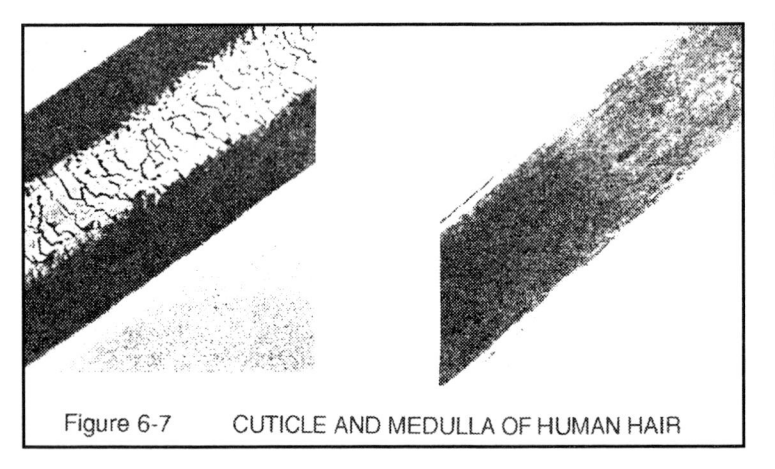

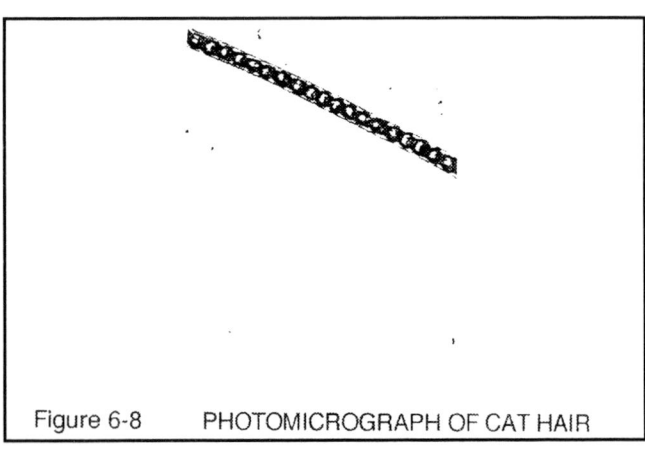

**Figure 6-7** CUTICLE AND MEDULLA OF HUMAN HAIR

**Figure 6-8** PHOTOMICROGRAPH OF CAT HAIR

Hair analysis can provide a positive conclusion that the hairs match and came from the individual whose hair exhibits the same microscopic characteristics as the matching hair. Another conclusion would be that the hairs are not similar and did not originate from the same individual or that no conclusion can be reached.

Hair found at a crime scene should be carefully removed with tweezers and placed in a clean container or folded into a clean piece of paper. Collection from both the victim and suspect is important since a comparison will have to be done in order establish a link between the victim and the suspect. Hair collected from the victim should include samples from the head (crown, temple, nape, beard, eyebrow), arm, underarm, chest, pubic region, and leg areas. About 40 hairs should be included from each area and they should be packaged separately. Hair should also be carefully removed and labeled which was near a wound. Hair collected from a living victim or suspect should be combed first and then pulled out by the root, if possible. About 20 hairs from each area listed above are collected. Standards should also be collected from pets which are part of the crime scene.

# FIBERS AND THREADS

Fragments of cloth evidence may yield individual as well as class characteristics. A common source can be verified when a portion of cloth is fitted physically with another piece of cloth (Figure 6-9). Fibers can be transferred by simple contact between two objects. Fibers may be found at point-of-entry, on furniture and rugs, on clothing and draperies or curtains, and hats. Cloth is comprised of small threads which are composed of tiny textile fibers.

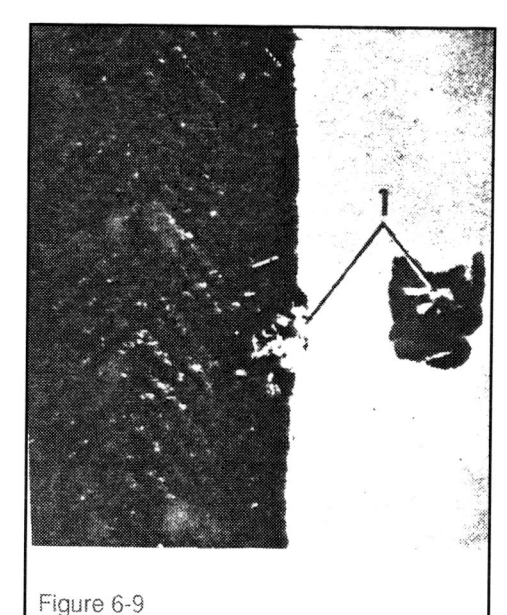

These fibers can be classified as mineral (glass and asbestos), animal (silk, wool, and fur), vegetable (cotton, linen, hemp, jute), or synthetic (rayon, nylon, Dacron, acetate). Fibers can be analyzed by a burn test, solvent/solubility test (using acetone, HCl, and sodium hypochlorite), stain test, and microscopic examination. By using a series of tests, the type of fiber can be determined. Burning fiber may give off a particular odor and leave a residue which is ash-like, brittle, or a hard bead. The solubility test determines if the fiber will dissolve in a particular solvent. The fiber identification stain will react in a predictable manner with different types of fiber. Finally, microscopic examination will reveal specific markings of the interior of the fiber, folding or twisting, and light transmittance quality (Figure 6-10 and 6-11).

Figure 6-9
FRAGMENT OF CLOTH FOUND ON VEHICLE MATCHES VICTIM'S CLOTH COAT

Figure 6-10 PHOTOMICROGRAPH OF COTTON FIBER

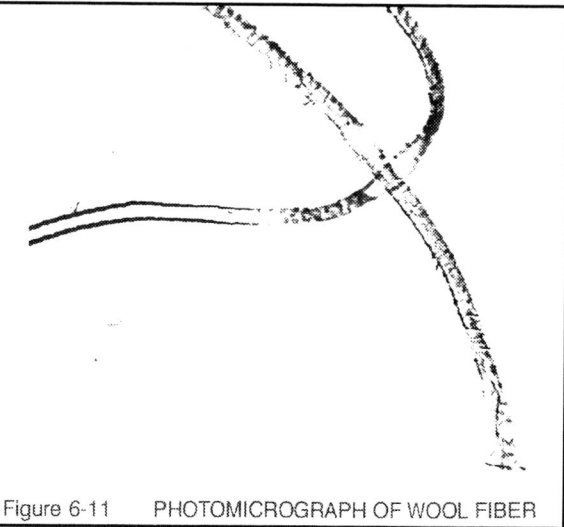

Figure 6-11 PHOTOMICROGRAPH OF WOOL FIBER

Fibers can provide important comparison evidence. When suspect's fibers are recovered from the clothing of a victim, the suspect can then be placed at the scene of the crime. Figure 6-12 shows the basic materials required to collect trace evidence: tape, disposable gloves, Petri dishes, and a marking pen. The forensic technician takes a five inch piece of tape and holds each end between the thumb and index finger (Figure 6-13). The technician then touches the tape to the surface and repeats this action for a number of times (Figure 6-14). The tape with collected trace evidence is then placed in a plastic Petri dish, covered, and labeled (Figures 6-15 and 6-16). One piece of tape is enough to cover one half of a victim's chest and abdomen or one half of a leg. Collected trace evidence is taken to the lab for analysis. Depending on the type of trace evidence, the local lab may elect to send some evidence out to speciality labs (hair and fiber analysis, for instance).

Fibers are also collected by sweeping or vacuuming through a special filter paper. The sweepings and filter paper are collected in an evidence bag. When fibers are located attached to a larger object, they should not be removed. The entire object should be packaged and submitted to the crime lab for analysis. If the object is too large, the fiber should be photographed and carefully removed and packaged for analysis. Although it is recommended to remove fiber at the crime lab, when removed at the crime scene forceps, cellophane tape, or vacuum

Figure 6-12
MATERIALS NEEDED FOR TRACE EVIDENCE

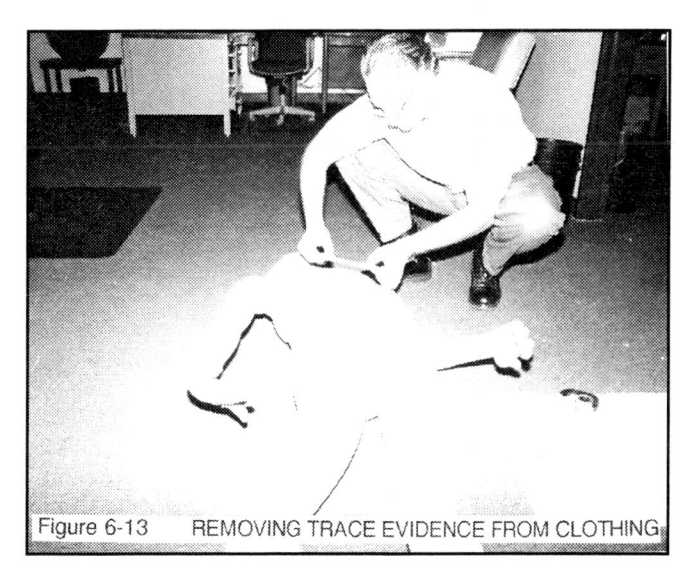

Figure 6-13  REMOVING TRACE EVIDENCE FROM CLOTHING

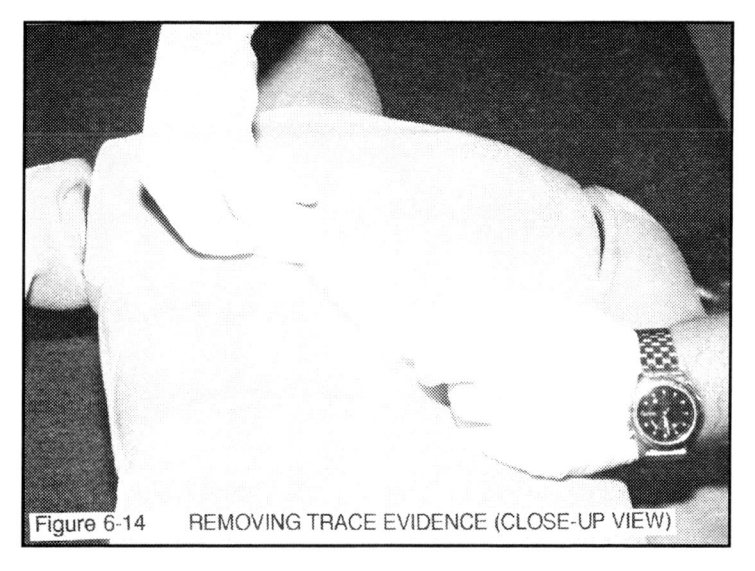

Figure 6-14  REMOVING TRACE EVIDENCE (CLOSE-UP VIEW)

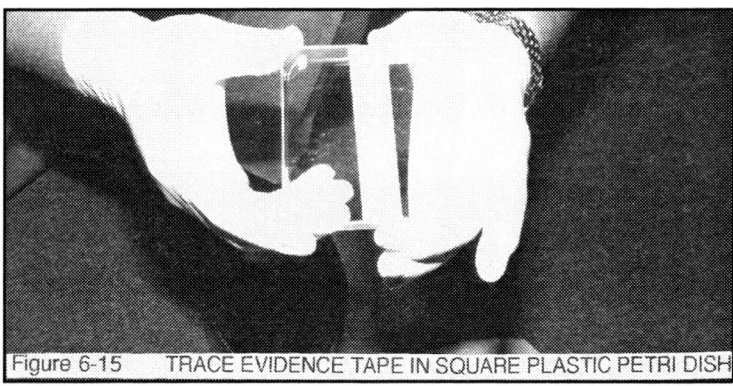

Figure 6-15  TRACE EVIDENCE TAPE IN SQUARE PLASTIC PETRI DISH

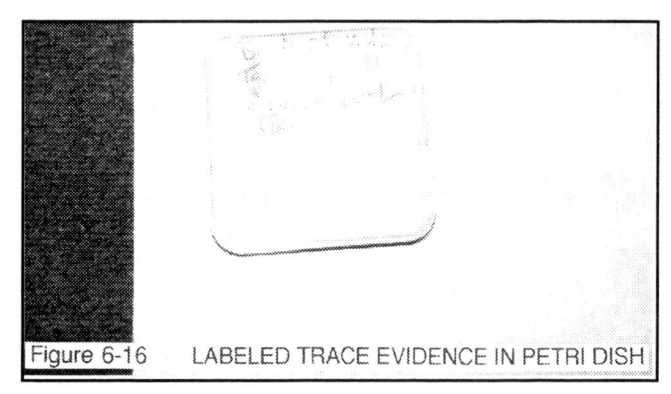

Figure 6-16  LABELED TRACE EVIDENCE IN PETRI DISH

sweeping with special filters are the procedures to follow. The cellophane tape method works well since it collects just the surface material while the vacuum method collects a lot of debris and the forceps method may miss unseen surface material.

Standards should also be collected from every area at the crime scene including rugs, drapes, and furniture. Each sweeping should be collected in a separate evidence bag. Fibers are identified as to type of cloth and color. Matching characteristics based on microscopic, micro chemical, and melting point are also considered in fiber analysis. Type of dye, direction of the fiber twist, and thread count are also useful in the description of evidence. Fiber matches alone are not positive evidence and corroborative evidence is required for the full evidence potential of fiber at the crime scene.

## STRING, ROPE, AND CONTAINERS

The main importance of these items is the trace material which may adhere to their surfaces. Rope used to strangle a victim may have traces of the victim's skin cells on its surface. Containers of these items, many times left behind at the crime scene, may possess latent fingerprints or even, as in some cases, the name and address of the criminal. Knots used should not be untied, if possible, since they might prove useful as evidence. Rope and string recovered from a suspect can be compared with samples discovered at the crime scene. Type of material, number of strands, the direction of twist and weave pattern, color, diameter, and even the weight per unit length can provide comparison evidence.

## SOIL, ROCKS, MINERALS, AND DEBRIS

Particles of soil, rocks, and other minerals may be found on the suspect's shoes, clothing or other personal items (including the vehicle). Soil is considered to be the top surface of the earth down to a level that the normal foot or tire impression would extend. Debris is the remains of any larger object that has been broken down which would include pieces of broken furniture or lamps or other building materials at the crime scene.

These materials by themselves don't provide identity. However, when matched to the crime scene or objects at the crime scene and the suspect, these materials provide solid evidence that the suspect was at the crime scene. The suspect might bring these materials into the crime scene from an outside source or the suspect might carry these materials from the crime scene to his vehicle, residence, or place of work on his shoes or clothing.

Collection procedure includes photography and casting (if necessary) before any samples of soil, rock, minerals, or other debris are collected. Additional samples are usually collected from the area around the first sample. Between four to eight samples are randomly collected from 3 to 20 feet from the original sample to be used as comparisons by the lab.

BUILDING MATERIALS

Brick, mortar, stucco, cement, wood, glass, paint, plaster, asbestos, insulation, and metal fragments can all qualify as trace materials at the crime scene. Any material small enough to be picked up on the clothing of a suspect or victim can qualify. Although mostly found on burglary suspects who collect these materials while in the act of breaking into a structure, these materials can become trapped onto an individuals clothing, skin, hair, and shoes during a physical struggle.

Tools and tool marks are associated with building trace materials and these will be covered in chapter 7. Building materials can be characterized by chemical, physical, and microscopic methods. Class characteristics can be proven, but unless the trace material is shown to be an exact 'fit' to an object or surface at a crime scene, it cannot be linked to a specific substance.

There are special chemical and spectrographical techniques which help to identify metal filings or shavings. However, as with the other building materials, only class characteristics can be proven. There are almost always tiny metal fragments left on the skin when metal is touched. The metal piece which holds the two wooden pistol and revolver grips will often leave such tracings. The trigger and trigger guard will also leave their pattern in the skin of the shooter. The test to develop these tracings is somewhat inaccurate due to the fact that the suspects own perspiration, among other factors, can limit the results.

WOOD AND PLANT MATERIAL

Wood splinters and dust can be an extremely important trace evidence material. Microscopic examination can reveal the type of wood, whether hard or soft wood, even the portion of the tree where it was once located. Tools used on wood will leave their own individual 'fingerprint' marks on the wood. Occasionally, wooden tool handles are chipped or splintered leaving their matching pieces at the crime scene.

Fragments of plants, leaves, bark, twigs, and pollen, brought onto the crime scene or picked up there and carried off by a suspect, can be classified as to type. As with other trace evidence, these can be valuable as circumstantial evidence.

**CRIME SCENE SCENARIO-"ACCIDENT, SUICIDE, OR HOMICIDE?"**
-PART FIVE: GSR AND TRACE MATERIAL-

The Victim was photographed at the crime scene. Each item of evidence was discovered, recorded, collected, and placed in marked containers as the search continued. The victim's skin, hair, and clothing were searched for hair and fiber, and other trace materials. This was accomplished with a taping technique. Each piece of tape was labeled and placed in a separate evidence envelope. Comparison samples of the victim's own hair and cloth fiber were also collected. Cuttings and scrapings from the victim's finger and toe nails were also collected, labeled, and packaged in plastic vials for analysis at the crime lab. A gunshot residue test was conducted on the victim's hands, chest, and t-shirt. Preliminary findings indicated that two distinctly different types of hair were found on the victim's red shorts and white t-shirt . These hairs were identified as both Caucasian: one dark brown, broken and not pulled, the other black, pulled out by the root. Fiber analysis indicated several brown silk threads found in the victim's t-shirt and two green polyester threads in the victim's shorts. The County Coroner placed the victim's body in a body bag at 1:36 pm to help preserve any trace evidence which might otherwise be lost in transit to the morgue.

Trace material analysis on the suspect, Steve Sorensen, revealed only two short fragments of dark brown hair on his jeans. Several green polyester threads were found on his jeans and two white cotton threads were found on his brown silk shirt.

An atomic absorption (AA) spectrophotometer (which is capable of measuring the amount of light transmittance and absorbance of different chemicals) was used to analyze the gunshot residue (GSR) on the victim's shirt and skin near the bullet entrance wound. A dilute solution of nitric acid on a cotton-tipped, plastic applicator was used to swab the victim's chest region, his hands, and his t-shirt. Each area swabbed was collected in a sealed plastic tube. The samples were processed and placed in the spectrophotometer for analysis. Particles of GSR from the bullet's primer were located on both the victim's t-shirt, and skin in the chest region. There was no GSR on the victim's hands. The same procedure was used on the hands and shirt of the suspect, Steve Sorensen. GSR particles were found on his left palm only (not the back of his hand) and on the inside of his shirt (not on the outside). The revolver and the single cartridge casing also tested positive for GSR particles.

The single cartridge casing was analyzed for latent fingerprints. The casing was placed in a cyanoacrylate fuming chamber. A whitish partial print was visible after thirty minutes exposure to the cyanoacrylate fumes. This latent print was dusted with a magnetic powder and lifted with a 3M tape and placed on a standard white 3 inch by 5 inch Latent Print Backing Card (Figure 4-7). Copies were produced and sent to state and federal fingerprint agencies for identification.

Detectives Dodge and Summer decided to visit Bill Morganson's high school. They needed to identify the victim and locate his family. They also needed to locate the family and residence of Steve Sorenson. As Dodge headed for the driver's side of the car, Summer turned to take one more look at the crime scene residence. As she was turning, she caught a glimpse of movement from the house next door to the right of the crime scene.

"Hey, Dodge!, didn't you tell me there was no one home on either side of the crime scene?"

"That's right, no answer from either side" replied Dodge. He had known his partner long enough to know that she never joked on duty. She was all business.

"I saw the living room curtain move" added Summer.

Dodge was now looking at the window in question and aware that he was straining his eyes to focus. "Could have been a pet playing with the curtains?"

"I don't think so, Dodge, we better check this out!" Dodge followed Summer to the house in question whispering that he needed to get his eyes checked for distance vision.

SUGGESTED READINGS-

Benedetti-Pichler, A.A. *Identification of Materials.* New York: Academic Press, 1964.

Brunner, M. and Coman, B.J. *The Identification of Mammalian Hair.* Melbourne: Inkata Press Proprietary, Ltd., 1974.

Burd, D.Q. and Kirk, P.L. "Clothing Fibers as Evidence." *Journal of Criminal Law and Criminology* 32:333, 1941.

Burton, J.F. "Fallacies in the Signs of Death." *Journal of Forensic Science* 19(3):529-534, 1974.

Dixon, K.C. "Positive Identification of Torn Burned Matches with Emphasis on crosscut and Torn Fiber Comparisons." *Journal of Forensic Science* 28(2):351-359, 1983.

Grieve, M.C. "The Role of Fibers in Forensic Science Examinations." *Journal of Forensic Science* 28(4):877-887, 1983.

Hicks, J.W. *Microscopy of Hair: A Practical Guide and Manual* . F.B.I., U.S. Government Printing Office, 1977.

Longhetti, A. and Roche, G. "Microscopic Identification of Manmade Fibers from the Criminalistics Point of View." *Journal of forensic Science* 3:303, 1958.

Pounds, C.A. "The Recovery of Fibers from the Surface of Clothing for Forensic Examination." *Journal of Forensic Science Society* 15(2):127-132, 1975.

Robertson, C.H. and Govan, J. "The Identification of Bird Feathers. Scheme for Feather Examination." *Journal of Forensic Science Society* 24(2):85-98, 1984.

# -CHAPTER SEVEN-
# TOOL MARKS

Crimes which involve forcible entry frequently involve the use of tools. The most common tools are screwdrivers, knives, chisels, crowbars, putty knives, probers, pliers, axes, cutters, and drill bits. Each tool has its own signature which is often left at the scene of a crime. The most common tool signature is produced when a criminal prys open a window or door with a metal tool. The metal tool is often harder than the surface used to pry against and tool marks are left behind as clues. Tool marks, then, can mean the mark produced by, the tool itself, or the trace materials that may be associated with either the mark or the tool. Broken metal objects will also be covered in this chapter.

## DEFINITION AND VALUE AS EVIDENCE

A tool is considered as any object that is capable of making an impression on another solid object. A tool mark is considered to be any impression, scratch, cut, abrasion, or gouge which was caused when a tool was brought into direct contact with the object. There are two general types of markings. The first involves a general form and size of the tool which makes positive identification very difficult, but does serve as a guide to help decide if a tool of the suspect could have produced such marks. The second type of mark shows specific surface injuries, irregularities, and other specific characteristics of the tool in question in the form of indentations and striations. These type of markings provide the best evidence value.

If the tool mark is pressed into a material it is classified as a negative impression. As the tool impresses its outline into a material, channels or furrows (known as stria or striations) are produced in the material which run in parallel lines. Bolt cutters knife blades, and screwdriver blades all produce negative impressions with these striations or lines. In most cases, the leverage action against the material by the tool will produce the tool mark. It is possible to microscopically identify and match the striations and impression made in the material with a specific tool recovered on a crime scene. This combination can be linked to identify a suspect only if fingerprints are also present on the tool.

## CHARACTERISTICS OF TOOLS

Tool marks and the associated impressions are able to reveal the class characteristics of the tool used in a crime. The class of the tool can help to identify if the tool was a screwdriver, a putty knife, a pocket knife, or a chisel. In short, the class of a tool mark can help to narrow the range of the search for a tool.

Just as the class of the tool mark can help to identify the kind of tool used in a crime, it should be noted that tools which are similar in class characteristics may have quite different individual characteristics. Methods of manufacture and the previous use of the tool produce individual markings on every tool which help to provide identity for that particular tool. Most tool and tool mark identification is done in the lab with special microscopic equipment and special lighting.

## CLUES WHICH CAN BE OBTAINED FROM TOOL MARKS

Many times tools used by burglars are damaged in the entry process. This damage is often reflected in the type and kind of tool mark made at the crime scene. This damage, then, becomes a signature of identity of the tool and if often used by the crime scene investigator to differentiate one tool to the exclusion of all others. Trace materials left in the impression and on the tool itself may include minute amounts of paint which can be analyzed and also used to match the tool mark with the tool.

## TOOL MARK COLLECTION

Doors, windows, or other openings at the point of entry as well as the possible route taken by the criminal at the crime scene are of prime importance in the search for tool marks. When tool marks are discovered they are photographed and recorded. Casts are made and, if necessary, the entire surface containing the tool mark is physically removed from the crime scene. A portion larger than the tool mark in the material is removed to provide a standard of comparison as well as to prevent splintering or breaking of the tool mark.

Mikrosil™, a very popular casting putty, can be used to develop tool marks in metal, wood, or glass (Figures 7-1 and 7-2). Since Mikrosil™ has a short setting time and good releasing ability, microscopic detail is preserved. The cast is then compared to the recovered tool to provide identity of the tool to the crime scene. Suspects can then be linked to the crime scene through their physical association with the recovered tool and marks from the crime scene matched to the same tool.

Plaster of paris can be used on larger marks, but there is a certain amount of shrinkage which would not occur with Mikrosil™ or dental casting powder. Plaster of paris will not mold the tiny, microscopic detail required to match tool scrapings or scoring. A knife held at right angles will produce a wider scoring pattern on a surface than the same knife held at an acute or obtuse angle. The direction of movement and right- and left-handedness can also be determined by examination of tool scrapings (Figure 7-3).

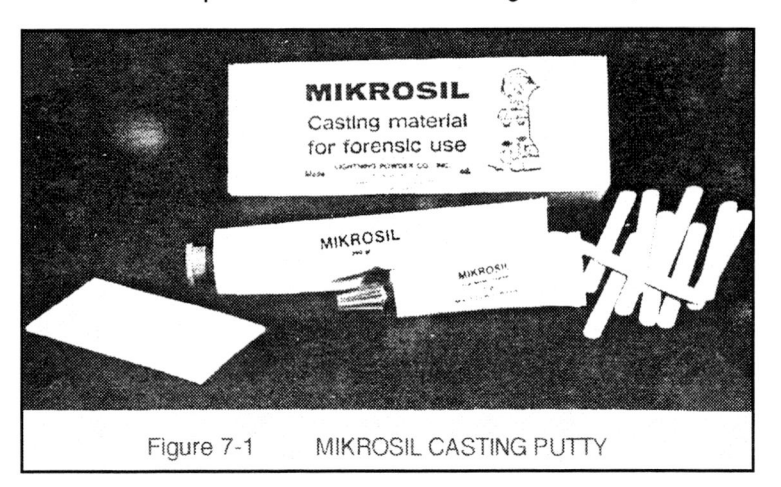

Figure 7-1    MIKROSIL CASTING PUTTY

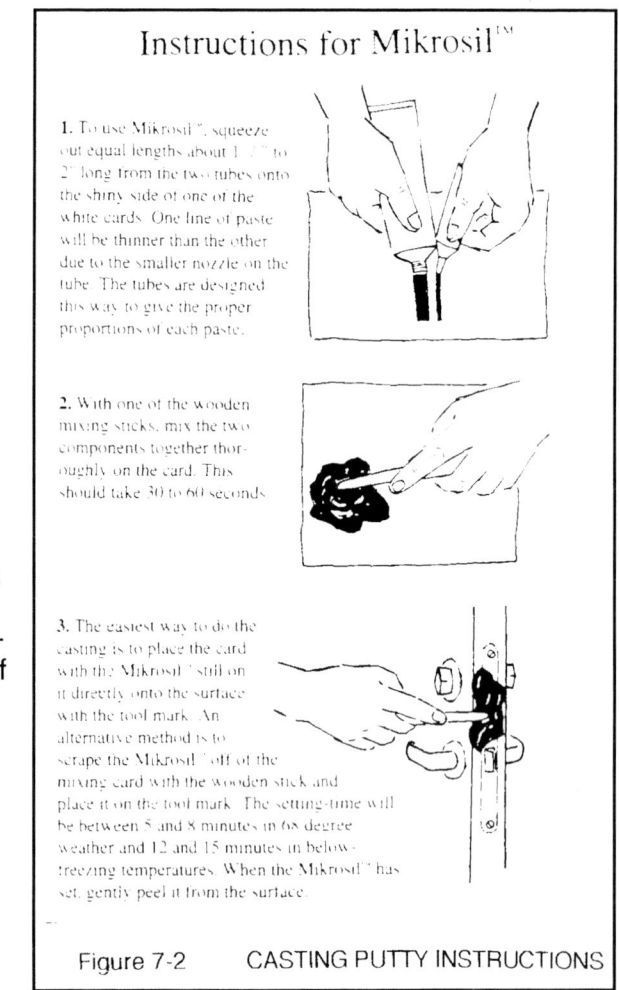

Figure 7-2    CASTING PUTTY INSTRUCTIONS

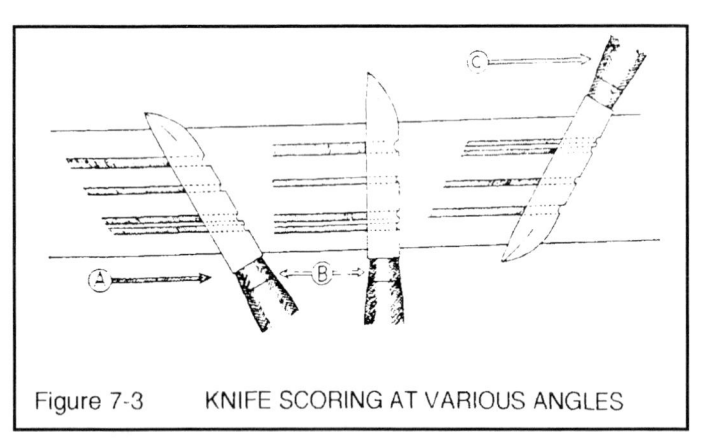

Figure 7-3    KNIFE SCORING AT VARIOUS ANGLES

If only class characteristics can be determined from a tool mark in wood, a close-up photograph including a scale is taken and a cast is made. Casting should be done only as a last resort since it can never equal the original tool mark. This is especially true when trying to produce a cast where there are scratches in paint. Even the best casting materials would not be able to adequately reproduce such scratches. However, a recovered tool can be compared with the original tool mark in the lab and photography used to record it for the court. There have been good results using silicone rubber or dental impression materials to produce fine, minute detail. The decision to cast a tool mark is difficult since there is always a chance of damaging the original.

The tool mark is left in the material. If the tool mark is in a metal surface it is generally considered of higher evidence value than tool marks in wood. The metal surface containing the tool mark is photographed and removed to be analyzed in the lab. If the tool mark in the metal is not immediately recovered, a thin film of oil should be placed on the mark to prevent oxidation. Once recovered, the tool mark should be protected against moisture, dirt , and other abrasive particles by packing the recovered piece of material in soft tissue or paper in a cardboard container.

Once the tool mark has been found, the search for a particular class of tool intensifies at the crime scene. The suspect is also searched for any tools, especially the area in which the arrest is made. Suspects will discard evidence once they feel the possibility of capture.

**Never try to 'fit' a recovered tool to a mark left at a crime scene!** The tool may impart additional marks to the impression which would then permanently destroy the original evidence. Trace materials adhering to the tool or the impression may be lost or contaminated by attempts to match a tool to a tool mark.

Protection of the tool and the tool mark for lab analysis is of prime importance. Each piece of evidence is labeled and wrapped separately to prevent contamination and damage. Notes, sketches, and photographs of the location of tools and tool marks are vital to accurately describe the evidence submitted to a court of law.

In the lab, a standard tool mark is made with the tool in evidence. This standard is then compared with the tool mark gathered from the crime scene in a side-by-side comparison. The photographer should be careful to keep the film plane parallel to the mark and should include a scale, evidence number, and color guide. The enlarging process can then produce an exact replica of the tool mark.

Trace materials such as wood, metal, paint, and glass can be as valuable as the tool mark itself. Many times the trace materials from the tool mark are also found on the tool and provide a second witness that the correct tool had been found. Tools have been identified by stains left behind where the tool was stored. Blood from a knife was found on the suspect's table cloth in the shape of the knife. Crime scene investigators should consider how the suspect was standing when the tool mark was being made. Often, an alert investigator can gain insight into whether the suspect being sought is left- or right-handed.

BROKEN METALS AND OTHER MATERIALS

Often, objects are broken at the crime scene. Pieces of metals or plastic left at the crime scene can often be matched to objects possessed by the suspect. The shape of the break and its match to the actual object are photographed in the lab. The broken object, for sake of identity, must be recovered from the suspect, his vehicle, or his residence in order to provide a positive link between the suspect and the crime scene (Figure 7-4).

Buttons are often broken during the act of committing a burglary or violent crime. Pieces of broken buttons can be matched to their mates for a positive identification (refer to Figure 3-1). Also, many times a piece of thread or fabric may be present with the recovered piece of button which would provide a more exact identification.

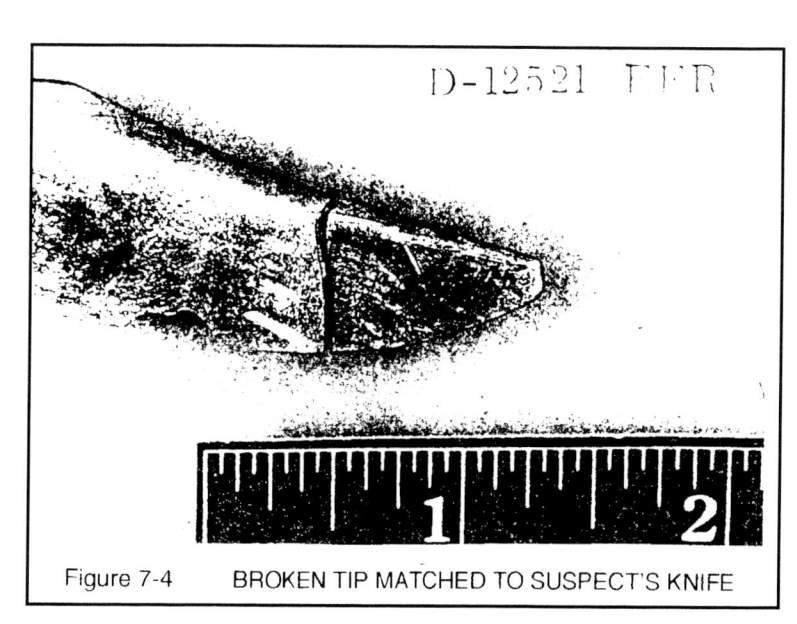

Figure 7-4    BROKEN TIP MATCHED TO SUSPECT'S KNIFE

**CRIME SCENE SCENARIO-"ACCIDENT, SUICIDE, OR HOMICIDE?"**
-PART SIX: TOOL MARKS AND THE GIRL NEXT DOOR-

The only fresh tool mark discovered at the crime scene was an indentation in the wood rail of the rear garage door just above the doorknob. The indentation was donut-shaped with measurements of 5/8" outside diameter, 1/4" inner diameter, and 3/16" deep. Most of the blue paint was missing. Photographs were taken, the tool mark was carefully wrapped with soft paper and tape and covered with a plastic bubble-wrap, and the entire door was taken to the crime lab for analysis.

The decision was made to produce a cast of the tool mark using a non-shrinking plaster powder mixed with a water solvent. Initial tests indicate that the barrel of the revolver was jammed almost straight into the door with a force heavy enough to produce an indentation 3/16" deep. Blue paint was removed from the revolver's barrel and the garage door and sent to an outside laboratory for analysis. Results showed a positive match in the color and chemical composition of the exterior coat of paint on the door and the paint removed from the revolver barrel.

Detective Summer had noticed some movement in the living room window in the house to the west of the crime scene residence. It was 1:40 pm and both Dodge and Summer were tired and hungry. Dodge thought his partner had seen a family pet moving the curtain since he had found no one at home while making a door-to-door inquiry. They were both silent as Summer knocked on the front door. As Summer was knocking a second time, the automatic garage door opener began to open the garage door and a white Honda Accord pulled up into the driveway. A woman, who appeared to be in her middle thirties, stopped the car in the driveway when she saw the two detectives at the door to her house. The woman quickly got out of her car and walked toward her front porch. "Can I help you with something/"

Detective Dodge always felt that he should open doors and do all the introductions for his partner. Although this bothered Kelley Summer, she had been thankful on several occasions when Dodge had been attacked by irate and dangerous individuals. This particular woman did not appear to be angry or dangerous.

"I'm Detective Dodge and this is my partner, Detective Summer," announced Dodge. "We're from the city police department."

"Has something happened to Laura?" demanded the woman. Her demeanor was changing from idle curiosity to a worried concern.

"Who is Laura?" demanded Dodge in his usual abrupt manner.

Summer, knowing the brusque manner in which her partner was accustomed to assume with strangers, interrupted her partner.

"I'm sorry, ma'am, if we startled you. Please excuse my partner's bluntness. There has been a homicide at the residence next door and we were in the process of conducting a house-to-house search.. . . ."

"Homicide?, next door?, You mean someone was killed?" interrupted the woman.

"Yes," answered Summer, "and as I was saying, we had noticed some movement in the curtains in your living room." "We were knocking to see if anyone had returned home."

"Returned home?" the woman seemed to continue repeating words spoken to her. "Where is my daughter?"

"I knocked on your door about an hour and a half ago and there was no answer," added Dodge.

"My daughter was sick this morning and stayed home from school. I have been to the pharmacy to pick up her medicine and then the grocery store." "I guess I've been gone for almost three hours." The woman walked to the front door, inserted her key, opened the door, and called her daughter's name. After a brief pause, a young girl ran across the living room and grabbed her mother with both hands. She appeared frightened.

"Oh, Laura, I'm was afraid you had been hurt!"

'I'm okay, mommy," returned Laura as she began to sob.

"Mommy's home now, everything will be fine." The woman turned to the two detectives. "I'm sorry, but you startled me. My name is Mrs. April Green and this is my daughter, Laura, and she is seven years old"

"Hi, Laura," replied Summer, "my name is Kelley Summer and this is Wilson Dodge."

The little girl had stopped sobbing. "Are you policemen?"

"Yes, we're detectives for the police department," answered Summer, "and we have been to every house asking questions." "Mrs. Green, do you mind if we ask Laura a few questions?"

Mrs. Green was obviously doing some heavy duty thinking. "Is Laura in any danger?"

"No," assured detective Summer, "we need to gather as much information as we can regarding this morning's incident."

Mrs. Green motioned the detectives toward the living room sofa and they all took seats. Laura chose to sit on the arm of the over-stuffed chair her mother had chosen to sit on.

"Laura," began Summer, "did you hear or see anything unusual this morning?"

Laura was beginning to lose her timidness around detective Summer. "I heard a loud bang this morning and it scared me."

"Where were you when you heard the loud band."

"I was going to our mailbox on the street by the maple tree to get our mail. Our mailman comes at 11:15 every morning. Mommy says he must have a built-in clock because he is never late and always on time. When I'm home from school I always watch for him out the window and I run out to say 'hi' to him."

"Did you say 'hi' to your mailman this morning?" asked Dodge.

Still a little afraid of detective Dodge, Laura directed her answer at detective Summer. "Yes, I met him at the mailbox and he handed me our mail."

"When did you hear the loud bang?" probed Summer.

"Right after the mailman left. It scared me and I ran into our house."

"Did you see anyone after you heard the noise?" Summer asked, searching for just the right words to say which wouldn't upset Laura.

"No!" exclaimed Laura, "I didn't see anything or anybody, honest, I didn't" She began to cry and leaned on her mother's shoulder.

"Laura hasn't been feeling very well, today, maybe we could continue this later on," suggested Mrs. Green, "I need to give Laura her medicine and make her some soup."

"Of Course," replied Summer, "forgive us for our abruptness." "We sometimes forget who we're talking to when we are on duty." The detectives excused themselves and left a card with their telephone numbers should Mrs. Green need to get in touch. On the way back to their car, Wilson Dodge was deep in thought.

"What's on your mind? asked Summer.

"I can't put my finger on it yet, but something is not quite right. Laura is scared. She must have seen or heard more than she is admitting!"

"Come on, Dodge, you're been watching too many movies."

Ignoring her comment Dodge added: "Let's get a bite to eat and try and make it to our victim's autopsy at 2:20."

SUGGESTED READINGS-

Bonte, W. "Tool Marks in Bones and Cartilage." *Journal of Forensic Science*. 20(2):315-325, 1975.

Cassisy, F.H. "Examination of Toolmarks from Sequentially Manufactured Tongue-and-Groove Pliers." *Journal of Forensic Science*. 25(4):796-809, 1980.

_____, "F.B.I. Laboratory Makes Tool Mark Examinations." *FBI Law Enforcement Bulletin*, Revised, 1975.

# -CHAPTER EIGHT-
# FIREARMS AND BALLISTICS

## INTRODUCTION AND COMMENTARY

The number of handguns in the United States has been estimated to be approximately 220,000,000. With the total population of around 258 million, the per capita rate is 0.853. These statistics (taken in 1996) are for permitted (legal) handguns. Great Britain has 409,000 registered handguns with a per capita rate of only 0.006 (total population is about 68 million). The next statistic is frightening: Great Britain had 77 murders by firearms in 1996 while the United States had 13,673 murders by firearms during the same time period. The rate of murders committed by firearms per 100,000 in Great Britain is 0.116 and 5.25 in the United States.

During March (1996) a young man walked into the Dunblane Elementary School in Dunblane, Scotland, and murdered 16 children and 1 teacher. Even though he used rifles to massacre these children, anti-gun sentiment was so strong that Great Britain has passed legislation which will remove all handguns (with the exception of the .22 caliber revolvers) from permitted owners. The people of Great Britain are determined to control the use of handguns involved in crime.

Gun control is always a prime issue at each election time, yet with all the press there seems to be a geometric increase in the number of handguns manufactured and sold (and that includes legally as well as illegally) in the United States. Various groups, such as the NRA (National Rifle Association) and firearm manufacturers, have very powerful lobbies in Washington, D.C. who have been used to prevent gun control in the United States. This is a very 'hot' issue and seems to reach to the very roots of our country. We have the right to bear arms guaranteed by our Constitution. There are some states which have passed legislation which allows citizens to carry weapons (handguns) concealed in public places. Although too early to predict, there is some indication that in states which allow citizens to carry concealed handguns there has been a decrease in violent crime (statistics vary depending upon who conducts the surveys). One deterrent may be that the criminal doesn't know if the intended victim is armed and so chooses to avoid the confrontation.

There could be as many as one million handguns in Los Angeles County alone. The bottom line is that there are many of today's youth who are able to possess illegal handguns. The rationale given by some teen boys was "we need to protect ourselves" and "I feel safe when I carry a piece". What do the statistics say about protection and peace of mind? One news commentator, in a special on handguns in our schools, conducted an interview with an unidentified youth. The youth was asked if it bothered him if his victim carried a gun. His reply was chilling: "If I'm robbin' someone and they pull out a gun. . .I'm gonna waste them right there. . .no if's about it." Experienced criminals, who carry guns, will use them without conscience if they suspect their victim capable of causing them harm.

The above reality is what the law enforcement agencies must face every day. They are sworn to protect the citizens under their jurisdiction which is becoming increasingly more difficult to accomplish. The crime scene investigator is also faced with ever increasing case loads of crime scenes to solve. The sad fact is that more and more of these crime scenarios involves the use of a handgun.

The ability of the crime investigator to make a connection between the spent bullet and the firearm that fired it can be traced back to 1835. The Bow Street Runners (Scotland Yard's predecessor) matched a ridge on a bullet (removed from a victim) to a gouge in molding at the suspect's home. After the suspect confessed, this ballistics success led to the science of ballistics.

Needless to say, crime investigators need to deal with firearms used at the crime scene. This chapter is devoted mainly to the forensics effort to identify, mark, and match the weapon with the bullet or spent slug recovered at a crime scene. Of course, once the spent bullet is matched to the firearm, fingerprints on the firearm and cartridge casing and analysis of gunshot residue may lead to the capture of the person who fired the shot.

## FIREARM SAFETY AND TERMINOLOGY

Firearms are classified into two basic categories: handguns and shoulder weapons. These may be a single shot (loaded manually, fired, unloaded manually, and reloaded), revolver (a specific number of cartridges are loaded into a cylinder which revolves each time the hammer is cocked), semi-automatic (a magazine, loaded with cartridges, pushes each new cartridge into the firing chamber automatically each time the trigger is pulled), and automatic (most military weapons, once the trigger is pulled, the magazine will automatically push each cartridge into the firing chamber and a repeat process of firing and reloading will occur until the magazine is empty).

Handguns can be classified into two groups. The term **pistol** refers to all handguns which do not have a revolving cylinder. A **revolver** is a handgun which has a revolving cylinder. Revolvers are divided into four main groups (swing out cylinders, break top, side load, and solid frame) and pistols are divided into two groups (automatic and semiautomatic). The barrels of handguns are machined with narrow, spiral grooves (called rifling) which produce a spin on the bullet to stabilize it in flight. Refer to Figures 8-1 and 8-2 which illustrate the relationship between the lands (actual bore or caliber of the gun barrel) and the grooves (the recessed indentations cut into the barrel in a spiral twist). Shoulder firearms are rifles, which also have rifling, and shotguns (referred to as 'smooth-bore' weapons with no rifling). When a live round is fired it produces two basic components: a spent cartridge case and a bullet which is projected from the cartridge case through the barrel of the gun toward a target

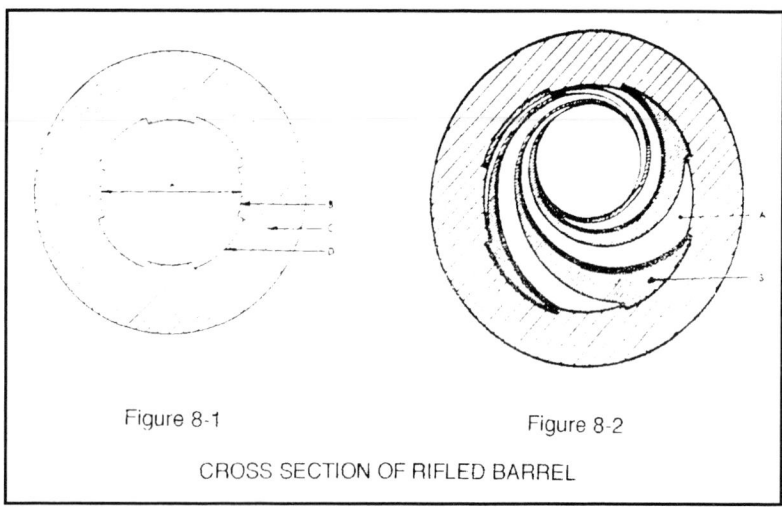

Figure 8-1    Figure 8-2

CROSS SECTION OF RIFLED BARREL

The ammunition for handguns can be classified in two general categories: rimfire and centerfire (Figures 8-3 and 8-4). A few older and larger caliber weapons and .22 caliber handguns use rimfire ammunition. Larger caliber handguns use the centerfire ammunition. Rimfire and centerfire are named for the location of the primer (in the base of the cartridge) used to ignite the gunpowder. The primer is located in the rim area of a rimfire cartridge and in the center of the centerfire cartridge. The revolver cartridge case has a straight lip on the rear of the casing. The semi-automatic and automatic cartridge case has an extractor groove indented in front of the straight lip at the rear of the casing (Figure 8-5).

The distance across the bore diameter is measured in hundredths, or in thousandths of an inch or in millimeters. This distance is called the caliber of the weapon. The caliber is usually an approximation of the actual bore diameter. Ammunition manufacturers work with dimensions specific for each make and model of weapon.

Figure 8-3    RIM FIRE .22 CALIBER CASING

The crime scene investigator, before picking up a handgun, should note the position of the hammer (if one is present), and record the position of the hammer (down, half cocked, or cocked). The safety and its position should also be noted. The weapon should not be disturbed until sketching, recording, and photographs are taken. The floor or surface below the weapon should be carefully studied for any marks or indentations which may indicate that the weapon was dropped from the shooter's hand. Traces of paint, wood, fiber, blood, hair, or other building materials should be protected until the weapon can be fully analyzed in the crime lab.

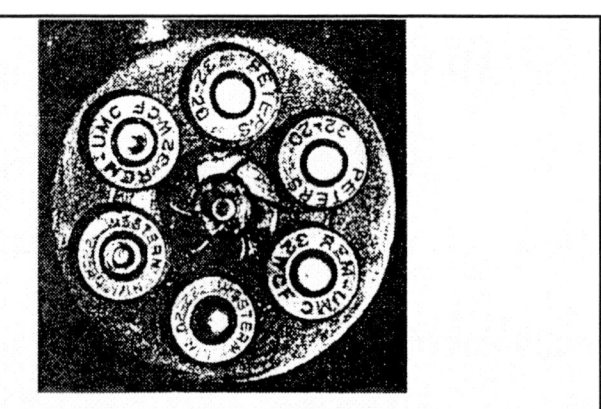

Figure 8-4    CENTER FIRE 32 CALIBER-3 SHOTS FIRED

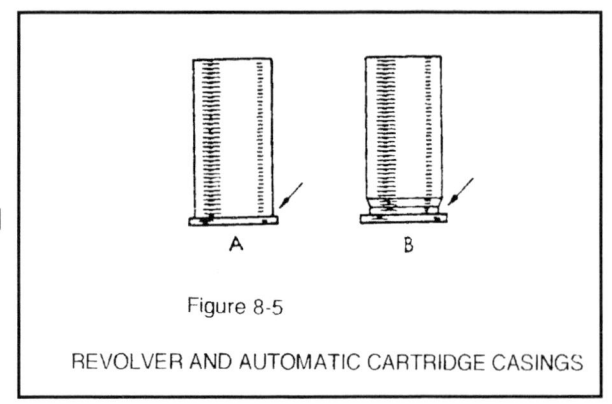

If the deceased is still holding the weapon, the crime scene investigator should make careful notes as to the exact position of the arm and hand of the victim as well as how the weapon is gripped. This is extremely important in cases where suicide is suspected. A murderer may have placed the weapon in the victim's hand after killing the victim.

The number and position of cartridge cases in the crime scene area should be recorded. The crime scene sketch should include the location of the handgun, its make, model, serial number, caliber, and any other descriptive information. The handgun should be picked up by using the index finger and thumb on the checkered portion of the grips (these areas will

Figure 8-5

REVOLVER AND AUTOMATIC CARTRIDGE CASINGS

not usually produce identifiable fingerprints). A handgun should **never** be picked up by inserting a pencil, pen, or stick in the muzzle end of the barrel as this might destroy clues. Weapons fired at contact range (touching the victim) often collect blood, hair, and fragments of cloth and fiber in the barrel. If the weapon has not been fired recently, dust, rust particles, and even spider webs may be present in the barrel (Figure 8-6). Care should be taken so as not to discharge the firearm while handling. The direction of the muzzle should be noted and all personnel cleared from that area in the event that the weapon should discharge when handled. The firearm should be unloaded and all ammunition fired or unfired should be recorded. The position of the cylinder and loaded and spent cartridges should be recorded with a revolver. In unloading a semiautomatic pistol, the number of rounds left in the magazine and whether a round is still in the chamber (ready to be fired) should also be recorded. This type of information may help the investigator determine whether the case is a homicide or a suicide.

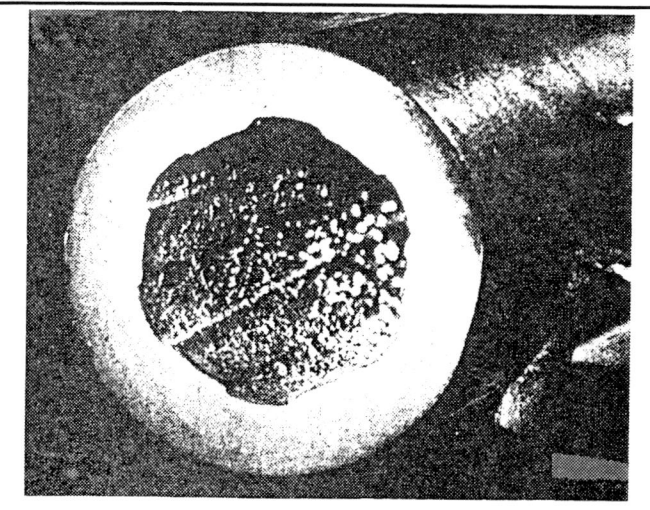

Figure 8-6  DUST DEPOSITS IN RIFLE BARREL INDICATE THAT WEAPON WAS NOT FIRED RECENTLY

In some cases, the recovered weapon is damaged or exposed to excess moisture. These should be sent to the crime laboratory in an evidence bag labeled in large red letters, "CAUTION, LOADED FIREARM." This type of firearm must be dried and thoroughly cleaned before it can be fired to produce a ballistics test.

Position of bullets discovered at the crime scene should be recorded and photographed. The path of the bullet is an important factor to determine the position of the shooter. The location of the spent cartridges may also prove helpful to determine the location of the weapon when it was fired. The bullets should not be removed from objects as they may become damaged by the tool used in their removal. The very fine markings (from the barrel rifling) may be destroyed. Instead, the bullet and its object, or the bullet and a portion of the surface it is embedded in, need to be collected as one piece, labeled, packaged, and sent to the crime lab for analysis.

## GUNSHOT RESIDUE (GSR)

When a firearm is discharged there are gases expelled from the muzzle of the weapon which contain particles of the primer and burning gunpowder. These particles are called gunshot residue (abbreviated GSR). During the discharge, gases also travel in a rearward direction toward the shooters hand. Gunshot residue is usually deposited on the outside of the hand since the palm area is protected from exposure to gunshot residue (Figures 8-7 and 8-8).

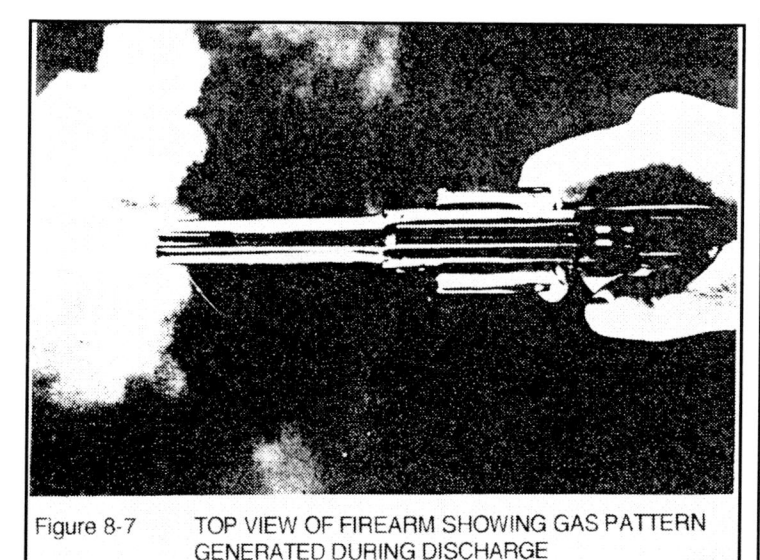

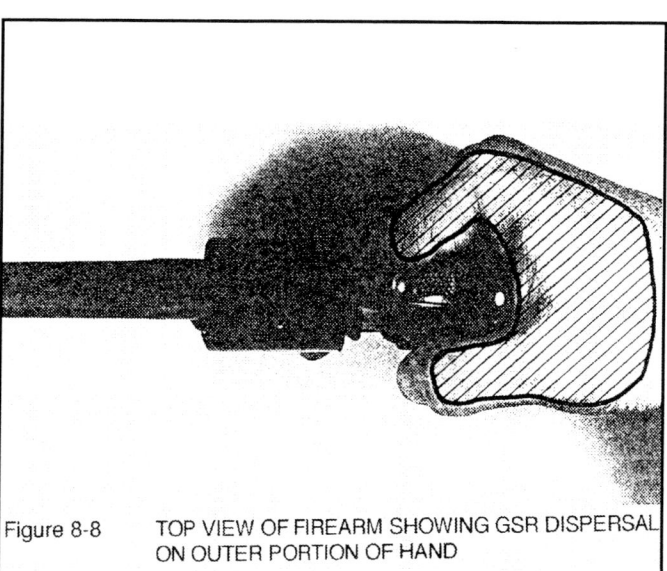

Figure 8-7  TOP VIEW OF FIREARM SHOWING GAS PATTERN GENERATED DURING DISCHARGE

Figure 8-8  TOP VIEW OF FIREARM SHOWING GSR DISPERSAL ON OUTER PORTION OF HAND

## POWDER RESIDUE TESTS

To determine the distance the weapon was from its target when discharged, the lab first examines the area struck by the bullet. For this example there was no gunshot residue found at the target site. The lab analyst then uses the same ammunition and the same gun involved in the case and fires it as the measured distance. It may then be noted that at a certain distance, say 5 feet, no residue is deposited on the test material. In this case the laboratory technician will conclude that the weapon was held 5 or more feet from the victim when it was discharged.

If the area struck by the original bullet has partly burned powder, some unburnt powder traces, or smoke and burning, the lab will be able to estimate the distance the gun was held from the bullet's point of impact. The limit on determining the distance that the firearm was held is the maximum distance that the unburned powder will travel from the muzzle of the gun.

Some very sophisticated methods have been developed such as neutron activation analysis (NAA), scanning electron microscopy/energy dispersive X-ray analysis (SEM/EDX), and atomic absorption (AA) to test for gunpowder residue (Figures 8-9 to 8-11). Since there is some uncertainty as to the 'best' method to determine powder residue, some crime labs have stopped conducting the powder test. However, many labs do this test and have been able to determine that a suspect who possessed powder residues on his person had recently fired a firearm. The atomic absorption (AA) spectrophotometer (used to analyze GSR) was discussed in Part 5 of the Crime Scene Scenario in Chapter 6.

The chemical components found in the primer are the object of the GSR testing. The hands of any suspects should be protected with paper sacks (not plastic which might cause perspiration to dilute the GSR's) Cotton-tipped plastic applicators are used in both the NAA and AA techniques to collect samples from skin and clothing (or other objects in question). The technician must wear latex gloves to prevent contamination of the surface to be tested. Special evidence collection kits are available which provide all the collection materials. A 5% nitric acid solution is either applied to the cotton swab and applied or sprayed first onto the skin or clothing and then collected with the cotton swab. The SEM/EDX technique uses small aluminum discs attached to double-sided cellophane tape. The discs are dabbed over the skin or clothing in question, placed in a plastic container, and sent to the lab for analysis (Figures 8-12 to 8-14).

## Gunshot Residue Test

The examination of gunshot residue can disprove an assumption made falsely or mistakenly. For example, in the case of an apparent suicide involving a handgun, a gunshot residue collection should be done on the hands of the deceased. If no residue is found, the case could actually be a murder made to look like a suicide.

To protect this residue it is suggested to put brown paper bags (NEVER white paper bags or plastic bags) on the suspected shooter's hands and tape them around the wrist. The collection should be done at the earliest possible moment. If the suspected shooter is deceased and the collection cannot be done immediately, it is recommended that the hands be covered with brown paper bags by the coroner or medical examiner prior to moving the body.

There are two types of laboratory analysis which can be done on the collected residue. One is an **Atomic Absorption** (AA) Analysis and the other is using a **Scanning Electron Microscope** (SEM). These collection kits come in three different styles. One kit is only for the AA process, one is only for the SEM examination and the third kit contains supplies for both types of collection.

The AA test supplies consist of cotton swabs in tubes and a liquid chemical. The liquid is put on the cotton swabs and rubbed on the suspected shooter's hands. The cotton swabs are then placed back into the tubes and sent to the lab for analysis. The SEM examination supplies consist of metal discs (or stubs) with adhesive on them. The discs are dabbed on the hands and the adhesive picks up the gunshot residue particles. The metal discs are then sent to the laboratory. Visible stains do not appear on the hands. The resulting data is obtained only by laboratory examination.

Figure 8-9    GUNSHOT RESIDUE TEST DESCRIPTION

Figure 8-10    GUNSHOT RESIDUE TEST KITS

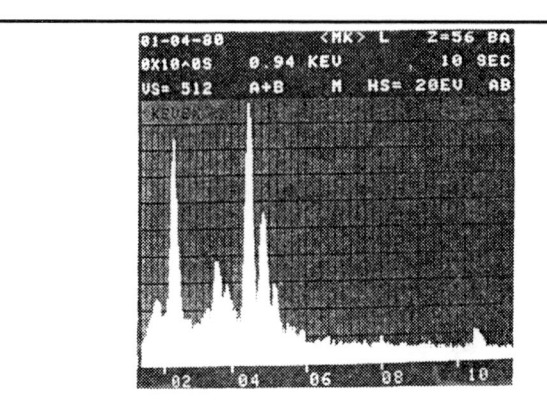

Figure 8-11    GSR TEST RESULTS SHOWING X-RAY SPECTRUM

A negative test result is interpreted to mean that a suspect either took evasive action that removed the GSR particles from the skin or did not fire a weapon. A positive test means that GSR particles are present and the suspect has fired or handled a firearm during the previous 6 hours. If the suspect's palms contain GSR particles (but not the back of the hands), there are two possibilities. The first is that the suspect held a recently fired weapon but did not fire the weapon. The second possibility is that the suspect fired a weapon that was extremely 'clean', in that, very little GSR's were released when it was fired. There is a 6 hour time-frame in which to test for GSR on both the victim and the suspect.

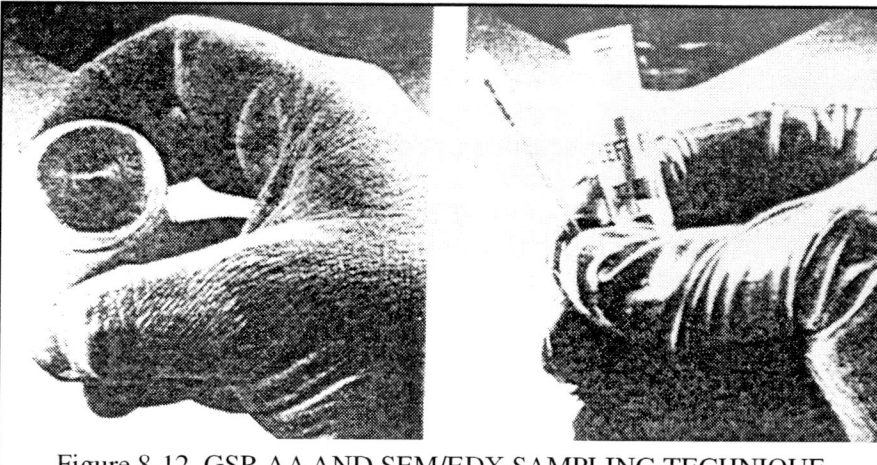

Figure 8-12  GSR AA AND SEM/EDX SAMPLING TECHNIQUE

FIGURE 8-13    AA/GRS TEST FORM

FIGURE 8-14    SEM/GRS TEST FORM

## LATENT PRINTS FOUND ON FIREARMS

After the firearm has been recorded and unloaded it is then dusted for fingerprints. This can be done at the crime scene (some investigators prefer to have this done at the crime lab) and the serial number should also be lifted from the firearm and recorded by rubbing a finger over the number and dusting the number with powder and lifting the number with tape. Serial number or other marking restoration can be accomplished with chemical and electrochemical etching techniques. Serial numbers which have been completely filed away have been restored using these techniques. The fingerprint tape is then attached to a fingerprint card and all the pertinent information included. A cyanoacrylic fuming technique to develop latent fingerprints is described in Chapter 4. A commercial rifle fuming chamber is shown in Figure 8-15.

If there are obvious trace materials of blood, fiber, hair, etc. on the firearm, it should be boxed and labeled and sent directly to the crime lab for analysis. Dried blood will normally not be harmed by fingerprint dusting, but the dusting procedure may contaminate and ruin other trace evidence. If latent prints and obvious trace materials are discovered on a weapon, the best procedure is to carefully package and label the weapon and send it to the crime lab for a detailed analysis.

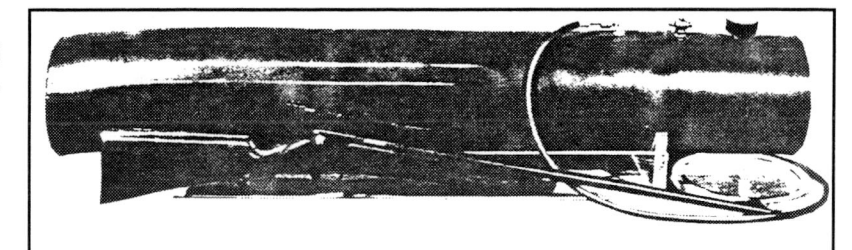

Figure 8-15 COLEMAN VACU-PRINT™ LONG (RIFLE) CHAMBER

## MARKING FIREARMS

An inconspicuous place should be selected on the firearm for marking. The firearm should also be tagged to show all important information. A solid frame revolver which does not have a swing-out cylinder or is not of the break-top type may be marked inside the trigger guard on the bottom of the frame. Revolvers with swing-out cylinders may be marked on the inside frame. Top-break revolvers are marked on the frame which is normally hidden by the cylinder. A semi-automatic pistol can be marked in the magazine well after the magazine has been removed.

The position of the safety (usually visible on pistols but not on revolvers), whether the weapon is cocked and loaded. On some automatic pistols this is difficult to see unless there is an indicating pin. On most pistols, the position of the rear portion of the bolt will reveal if the weapon is cocked. The evidence tag should also include whether the bolt is closed, partly open, or fully open. Also, the record should include if a cartridge case is jammed in the ejection port and if the magazine (which holds the cartridges) is loose or locked into firing position.

## MARKING CARTRIDGE CASES AND BULLETS

Bullets discovered at the scene of a crime are marked on the nose or the base. No marks should be made on the surfaces marked by the barrel of the gun since these will be matched with a lab tested bullet from the same gun to test for a match. After a bullet is marked it is rolled in a piece of paper and placed in an appropriate container. Care must be taken so as to not damage the surface of the bullet.

Bullets removed by a doctor should be marked by the doctor as well as by the crime scene investigator. Doctors, when working on live victims, try not to mar a bullet when removing it, however, the safety for the victim is of first consideration. Bullets covered with body fluids or other moisture should be allowed to air dry before they are marked and packaged. Trace materials and blood samples can be preserved in this manner.

Cartridge cases should be marked inside the mouth of the cartridge. If the cartridge is crushed flat, the mark should be made near the mouth and never near the rim (closed end) of the cartridge. Cartridge casings are normally found at crime scenes where semi-automatic pistols are used since they are ejected after each shot is fired. Many times the ejection pattern of the casings can help establish the relationship of the position of the suspect to the victim

A file is maintained in the FBI National laboratory of many unsolved crimes where bullets and cartridge cases have been recovered. There have been recent crimes where the ballistic test matches an older, unsolved crime. A suspect can then be linked to both crimes by the use of this ballistics comparison. Bullets are filed as to particular caliber and number of groove impressions (rifling), and the direction of their twist (inclination). Each gun that is submitted is then fired. The spent bullet is then compared with all unsolved bullets to see if there is a match and possible match with a suspect to a previous, unsolved crime.

## BALLISTICS

Ballistic lab analysis centers on the matching process between spent bullet and recovered firearm from the crime scene. The firearm must be test-fired with the same ammunition (only after all other forms of identification and lab testing have been completed), from a distance determined to match the original distance and into a similar material. The test-fire process should be conducted in a chamber (loaded with water or commercial components) which will prevent any damage to the spent bullet (Figure 8-16). This new spent bullet is then microscopically examined and matched to the original crime scene bullet. There are rifling (tiny groove and land markings) in the barrels of handguns and rifles (not in shotguns) which leave a fingerprint-type mark on the bullet as it leaves the barrel of the gun. It is these marks which can be matched since a gun will always produce the same markings on every bullet it fires (Figures 8-17 and 8-18)

When a weapon is discharged, the firing pin strikes the base of the cartridge which detonates the primer. The ignited primer, in turn, ignites the gunpowder which causes a rapid expansion of gas. The cartridge casing is forced against the breech (region of barrel where cartridge is located) which resists any further expansion. This chain reaction then pushes the bullet forward, down the barrel. As the bullet is propelled down the barrel, it picks up the barrels distinct rifling pattern as well as any tiny imperfections of the lands and grooves. Specific markings result from the physical loading, chambering, and firing of the cartridge. Specific markings also result from the extracting and ejecting process utilized in semi-automatic pistols. These markings are impressed on the bullet and casings and can be used by comparison to exhibit identity.

Figure 8-16    BULLET CATCHER

Bullets and casings may be used to determine the type, make, and even the model of weapon used at a crime scene. The marks made on the cartridge cases by the extractor and ejector of automatic weapons can also lead to a comparison identity. Cartridge cases are never placed in the chamber of a crime scene weapon since old markings on the casing may be destroyed and new marks made.

Bullets are basically composed of lead. They may be solid lead (mostly used in revolvers), semi-jacketed with another metal surrounding a lead center leaving a soft nose, or full-jacketed with another metal surrounding the nose of the bullet leaving only lead at the end of the bullet (usually associated with automatic pistols). The semi-jacketed bullet will break apart if it strikes a hard surface (such as bone). The full-jacketed bullet will often remain undamaged or slightly damaged when it strikes a harder surface such as bone. The degree of hardness varies in regular lead bullets with no metal jackets. The amount of damage to these bullets varies with the amount of hardness. There are exceptions to the type of bullet used in various handguns which means there is no hard and fast rule. The crime scene investigator needs to keep an open mind when hypothesizing the type of bullet and weapon used.

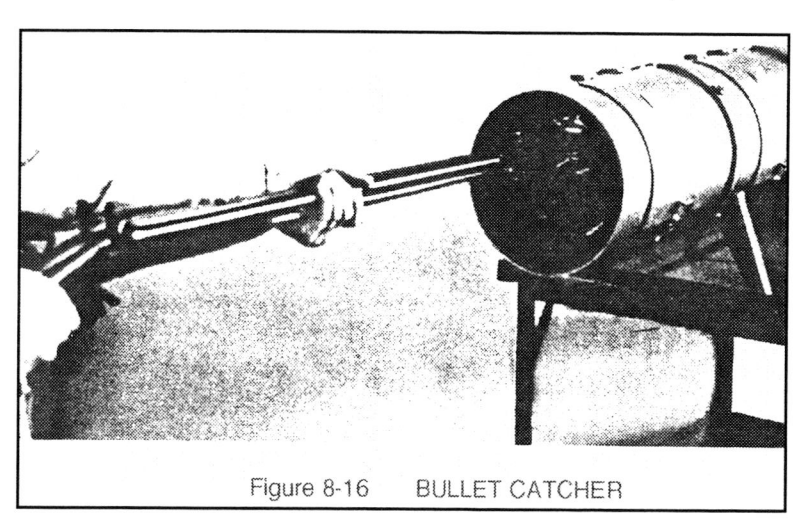

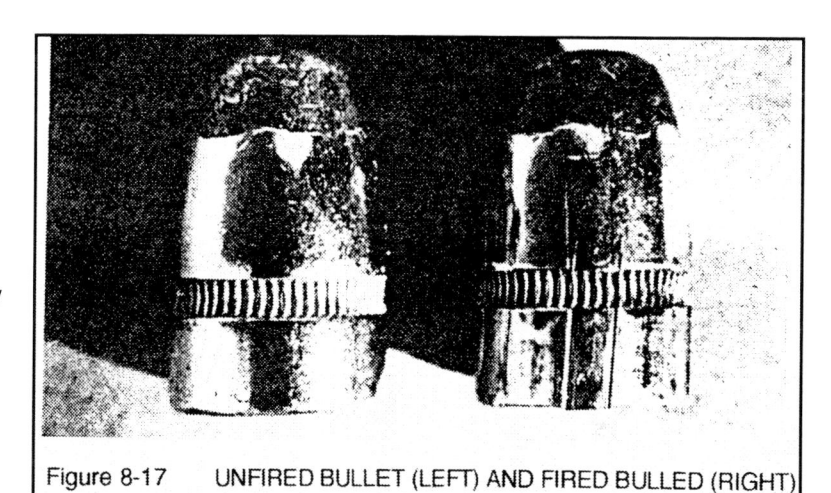

Figure 8-17    UNFIRED BULLET (LEFT) AND FIRED BULLED (RIGHT)

Figure 8-18    BULLET STRIATIONS IN GROOVE IMPRESSIONS IN MATCHING BULLETS FIRED FROM SAME WEAPON

# CRIME SCENE SCENARIO-"ACCIDENT, SUICIDE, OR HOMICIDE?"
## -PART SEVEN: WEAPON AND THE MORGUE-

The .357 magnum, 6-shot revolver (Smith and Wesson, model M-13), recovered in the neighbor's backyard, contained no cartridges in the cylinder (Figure 8-19). The revolver has been thoroughly checked for trace materials and blue paint fragments were removed from the end of the barrel. There was no trace of blood, skin, hair, or cloth fibers found on the weapon. GSR residue was discovered on the barrel, on portions of the cylinder, and on the trigger guard.

A search was conducted of the alley adjacent to the location where suspect #1, Steve Sorensen, was apprehended. One box of .357 magnum centerfire lead revolver cartridges were recovered from a plastic trash container. One cartridge was missing from the box. The cartridges were examined for fingerprints. These were labeled, packaged, and sent to the crime lab for analysis. A further search of the area failed to recover any related evidence.

The victim, still unidentified on the afternoon of day one of the shooting, had been taken to the city morgue by the county coroner where a local pathologist was ready to perform an autopsy. Detectives Dodge and Summer arrived at 2:20 pm at the County Morgue. They grabbed some fast-food while in route from the crime scene.

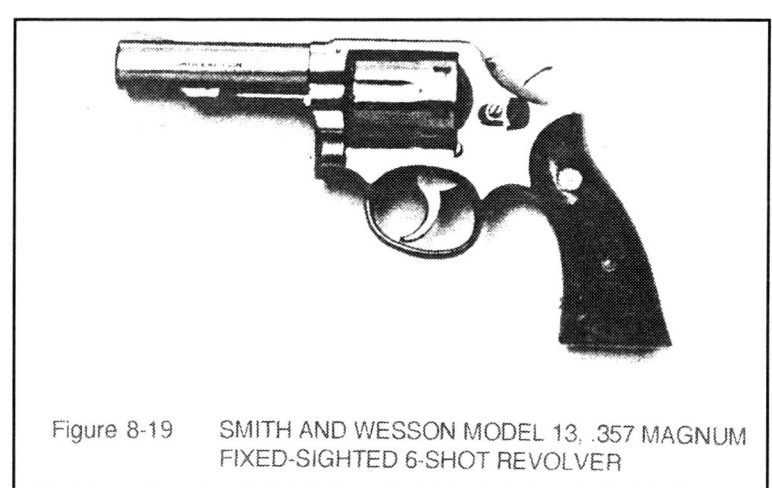

Figure 8-19   SMITH AND WESSON MODEL 13, .357 MAGNUM FIXED-SIGHTED 6-SHOT REVOLVER

Dodge was still eating a hamburger when they entered the morgue.

"Hey!, no eating in the morgue!" shouted Dr. Kramer, who was filling in for the regular coroner, Dr. Robert Sawyer.

"Yeah! Dodge, doesn't it bother you to eat in here?" added Summer.

"I'm hungry!" Dodge exclaimed, defending himself.

"Well, if you must, finish eating out in the hallway!" answered the irritated doctor. Dodge left the morgue laboratory to finish his meal while Dr. Kramer conducted his examination of the victim.

The following is the autopsy report prepared by Dr. Kramer. The victim was a male, Caucasian, approximately 16 to 18 years of age, short blond hair, brown eyes, 5' - 6" tall, 150 lbs., with a single gunshot entry wound to the upper left chest region. There was no identification found on the victim's clothing. The bullet had entered the upper left chest cavity on a plane perpendicular to the plane of the victim's chest. The bullet penetrated the left side of the chest through the fourth rib (at its juncture to the sternum) and passed directly through the left ventricle to lodge in the 5th thoracic vertebra. X-rays were taken before entry into the chest cavity to verify the pathway and resting position of the bullet. Death had been instantaneous by extreme trauma to the heart and subsequent loss of blood volume. Internal bleeding was extensive in the heart and lung cavities. The bullet's entrance into the 5th thoracic vertebra resulted in the instant expansion due to heated gases and the resultant devastation of spinal tissue. The bullet was carefully removed and placed in a labeled plastic vial, sealed, and sent to the ballistics lab for analysis. There was no exit wound. There were no other wounds or bruises other than the bruises which surrounded the bullet entry wound area. The victim had no scars or tattoos. A diamond shaped reddish birthmark was located just beneath and behind the victim's right ear at the natural hair line. The victim's blood was type O positive. Dental impressions were taken and sent to a dental lab for processing. A forensic odontologist has been called in to assist in identification.

A ballistics test was conducted by firing a similar cartridge from the .357 revolver into a commercial bullet catcher. The bullet's groove and land fingerprint matched perfectly to the bullet recovered from the victim.

A door to door neighborhood search was conducted on day one of the shooting with negative results as to the identity of the victim or the whereabouts of Bill Morganson (now classified as suspect #2). The search was continued at the local high school where the assistant principal and several teachers were able provide the names of several friends of Bill Morganson. Bill Morganson's teachers did not recognize a picture of the deceased victim.

At 3:10 pm Dodge and Summer arrived at Bill Morganson's high school to interview school officials. Two of Bill's teachers gave the detectives the names of three students who were Bill's friends. Andrea Coleman and Taylor Sampson, who were still at school, had not seen nor heard from Bill since they saw him at school the day before the shooting. The third name supplied by Bill's teachers was Matt Kenney.

Matt was home with his parents when interviewed by Detective Dodge and Summer at 4:05 pm on day one. Matt seemed extremely nervous and agitated when asked about his friend. He gave an account similar to that of Andrea and Taylor in a very unconvincing manner. Even Matt's parents noticed unusual behavior in their son. Dodge had interviewed hundreds of people and had become an excellent observer. When shown a picture of Steve Sorenson, Matt'a behavior was noticeably changed. He began to insist that he had never seen that person. He began to talk faster and in a higher tone of voice.

As Dodge and Summer were leaving the Kenney residence, Summer commented to Dodge: "Matt Kenney knows more than he will admit."

"He's scared," observed Dodge, "and I'm not exactly sure what he is afraid of."

"Do you think Bill threatened him?" asked Summer.

"Too early to tell, let's give him some time to show us what he knows." Dodge radioed the police dispatcher from their car. He requested surveillance of the Kenney residence.

SUGGESTED READINGS-

Andrasko, J. and Maehly, A.C. "Detection of Gunshot Residues on Hands by Scanning Electron Microscopy." *Journal of Forensic Science* . 22(2):279-287, 1977.

Barnes, F.C., and Helson, R.A. "An Empirical Study of Gunpowder Residue Patterns." *Journal of Forensic Science* . 19(3):448-462, 1974.

Burrard, G. *The Identification of Firearms and Forensic Ballistics* . New York: A.S. Barnes and Co., 1962.

David, J.E. *An Introduction to Toolmarks, Firearms and the Striagraph* . Springfield, Illinois: Charles C. Thomas, 1958.

DiMaio, V.J.M. *Gunshot Wounds—Practical Aspects of Firearms, Ballistics and Forensic Techniques* . New York: Elsevier, 1985.

DiMaio, V.J.M. , et. al. "An Experimental Study of Powder Tattooing of the Skin." *Journal of Forensic Science* 21(2):373-377, 1976.

Josserand, M.H. and Stevenson, J.A. *Pistols, Revolvers, and Ammunition* . New York:   Bonanza Books, 1972.

Lowry, E.D. *Interior Ballistics: How a Gun converts Chemical Energy into Projectile Motion* . Garden City, New York: Double Day and Company, Inc., 1968.

Matricardi, V.R. and Kilty, J.W. "Detection of Gunshot Residue Particles from the Hands of a Shooter." *Journal of Forensic Science* . 22(4):725-738, 1977.

Nesbitt, R.S., et. al. "Detection of Gunshot Residue by Use of the Scanning Electron Microscope." *Journal of Forensic Science* . 21(3):595-610, 1976.

Stone, I.C., et. al. "Gunshot Wounds: Visual and Analytical Procedures." *Journal of Forensic Science* 23(2):361-367, 1978.

Wolten, G.M., et. al. "Particle Analysis for the Detection of Gunshot Residue I: Scanning Electron Microscopy/Energy Dispersive X-ray Characterization of Hand Deposits from Firing." *Journal of Forensic Science* . 24(2):409-422, 1979.

# -CHAPTER NINE-
# LEGAL AND ILLEGAL DRUGS

## INTRODUCTION

Crime scene investigators should be familiar with basic pharmacology since legal as well as illegal drugs can be closely linked with crime. Drugs are often discovered in bulk form or in specimens of blood and urine at the crime scene. The presence of drugs is very common in traffic accidents and driving under the influence of alcohol as well as in their illegal manufacture in home-based laboratories. The term drugs refer to the solid or liquid form and are sometimes called bulk drugs. The term toxicology refers to the study of the type of drug, amount present, and its physiological effect on the body. The toxicological specimen, then, is the sample of blood or urine taken from a suspect or victim involved at the crime scene under investigation. Investigators should also be aware of how certain drugs affect an individual. One misconception is the term narcotic. **Narcotic** refers only to those drugs (extracted from the opium plant and the leaves of the coca shrub) which can cause addiction. The term **controlled drugs** or **controlled substances** refers to all drugs (including narcotics) which are covered by law and are restricted in some manner (most of which are addictive).

## IMPLICATIONS AT THE CRIME SCENE: DRUG ADDICTION AND ABUSE

**Addiction** is primarily a matter of physical dependency of the user on the drug. Once the addiction stage is reached, the user will become physically ill if he/she is deprived of a specific dosage of the drug. Some drugs do not produce a physical dependence, but most do. According to professionals in psychiatry, there is usually a psychological maladjustment which precedes the addiction stage of drug abuse. There is also a strong physical dependence which occurs in many individuals after the initial physical rejection has occurred in the body.

Marijuana is a drug which is not physically addictive. However, there are strong indications that the frequent user can become psychologically and emotionally dependent on marijuana. The drug user will feel an unusually strong compulsion to continue taking the drug. The means of obtaining the drug become less important as this desire for the drug increases and this can lead to criminal behavior. As the user of the drug begins to develop a tolerance for the drug, the body tries to compensate and accept the foreign substance. The usual 'high' or feeling of well-being becomes lessened as tolerance occurs. The user is forced to take increasingly larger doses of the drug in order to obtain the original effect of the drug.

People take drugs for a number of reasons. One of the most documented reasons for drug use is the ability to shut out problems and release anxiety. Drug use is not restricted to any age group, race, or culture, but is widespread throughout a wide cross-section of our society.

**Street drugs** (drugs produced by unqualified individuals in home-labs) are especially dangerous to the user. There is no quality control or guarantee which the large pharmaceutical companies provide. On many occasions, street drugs are sold which contain lethal substances. There is also no guarantee of dosage so the user is in danger of overdose with each use. Because there is no content guarantee, an apparent poisoning, an accidental death, a homicide, or a suicide can all be the result of street drug consumption.

**Drug abuse**, then, applies to any use of a drug, whether or not legally possessed, so that the user has been or is likely to be adversely affected by the drug. **Controlled substances** (which require a medical doctor's prescription) and **over the counter** drugs (sometimes called legal or non-controlled drugs which do not require a doctor's prescription) are two terms which are commonly used by crime scene investigators. Even very low levels of certain over-the-counter drugs by some individuals could qualify as drug abuse. Many drugs which are widely recognized for their medicinal value by doctors which are legally prescribed for patients are also widely abused by some individuals.

There are various classifications used to describe a general category of drugs. Depressants and stimulants (drugs which affect the central nervous system), marijuana, hallucinogenics, designer drugs, nonprescription drugs, and inhalants are all potential crime scene evidence

## THE COMMONLY ABUSED DRUGS

## DEPRESSANTS

Normally, narcotics are prescribed by doctors for their pain-killing (analgesic) effect. Narcotics, however, have an extremely high potential for abuse. The opiate alkaloids are derived from the opium poppy (*Papaver somniferum*) and include raw opium, morphine, and codeine. The synthetic narcotics are Demerol, dialudid, heroin, methadone, and Percodan.

Heroin is a derivative (that means it has been extracted from the opium poppy plant and further synthesized in the laboratory. This drug can cause an extremely high physical dependency. Heroin is mostly injected into the blood stream for an instant effect. It can also be sniffed. It has a very bitter taste so it is difficult to take orally unless encapsulated. It is sold in 'decks' or in clear gelatin capsules. The powder is dissolved in water and heated to boiling and taken up into a medicine dropper or syringe. The liquid is then injected into the blood stream.

Crime scene investigators look for the various equipment required to administer the heroin. The heroin user will take extreme care in protecting their heroin supply and equipment. The drug is sometimes stored in condoms. If the user is caught, they will swallow the drug in the condom and later recover the drug from their own feces. Women have been known to hide heroin decks or capsules in their vagina. All recovered heroin should be labeled and placed in clean envelopes or paper bags, sealed, and sent to the lab for analysis. These narcotics have a very similar white powdery appearance and the investigator will probably not be able to classify the substance at the crime scene. The investigator should refer to these as controlled

A second type of depressants, the barbiturates, are referred to as the sedative-hypnotic depressants which are normally prescribed to treat insomnia (lack of sleep) and tension. These have a very high potential for abuse and addiction. These drugs are the barbituric acid derivatives such as amobarbital, phenobarbital, and secobarbital. Barbiturates act on the central nervous system as a sedative or sleep-producing drug. These are taken orally and sometimes intravenously or rectally. These are prescribed by doctors and are fairly widespread. It should be noted, however, that barbiturates are commonly used in non-violent suicides. Barbiturates are legally manufactured by pharmaceutical companies in the form of tablets, capsules, suppositories and liquids. Abusers will use up to 40 pills each day so quantity found at a crime scene is important. Coupled with the use of barbiturates is the use of amphetamine drugs which are used to speed up an individual who has been taking barbiturates. The use of alcohol with the barbiturate can result in a 'quick drunk' where death from respiratory failure may occur. Alcohol and barbiturates are both depressants and their actions are additive.

Other nonbarbiturates include chloral hydrate, glutethimide (Doriden), and methaqualone (Quaalude). Even the drug PCP (phencyclidine, also known as 'angel dust') is classified as a sedative but is placed under the category of hallucinogenic drugs because of its hypnotic effect.

Drugs prescribed for their tranquilizing effect (chlorpromazine, prochlorperazine, trifluoperazine, meprobamate, chlordiazepoxide or Librium, and diazepam or Valium) are all used to treat psychological disorders and are considered addictive.


STIMULANTS

A drug which affects the central nervous system as a stimulant is cocaine. This narcotic drug is obtained from the leaves of the erythroxylon coca tree found in South America. It is a white, odorless, fluffy, crystalline powder and resembles heroin. Medically, cocaine is used as a local anesthetic in certain facial (eye, nose, and throat) surgical procedures. Unfortunately, its illegal use in rising in the United States.

Cocaine is injected and sniffed. A cocaine addict may inject the drug as many as 10 times in one day. It has been argued that an individual on this high dosage of cocaine would not be able to plan and carry out a deliberate crime. These individuals may, however, commit crimes out of imaginary fears of imminent danger. According to cocaine users, an individual taking cocaine can experience a sense of extreme muscular strength and a heightened awareness through their five senses.

A second category of stimulants is the amphetamines. Amphetamine (Benzedrine), methamphetamine (Desoxyn), dextroamphetamine (Dexedrine), and the nonamphetamine stimulants (Ritalin and Preludin) are often prescribed for patients who suffer from fatigue, hyperkinesia (in some cases ADD or attention deficit disorder), and narcolepsy (brief attacks of deep sleep). Amphetamines are used to stimulate the central nervous system which produces excitation, alertness, and wakefulness. The stronger the dosage, the stronger the effects. These are taken orally and can be injected. They are available only by prescription. When found on the crime scene, the bottle and pills should be collected in a clean envelope or paper bag. The color of the capsule and shape should be noted and recorded. Any markings on the tablets should be recorded carefully. Some examples of amphetamine drugs are amphetamine sulfate, long-acting amphetamine sulfate capsules, and dextroamphetamine sulfate. Methamphetamine (commonly known as 'speed') has more effect on the central nervous system than the amphetamines do and less effect on blood pressure and heart rate. Methamphetamines are taken by injection and causes an extreme physical dependence. Available by prescription, it is also manufactured in hidden labs and is sold illegally as a crystalline powder in tablet form as well as in a variety of liquid forms.

A third category of stimulants are the xanthine alkaloids (theophylline, theobromine, and caffeine) which are psychoactive drugs. Caffeine, widely used in soft drinks, coffee, and a number of food items has been shown to produce a strong stimulant effect upon the human physiology. This category of drugs is not presently related to law enforcement problems.

## MARIJUANA

Marijuana is a mixture of the leaves and flowers of the hemp plant *Cannabis sativa*. This drug is in widespread use today. Some of the short-term effects include muscle relaxation with some impairment of judgment and coordination, increased appetite, and a blurred perception of time.

Investigators should be looking for either the dried form or the live plants. There are usually 5 to 7 serrated blades to each leaf (but as many as 21 blades per leaf have been found). When this drug is discovered at the crime scene, the drug and its container should be placed in a clean paper bag, sealed, and marked.

Marijuana is usually smoked by the user. It is rolled in two or three cigarette papers. In some cases regular cigarettes are emptied and marijuana is replaced where the tobacco was located. Various forms of pipes are used to smoke marijuana. These range from the conventional tobacco pipe to the hookah (a type of water pipe). When this drug is burned, it gives off a sweet and very pungent odor. It can be mixed with tobacco, catnip, dried leaves, and oregano. There have been cases where the marijuana has been 'laced' (mixed) with addictive drugs such as heroin. This is a method used by the drug dealer to 'introduce' the novice drug user to more expensive and dangerous drugs.

Identification of marijuana in the field requires an experienced investigator. The drug is green to a greenish-brown in color depending on its state of dryness. It is recommended that the investigator describe this substance as a controlled substance until further analysis by the lab.

Hashish is much more potent and dangerous to the user than marijuana. Hashish is a brownish powder and can come in pressed brick-like blocks or small pieces which are wrapped in tinfoil packets. Hashish has been found mixed with instant coffee at crime scenes as a means of disguise. Hashish may be eaten or smoked. The search format is the same as for marijuana.

## HALLUCINOGENIC DRUGS

LSD (d-lysergic acid diethylamide), DMT (dimethyltryptamine), and PCP (phencyclidine) are the most commonly abused hallucinogenic drugs. They act on the central nervous system and on psychic and mental functions and have ho accepted medical use. They have been known to produce visions, images, and dream-like frightening thoughts. The user may have difficulty distinguishing between fact and fantasy and experience varying emotional changes. LSD is sold in foil packets, small tablets, or small vials of liquid saturated sugar cubes, cookies, and chewing gum. Foil is said to protect LSD from light exposure which reduces its potency. Since all hallucinogens are easily absorbed through the skin, the crime scene investigator should take the necessary precautions in handling this dangerous drug.

Other hallucinogens include psilocybin (from the mushroom *Psilocybe mexicana*), mescaline (derived from the cactus *Lophophora*), and diethyltryptamine (DET).

## DESIGNER DRUGS

Designer drugs are synthetic drugs synthesized in illegal drug laboratories by skilled chemists. Mostly found in California are fentanyl analogs, meperidine analogs, and 3,4-methylenedioxymethamphetamine (MDMA). MDMA is known on the street by the names of Adam, Ecstasy, MDM, and XTC.

These chemists perform pharmaceutical research to develop new psychoactive drugs. Unlike the bonafide pharmaceutical companies, these unscrupulous individuals do not provide any quality guarantee or testing to determine possible harmful side effects from the drugs.

Since large amounts of money are involved, these manufacturing activities are often the center of crime scene investigations. There is also, as in home-labs, a high element of danger from fire and explosion. Fire department arson investigators often discover these crime scenes first.

## NONPRESCRIPTION DRUGS

Nonprescription drugs include sedatives, antihistamines, and sleeping pills. These are capable of relaxing the user and producing drowsiness. These are rarely involved in law enforcement matters and are usually associated with traffic accident fatalities and driving while under the influence. Many times, alcohol is also involved with the use of nonprescription drugs.

## TOXIC VAPORS

Certain individuals smell or inhale drugs in the hope of achieving a condition of intoxication or euphoria (which is a feeling of well-being or elation). Model airplane glue as well as gasoline, paint thinner, carbon tetrachloride, fingernail polish, acetone, and toluene all produce fumes which individuals inhale deeply. Some symptoms include blurring of vision, intoxication, and possible suffocation. Search for plastic or paper bags, rags, handkerchiefs, or other objects which might be used to help the user inhale these chemicals.

## RULES FOR COLLECTING DRUG SUBSTANCES

1. If an illicit lab operation is encountered and a scientist from the crime lab is not present, do not attempt to shut down the lab. Ventilate the area and call for assistance.
2. Never taste any material suspected of being a controlled drug.
3. Never smell materials suspects of containing controlled drugs.
4. Do not handle controlled drugs more than is absolutely necessary. After drugs have been handled, wash hands thoroughly as soon as possible.
5. Handle all chemical materials recovered with care. They may be highly flammable, caustic (will burn the flesh), or susceptible to explosion.
6. Use care in searching a drug suspect, an automobile suspected of containing drugs or any area where it is possible that hypodermic syringes or makeshift needles may be hidden. Even slight pricks in the skins from such needles can be dangerous if the drug user has a communicable disease. Infectious hepatitis is common among persons who 'shoot' drugs. If the skin is punctured, wash the area with soap and water and get medical attention.

## CRIME SCENE SEARCH

The laws regarding search and seizure must be upheld if seized physical evidence is to be accepted in the courts. Many times the illegal drug is hidden on the suspect or stashed in a hiding place in the suspect's residence or vehicle.

The suspect's clothing and other personal articles should be carefully examined for hiding places. Any object or pocket has a potential recess or hiding place where drugs can be concealed from view. The suspect is also capable of swallowing the drugs or hiding them in a body cavity (such as the mouth, ears, nose, rectum, or vagina).

When searching the suspect's residence or vehicle, an organized approach is the most successful. The crime scene investigator should look for names, addresses, and phone numbers, money, and stolen property. Items which appear to be out of place or damaged areas should be recorded and thoroughly searched. Any area which might hide drug contraband should be searched. The backs and bottoms of television and radio sets, the tops and sides of doors, light switch and electrical receptacles, curtain rods, and almost

Figure 9-1

COCAINE HIDDEN IN COMMON HOUSEHOLD ITEM

anything that has a hollow space is suspect and should be searched (Figure 9-1). Accurate sketches and written notes recording each item of evidence recovered should be taken. Photographs should also be taken of all recovered drug evidence with their respective locations. The suspect's vehicle should also be systematically searched. The front end (grill, radiator, bumper, fenders areas, air filter and body frame), interior (seats should be removed and searched, dashboard, door side panels, head liner, and any recesses in the floor region), and the rear or trunk of the vehicle (rear fender area, spare tire well and spare tire, bumper, and the undercarriage) are all potential areas in which to conceal drugs.

Home-based laboratories are discovered when neighbors complain, odors are detected by passers-by, and when fire and explosion bring the fire department to the residence or structure (Figure 9-2). On many occasions, the Hazardous Materials department is called in to seal off a potentially dangerous home-based lab. Together, with the fire and police departments, they help supervise the safe clean-up and removal of life-threatening chemicals. Some police departments have their own hazardous materials division which handle chemical spills and the disposal of toxic substances.

Extreme caution should be used when searching a home-based lab. They may be 'booby-trapped'. After adequate ventilation of the lab has been provided, investigators should eliminate any potential fire hazards. Avoid using light switches which may spark and ignite explosive chemicals (Figure 9-3). Before any evidence is removed, the lab should be thoroughly photographed. Next, fingerprints should be dusted and recovered. All other evidence (including recipes and lab notes and sketches, sales receipts, all raw materials, intermediate, and finished products) should be collected and safely packaged for crime lab analysis.

Accurate weights of all recovered materials including numbers of pills, tablets, and packets should be recorded. The chain of possession of all evidence should be accurately recorded to provide the guarantee of the integrity of the evidence from the time it was legally seized until its use as evidence in a court of law.

When blood and urine samples are collected, certain criteria should be followed. Blood should be collected with a syringe cleaned with a nonalcohol cleansing agent such as aqueous zephiran. When urine is collected, the suspect should first void any urine in the bladder. After 20 minutes, a 25 ml sample of urine should be collected in a container with a preservative in the presence of an officer. All specimens should be labeled and sealed and sent to the medical lab for analysis. In homicide cases, blood and urine specimens are collected from the suspect to eliminate the possibility that the suspect had a 'diminished capacity' due to intoxication. This screening process determines if alcohol or drugs were present in the blood and urine of the suspect shortly after committing the crime.

There are a variety of test kits produced commercially which will test for specific drugs. The presence of cocaine can be detected with an identification swab which will turn from white to a specific indicator color (Figure 9-4). Disposable tube- and Pouch-Style drug test kits will detect samples of drug small enough to fit on the end of a flat tooth pick (See Figures 9-5 and 9-6 for test kit instructions). These kits provide a quick analysis of drug classification at the crime scene. Samples of all drugs, however, are collected and sent to the drug lab for official analysis and verification.

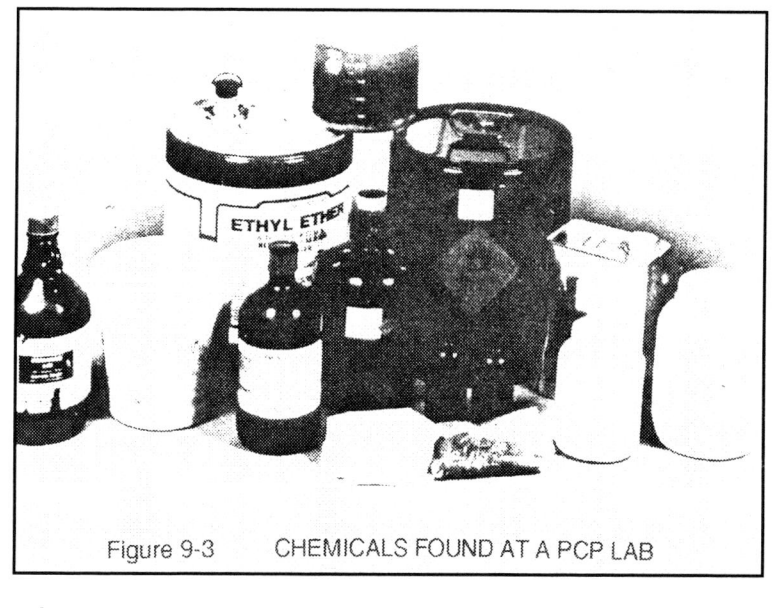

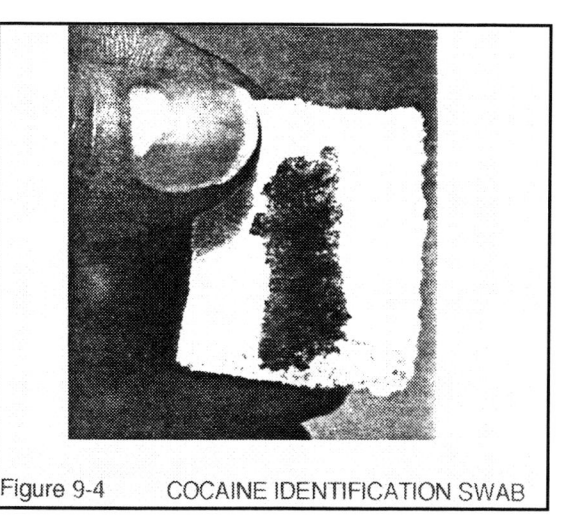

Figure 9-2   ETHER EXPLOSION DESTROYS THIS PCP CLANDESTINE LAB

Figure 9-3   CHEMICALS FOUND AT A PCP LAB

Figure 9-4   COCAINE IDENTIFICATION SWAB

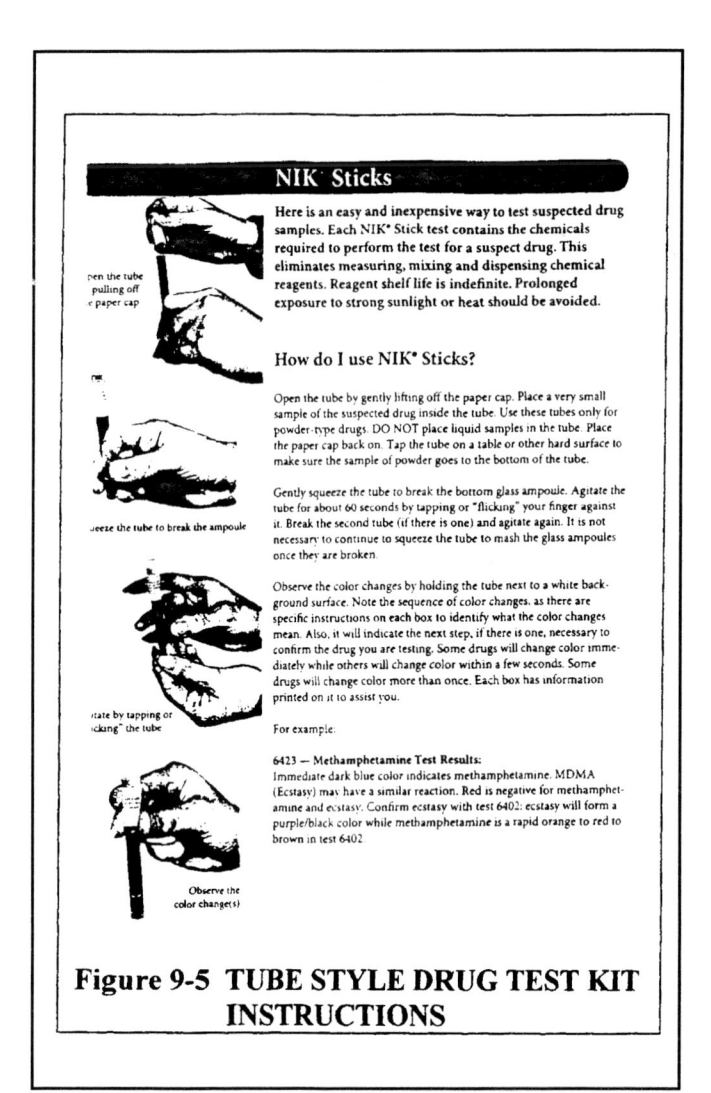

**Figure 9-5 TUBE STYLE DRUG TEST KIT INSTRUCTIONS**

**Figure 9-6 POUCH-STYLE DRUG TEST KIT INSTRUCTIONS**

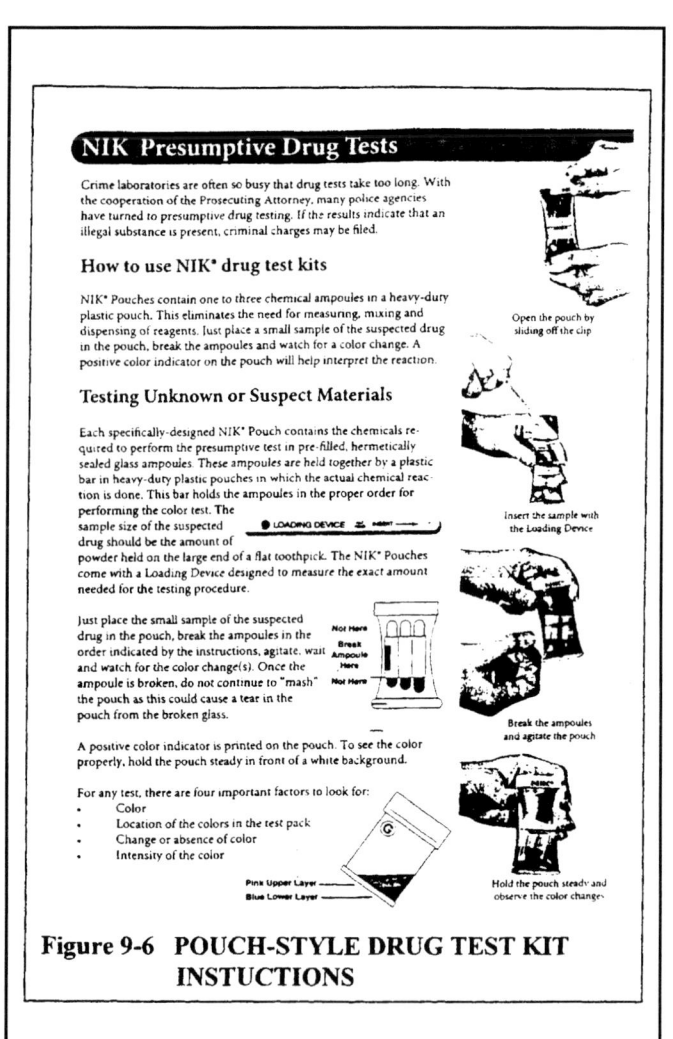

## CRIME SCENE SCENARIO-"ACCIDENT, SUICIDE, OR HOMICIDE?"
### -PART EIGHT: BILL'S TESTIMONY-

Detectives Dodge and Summer had spent the morning of day two testifying on a separate case in court. On the afternoon of day two at 2:30 pm, a phone call was received from the Mr. Kenney, the father of Matt Kenney. According to Mr. Kenney, Matt Kenney was ready to make a statement regarding Bill Morganson's whereabouts. An appointment was made for 3:30 pm. Matt Kenney was obviously scared. His hands shook while he gave a short statement. According to Matt Kenney, Bill Morganson was hiding in an old, abandoned water tower on the south end of town. Matt and a couple of his friends had brought food and supplies on several occasions. Matt had no knowledge of Bill's plans. Police units were dispatched to the location provided by Matt Kenney and Bill Morganson was arrested at 4:04 pm and brought into custody for booking without further incident. Bill Morganson was read his rights and issued no statement.

The white powder found on the shoes of Steve Sorensen and the bare feet of the victim was sent to the toxicology lab for analysis. Although drugs were suspected, the white powder was analyzed as laundry detergent. These samples also matched the white powder found on many places on the garage floor as well as the box of laundry detergent found on the shelf above the washing machine in the garage.

Bill Morganson was placed in a holding cell pending arrival of the juvenile authorities and his parents. A warrant was obtained to search and examine Bill for evidence related to the shooting incident. Clothing, fingernail clippings and scrapings, and hair samples were collected, labeled, packaged, and sent to the crime lab for analysis. Blood and urine samples were also collected by a medical technologist and taken to a medical lab for analysis. Bills hands were checked for gunshot residue. A back-pack, $375.00 in cash, some items of food, a flashlight and portable radio, sleeping bag, pocket-knife, and maps of the near-by towns were collected from the water tower where Bill Morganson was arrested.

In the presence juvenile authorities, his parents, and an attorney, Bill Morganson gave a short statement at 5:20 pm on day two. According to Bill, he, Steve Sorensen, and another youth he knew only as Joey Adams, were 'messing around' in his garage on the day of the shooting. Bill stated that he had 'ditched' school on this and several other occasions to be with Steve and Joey. "Steve would bring some beer and we would listen to some music and work out with the weights in the garage. On the day of the shooting, Steve produced a handgun he claimed belonged to a friend. Steve pulled out a box of cartridges and loaded the revolver with six cartridges. He then spun the cylinder and said 'Hey, I've got an idea.' He then took out five of the six cartridges and placed them in his front jean pocket. He spun the cylinder and pointed the gun at Joey and pulled the trigger. It all happened so quickly. The gun fired and the bullet hit Joey right in the center of his chest. The force of the bullet knocked him off the weight bench onto the floor. Joey didn't move. Steve ran out the back of the garage and I panicked and ran out the front of the garage down the street. I was afraid and mixed up and didn't know what to do."

When asked where Joey lived, Bill said he thought Joey lived with his grandma on the south side of town. No address was given. Bill also had little knowledge of Steve Sorensen. Both Joey and Steve were new friends he met about a month prior at a video store in town. He thought they attended the city's other high school across town.

Bill was returned to the custody of the juvenile detention officer. Detectives Dodge and Summer explained to the Morganson's and their lawyer that formal charges would not be filed until further analysis of recently obtained evidence.

Summer grabbed ahold of Dodge's coat on the way out of the station. "Not so fast, Dodge."

"Yeah, I know! exclaimed Dodge, "Bill's story doesn't quite match some of our evidence." "We need to get a statement from the Sorenson youth."

"We also need to get a positive ID on Joey" added Summer. "Maybe the blood lab analysis will be in on Morganson?"

"Tomorrow's another day, as they say," recited Dodge. He was hoping there would be no more night calls. He needed some time to consider the clues they had gathered during the past two days.

SELECTED READINGS-

Cravey, R.H., and Baselt, R.C. *Introduction to Forensic Toxicology*. Davis, California: Biomedical Publications, 1981.

Fasanello, J.A. and Henderson, R.A. "Vacuum Searches in Narcotics Cases." *Journal of Forensic Science*. 19(2):379-383, 1974.

Garriott, J.C., and Latman, N. "Drug Detection in Cases of 'Driving Under the Influence'." *Journal of Forensic Science*. 21(2):398-415, 1976.

Lundberg, G.D., et. al. "Drugs (Other an or in Addition to Ethyl Alcohol) and Driving Behavior: A Collaborative Study of the California Association of Toxicologists." *Journal of Forensic Science*. 24(1):207-215, 1979.

Turk, R.F., et. al. "Drug Involvement in Automobile Driver and Pedestrian Fatalities." *Journal of Forensic Science*. 19(1):90-97, 1974.

# -CHAPTER TEN-
# CHEMICALS

## INTRODUCTION

The use of chemicals in poisoning, explosions, and fires can pose some difficult problems for investigators. Crime scene investigators are sometimes faced with chemical evidence that is very hard to make a clear cause and effect determination. Certain poisons produce symptomology of specific diseases. It may be difficult to determine if a crime has been committed. However, the fact needs to be established that there are crimes which involve the use of various chemicals and there are laboratory specialists who can help establish the identify of those chemicals.

## POISONS

Medical examiners (coroners) and crime scene investigators are occasionally faced with cases of suspected poisoning. Since many poisons are able to produce similar symptoms to various diseases, it may be difficult to prove whether a crime has even been committed. If the crime scene investigator has any reason to suspect poisoning, the investigation should be conducted along the possibility of possible homicide, suicide or accidental death until the death of the victim can be attributed to natural causes.

Even though the movies and mystery fiction novels portray poison as a major method of homicide, poisons are seldom used in real life homicides. The intended victim would be aware of any alteration in their medicine. Laboratory specialists are also able to detect most poisons which would uncover any intended homicide.

Suicides and accidental deaths by poisoning are difficult to distinguish from homicides by poisoning. Alcohol, when taken with certain medications, may produce an accidental death caused by respiratory failure. This same scenario may also produce a suicide death. When the lethal dose of alcohol reaches about 50%, most individuals will pass out. But if the individual has taken some amphetamines while they were drinking alcohol, they might not pass out and continue drinking until a lethal dose of alcohol has been ingested.

The manifestations of systemic poisoning are vomiting, convulsions, diarrhea, rapid or slow breathing, paralysis, changes in skin color, contracted or dilated pupils, or difficulty in swallowing just prior to death. Not all poison victims experience all of these symptoms. However, most will experience enough of these symptoms for a witness to have noticed some of them, which makes a witness the best source of information. Physical evidence at the crime scene, if a witness is not available, is the next place to gather information. The crime scene investigator should determine what medication the victim normally took, what meals were eaten during the past three days (especially the last meal), and a prior medical history from the victim's doctor.

Toxicologists are specially trained in the identification, recognition, and antidotes of poisons. Since most crime laboratories provide a somewhat limited toxicological expertise, they rely on a combination of the capabilities of hospital and medical personnel as well as the laboratories of the coroner and toxicological specialists. A table is provided which lists some common poisons and their associated symptoms:

| TYPE OF POISON | SYMPTOM |
| --- | --- |
| Ammonia, vinegar, lysol | Distinctive odors |
| Arsenic, Mercury, Lead salts | Diarrhea |
| Carbon monoxide | Reddish pink patches on thighs and chest |
| Caustic poison from lye | Burns around lips and mouth of victim |
| Copper sulfate | Blue-green vomit |
| Cyanide | Burnt almond odor in air |
| Hydrochloric acid | Brownish-green vomit |
| Isopropyl alcohol | Nausea, vomiting, unconsciousness |
| Methyl (wood) alcohol | Nausea, vomiting, unconsciousness |
| Nitric acid | Yellow vomit |
| Phosphorous | Dark brown vomit with onion or garlic odor |
| Silver salts | White vomit which turns black in sunlight |
| Sulfuric acid | Black vomit |

The task of poison identification is made more quickly if the crime scene investigator is able to find a container for the medication or poison during the crime scene search. The container will be in a close proximity to the victim in the case of suicides or accidental poisonings. The container should be processed for fingerprints and trace materials before it is marked, packaged, and sent to the crime laboratory. All other items which could also be connected to a poisoning (dishes, glassware, contents of trash boxes, envelopes, and medicine containers) should also be sent to the crime laboratory for further analysis.

ALCOHOL

Alcohol may play a significant part in almost any type of crime investigation. Since beverage alcohol serves as a good solvent and taste masker, there is good reason to suspect its use in cases of poisoning.

In all cases of suspected alcoholic poisoning, the laboratory should include a blood alcohol analysis to determine the blood alcohol content in the victim's blood. If a mixed drink is found at the crime scene, any ice should be removed to prevent excessive dilution of the alcohol and any poisons which may be present in the drink. The liquid should then be transferred to a clean glass container and tightly sealed. The glass containing the drink should be sent to the laboratory for further chemical analysis as well as fingerprint analysis. Blood should be drawn by a qualified medical technician (about 3 to 5 ml is usually ample to determine the blood alcohol level). An anti-coagulant is added to the victim's blood sample to prevent the blood from clotting.

CHEMICALS RESULTING FROM EXPLOSIONS

Diffuse explosions usually occur as a result of the ignitions of natural gas, vapors from volatile liquids, or dusts from cotton or grains in an enclosed area. Most of these occur accidentally. After the explosion there may be a fire. If the walls of the structure are pushed out toward the top of the structure (causing the ceiling to collapse), the explosion was caused by vapors which were lighter than air (such as natural gas). When there is an explosion caused by vapors which are heavier than air (from chemicals like gasoline and kerosene) walls will be blown out from the bottom of the walls. The primary force in a diffuse explosion is the most significant portion of the explosion. There is very little 'return' force or implosion that is associated with explosions arising from more concentrated chemical form.

Concentrated explosions (unlike diffuse explosions) have a two-part explosion. The initial outward force of the explosion is followed by a more powerful return force called an implosion. The first force of the explosion may weaken the structure, but the implosion will cause it to collapse. Black powder, smokeless powder, nitroglycerin, dynamite, TNT, and C4 (plastic explosive) can all produce concentrated explosions (Explosive devices will be covered in Chapter 14). Oxygen is not necessary for the ignition of these materials. The characteristics of this type of explosion are local shattering and the production of a crater since the explosion expands in all directions. The hot gases released in large volumes during an explosion will cause solid objects to shatter.

Black powder and smokeless powder explosions usually leave behind detectable amounts of unburned powder and portions of the detonating devices. All recovered materials should be marked and placed in plastic containers and sketches should be made of the entire area.

Dynamite, TNT, and C4 require a detonating device (electronic) or a blasting cap. The search should be made for these items. Soil from the crater should be collected, marked, and placed in air-tight containers for lab analysis.

A suspects hands may be treated with acetone or methyl alcohol to determine the presence of dynamite. A trace material collection from the suspect's hands and clothing may reveal trace amounts of explosives which may be used to provide a link of the suspect to the crime scene area.

BOMBS

A bomb consists of a power source, an initiator, and an explosive substance. Once the power source is activated it takes only a microsecond for the explosion to occur. Bombs don't have to be aimed like a gun, or administered like a poison. They are a weapon of chance. They range from a firecracker to a nuclear weapon. The threat of bombings is growing steadily in the news. A lab chemist found residue left from a dynamite explosion aboard United Airlines Flight 629 in 1955. That led to the development of specific laboratory testing to determine if explosive residues were present in suspected bombings. Over 95% of a bomb will survive the blast. The problem arises in locating the thousands of pieces scattered in the debris. Finding those pieces is essential to the forensic explosives unit in order to determine who built the bomb. The pitting or cratering in metal fragments, the color of the flash and smoke, the odor, the sound of the explosion, the type and extent of the structural damage are all extremely important to the explosives unit. Fine mesh screens of decreasing size are used to 'sift' the bomb scene for evidence which is an extremely tedious job.

## FIRE AND ARSON

The first determination to be made by the crime scene investigator is whether the fire was accidental or intentionally set. Arson, although committed for a number of reasons, is usually conducted to cover other crimes. It is also used to defraud an insurance company. Arson can also be the vengeful tool of a malicious or psychopathic act by an individual upon others.

Most combustible materials will have been destroyed in a fire. This does not rule out the possibility of a thorough crime scene search uncovering vital pieces of evidence. Solid materials may be found which are foreign to the crime scene. A metal fuel container in a residential living room would be an unlikely place for that object. This same object in a garage would not offer as much arson evidence unless it could be shown that the container had been tampered with in some way.

The best evidence in a fire centers around the area of the origin of the fire. The fire investigator must take into account drafts, prevailing winds, and the fact that in the absence of air currents or drafts a fire will travel upward more rapidly than it will in a lateral direction. Secondary fires will begin when material falls from the original fire (charring will be less around these secondary fires than at the initial origin of the fire).

Evidence of several points of origin is usually reasonable grounds to assume that an arson has been committed. Investigators look for rags coated with volatile chemicals (gasoline, benzene, rubber cement, etc.) and their sense of smell is a good tool in finding these materials after a fire. These materials need to be collected in glass containers which are able to be tightly sealed. Many fire departments have specially trained dogs which can smell various flammable residue in concentrations of parts per billion. These animals can lead the fire investigator to minute amounts of flammable residue evidence saving hours of labor and money on expensive lab testing procedures on samples with no evidence value.

Igniters such as cigarette lighters or soldering irons are often used as well as matches, candles, and cloth wicks. All ignition devices are photographed and sketched thoroughly before being removed for laboratory analysis.

Burned documents are collected in the form of undisturbed paper ash. These are collected very carefully and placed in large container to prevent any further destruction. There have been many cases where burned document analysis has revealed important motive information in arson investigations.

## CRIME SCENE SCENARIO-"ACCIDENT, SUICIDE, OR HOMICIDE?"
### -PART NINE: STEVE' TESTIMONY-

At 9:30 am on the morning of day three since the shooting of Joey Adams, Steve Sorensen, with his parents present, was prepared to make a statement. Steve and his parents were appointed an attorney since they were financially unable to hire their own attorney. Detectives Dodge and Summer were also present. Steve had written his statement on a piece of notebook paper and had some difficulty reading his own handwriting. He did not appear nervous or excited.

According to Steve, he and Joey had met at the corner park where they waited for Bill to pass by on his way to school. It took no convincing for Bill to ditch school. After waiting at the park for about an hour, to make sure that Bill's parents had gone to work, the three boys walked to Bill's home. Once inside the house, they played some CD's in Bill's bedroom. Steve volunteered to go buy some beer from a local convenience store. When he returned, Bill and Joey were still listening to music in the bedroom. They drank the beer (two six packs) and decided to lift weights in the garage.

Once in the garage the boys took turns lifting weights and telling jokes for about an hour. Joey reached into his back pack and pulled out a revolver to show it off. Bill grabbed the weapon out of Joey's hand and pointed it at Joey's head. Joey pushed the barrel of the revolver away from his head and told Bill to stop fooling around. Bill reached into Joey's back pack and pulled out a box of cartridges and said he had never held a loaded handgun before. Joey grabbed the revolver and box of cartridges out of Bill's hands. He opened the cylinder and placed one cartridge in the cylinder. He spun the cylinder and swung it shut. He pointed the barrel of the gun at Steve's chest and pulled the trigger. There was a loud click as the hammer of the gun crashed forward and closed against the cylinder. The gun didn't fire. All three laughed. The game had begun.

Joey handed the revolver and box of cartridges to Steve and pointed toward Bill. Steve took the weapon and swung out the cylinder. He spun the cylinder hard and closed it. He pointed at Bill's chest and squeezed the trigger. Again, a loud click, and more laughing, almost hysterical now. Steve handed the gun to Bill and said "your turn, Billy, see how Joey's luck is holding out". Bill hesitated for a short time, then swung out the cylinder. He carefully spun the cylinder about one half turn and then closed it. He aimed at Joey's chest, and pulled the trigger. There was a flash of light and lots of smoke. Bill was holding the gun with one hand and the recoil pushed his arm up and back. Steve recounted how the loud gunshot seemed to ring in his ears. The rest seemed to happen in slow motion as Joey flew off the weight bench and onto the floor. He didn't move. Bill panicked and dropped the revolver on the floor. He ran out the front of the garage and down the street. Steve picked up the gun from the garage floor and ran out the back door to the garage.

Steve claimed he dropped the gun somewhere as he was running. After walking for about an hour, he was picked up by the police. Detective Summer was the first to speak.

"Who was with you just before the police arrested you?"

"I was by myself"

"The police saw another youth running off down the alley when they spotted you" added Dodge.

"I don't know what you're talking about."

"You said that it was Joey's idea to play Russian roulette?" asked Summer.

"Yeah, that's what I said!" Steve was becoming noticeably irritated.

"Did you ever have arguments with Joey or Bill?" Dodge was now leaning forward.

"We had some disagreements," said Steve.

"Were any threats made?" asked Dodge, still probing for signs of weakness.

"What do you mean by threats?"

"You know what a threat is, Steve. It's when you express an intention to injure someone who is annoying you." Steve had regained control of himself. "Joey liked Bill's girlfriend and Bill seems to be the jealous type."

"You mean Andrea Coleman?"

"Yeah, she flirted with Joey to make Bill pay more attention to her."

"Do you think Bill could have spun the cylinder to purposely place a bullet in firing position?" Dodge was carefully watching Steve's face and eyes.

"What are you saying?" cried Steve. "It all happened so fast. There wasn't enough time to plan something like that!"

Steve was taken back to the holding cell. Dodge and Summer left the jail at 10:06 am and drove back to police headquarters. They hadn't said a word since the interview. Summer spoke first.

"Their stories conflict, one of them is lying!"

"Or both of them," added Dodge.

"Yesterday, Bill said that Steve shot Joey and today, Steve said that Bill shot Joey. Are they trying to cover up something?"

"Do you think it's possible that Joey shot himself?" asked Dodge.

"He could have accidentally shot himself."

"We need some more tangible evidence before we rule out a possible suicide."

The blood alcohol analysis came in while the detectives were in their office. Blood alcohol analysis of Steve Sorensen and Joey Adams revealed a blood alcohol level of 0.25% and 0.16, respectfully. There was no alcohol found in the blood of Bill Morganson. The blood lab had typed Bill Morganson's blood as B negative.

No record of Joey Adams was found at Bill's high school. Steve Sorensen claimed Joey attended two of his classes at his high school. Dodge and Summer took a trip to the cross-town high school in an attempt to identify Joey. Two teachers recognized a picture of Joey Adams shown by the detectives and identified Joey as Wayne Adams. He had only attended school for about one and a half months. School records indicated that Joey lived with his grandma at 1457 Pocoima Ave.

SUGGESTED READINGS-

_____. *Alcohol and the Impaired Driver. A Manual on the Medicolegal Aspects of Chemical Tests for Intoxication*. Chicago, Illinois: American Medical Association, 1970.

Garriott, J.C., et. al. "Incidenceof Drugs and Alcohol in Fatally Injured Motor Vehicle Drivers." *Journal of Forensic Science.* 22(2):383-389, 1977.

Mason, M.F. and Dubowski, K.M. "Alcohol, Traffic and Chemical Testing in the United States: A Resume and Some Remaining Problems." *Clinical Chemistry* 20:126, 1974.

# -CHAPTER ELEVEN-
# CASTING AND COLLECTION OF RESIDUAL PRINTS

## INTRODUCTION

Since the criminal will leave behind various forms of evidence, most of which he/she is not aware of, the crime scene investigator must have various techniques, methods, and procedures to process and identify the evidence. There are a variety of types of impression evidence frequently left behind by the criminal at a crime scene. The most common types of evidence are footprints, tire marks, tool marks, and teeth marks. It is possible to make impressions or casts of these different forms of evidence which can be matched to the actual shoe, tire, tool, or set of teeth. It is then possible to either establish or to disprove identity depending upon whether there is a match. It should also be noted that many forensic technicians are now relying heavily upon photography as well as actual impression casting to provide identification. If there is reason to believe that particular impressions can be linked to known suspects, casts will be made as well as picture taking to provide a positive match-up with recovered evidence from a suspect.

Any object capable of making an impression or a scraping is called a tool. Tools can represent objects used to enter a residence, shoes, tires, and even teeth. A compression mark is left when an object or instrument is forced into material which is capable of retaining the impression. Tool, tire, shoe, tooth, and fabric impressions are some examples. A scraping occurs when an object is slid across a material engraving tiny (sometimes microscopic) lines. Examples of scrapings include lines on fired bullets, lines on materials left from the movement and force of tools, and lines left in objects caused by teeth marks.

Since tools and tool marks have been covered in chapter seven, the following discussion includes footprints, tire marks, fabric marks, and teeth marks.

## FOOTPRINTS

Footprints (referred to as shoeprints by some investigators) may provide conclusive evidence that a particular suspect was present at a crime scene. This is especially true if a trace material (found at the crime scene) is also recovered on the shoes of the suspect. Retrieving and preserving footprints, however, is an extremely difficult task for the crime scene investigator. The footprint is determined by the weight placed on the foot (more at the heel and toe areas), the rate of movement (more speed adds to the amount of slipping and smudging), and the type of material upon which the footprint is made.

Also of importance is the gait pattern which is determined by examining a series of footprints made by the suspect. The gait pattern includes the direction line (path of suspect), gait line (distance and direction between steps from one heel to the opposite heel), foot line (the line showing the direction of the foot), foot angle (the angle formed between the direction line and the foot line), principal angle (the sum of the two foot angles), length of step (the distance from one heel to the opposite heel along the direction line), and width of step (distance between the outer portion of both feet in the gait pattern). These components of the gait pattern are illustrated in Figure 11-1. Injured or sick suspects may walk with a broken gait pattern. The foot angle can help to determine if the suspect is running or carrying a heavy load. The length of step may determine the speed of movement and size of the suspect. In general, if the footprints are 20 inches apart, the suspect is walking slowly. Footprints 35 inches apart could indicate that the suspect was running. A good crime scene investigator is also able to tell if the suspect is moving backward (in an attempt to mislead investigators) as the gait and foot angles would be irregular.

It is important to make the distinction between footprint and foot impression. A footprint is produced when the shoe picks up foreign matter (dust, dirt, blood, moisture) and leaves it behind on a hard surface (mostly indoors). A foot impression occurs when the shoe leaves its imprint in a moldable material (soil, sand, clay, and snow) usually found outdoors. Foot impressions pose the greatest challenge to recovery (especially in the snow) since the outdoor environment may totally eliminate the impressions. Footprints indoors may be spotted by turning off all lighting and shining a flash light at a very low angle with the floor across the surface of the floor. Immediate

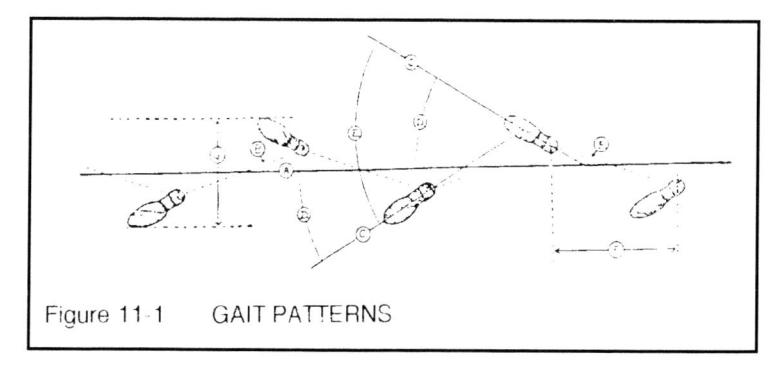

Figure 11-1    GAIT PATTERNS

action must be taken (upon discovery of footprints) to sketch, photograph, and cast or lift the footprints before they are destroyed. Figures 11-2 and 11-3 illustrate a dustprint recovered from a hard interior surface using a mylar coated foil and an commercial electrostatic dust print lifter.

Figure 11-2  SHOE DUSTPRINT RECOVERED INDOORS FROM A HARD SURFACE

Figure 11-3  ELECTROSTATIC DUST PRINT LIFTER

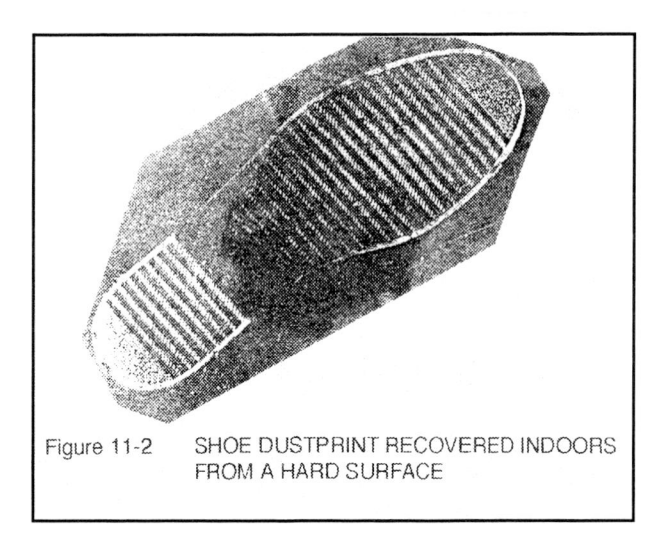

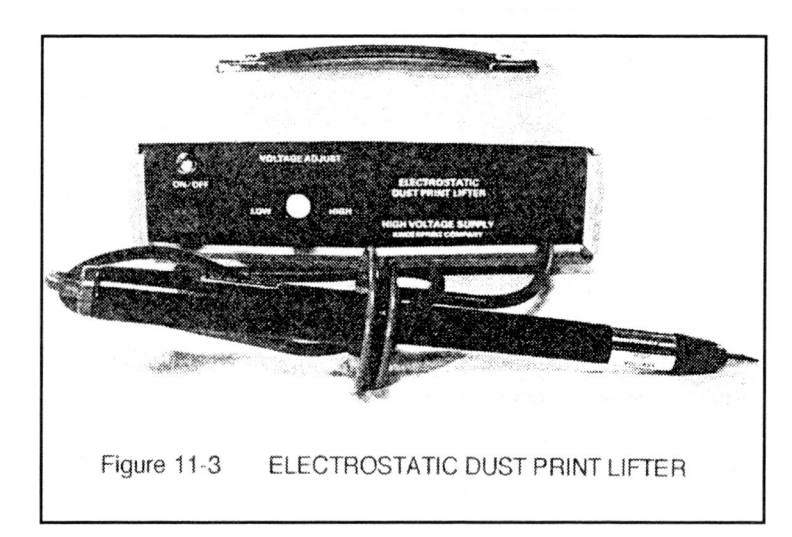

Photography of footprints should be taken on a vertical plane and include, if possible, the gait pattern. A color sample and a scale to indicate size should also be included. Trace materials in the footprints should be recovered and preserved for comparison should the shoe of the suspect be recovered. Footprints are lifted by using a 'lifter' which is a sheet of black rubber with a sticky surface. When a lifter sheet is not available, photographic paper is used to press against the footprint (with emulsion side down against the footprint). The photographic paper is beaten and forced against the footprint and allowed to dry. The lifted footprint is then photographed at an oblique angle which often provides a excellent replica of the original print.

Footprints of the recovered shoes of a suspect may be made by coating the shoes with a dust and pressing the shoes onto a paper on a hard surface. The newly made testprint is lifted and used as a comparison footprint (Figures 11-4 and 11-5). When gait patterns are required, the suspect must walk or run on a dusted paper wearing the recovered shoes to provide the proper forces and angles for identification.

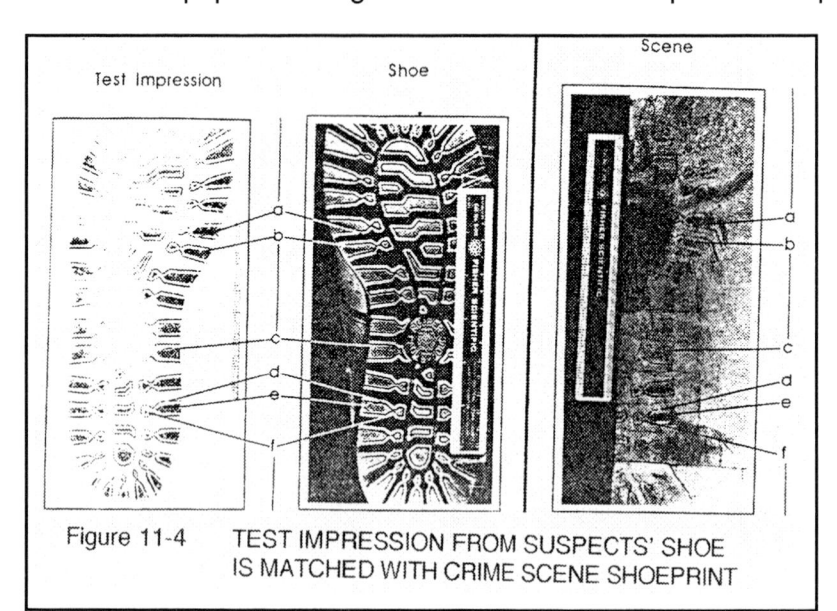

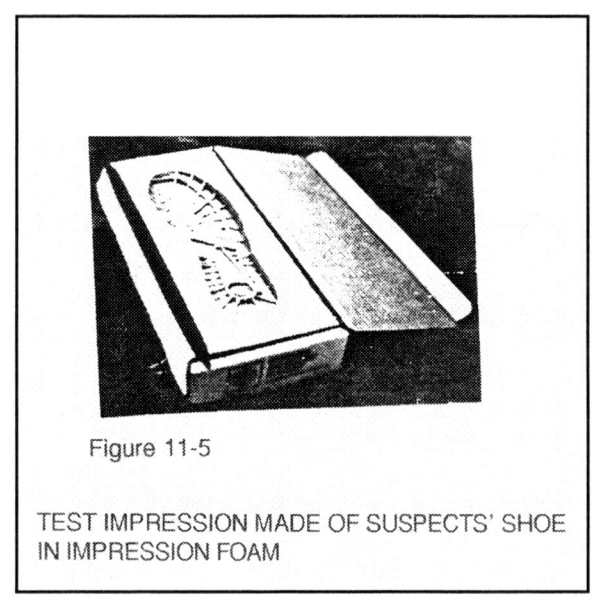

Figure 11-4  TEST IMPRESSION FROM SUSPECTS' SHOE IS MATCHED WITH CRIME SCENE SHOEPRINT

Figure 11-5  TEST IMPRESSION MADE OF SUSPECTS' SHOE IN IMPRESSION FOAM

Foot impressions are first photographed vertically with a camera using large negative films (4 X 5, or 120 film) to obtain better detail. A scale should be included. In deep impressions (those made in the snow), the scale should be placed at the bottom of the impression to eliminate any size distortion. Natural sunlight during the day and artificial light (during cloudy days or at night) help to provide the contrast needed to show the impression detail.

## TIRE MARKS

Tire marks can reveal the direction a vehicle moves. Only the rear tires leave a tire mark if the vehicle is traveling in a straight line. The tire tread pattern, distance between the two rear tires, and wheelbase of a vehicle (if the vehicle had stopped) are all potential evidence from analysis of tire marks. Many times, the make and brand of the tire and the vehicle can be determined. As with footprint analysis, tire marks can be very difficult to isolate and recover. On many occasions, there are many different tire tracks at the crime scene made at different times. Tire mark analysis requires many hours of painstaking measurements and photographs before any casting is performed.

Skid mark analysis is important to determine the velocity of the vehicle in question, the distance traveled before the brakes were applied, and the actual braking distance before impact. The trained technician would make all the necessary measurements and utilize the coefficient of friction, weight of the vehicle, and road conditions before making any conclusions.

Methods of photography are similar to those used in footprint recovery. Vertical photographs are taken (when possible) and oblique angle pictures are taken with various forms of lighting to capture the 3-dimensional aspect of the tire marks.

## FABRIC IMPRESSIONS

When a fabric is pressed against a hard, smooth surface, a latent print may be imprinted on that surface. This is especially true if the fabric or the hard surface was coated with a moist material such as blood, paint, soil, or even dust particles (Figure 11-6). This type of evidence is found in hit-and-run accidents where the fabric pattern of the victim is found imprinted on the bumper or fender of the suspected vehicle.

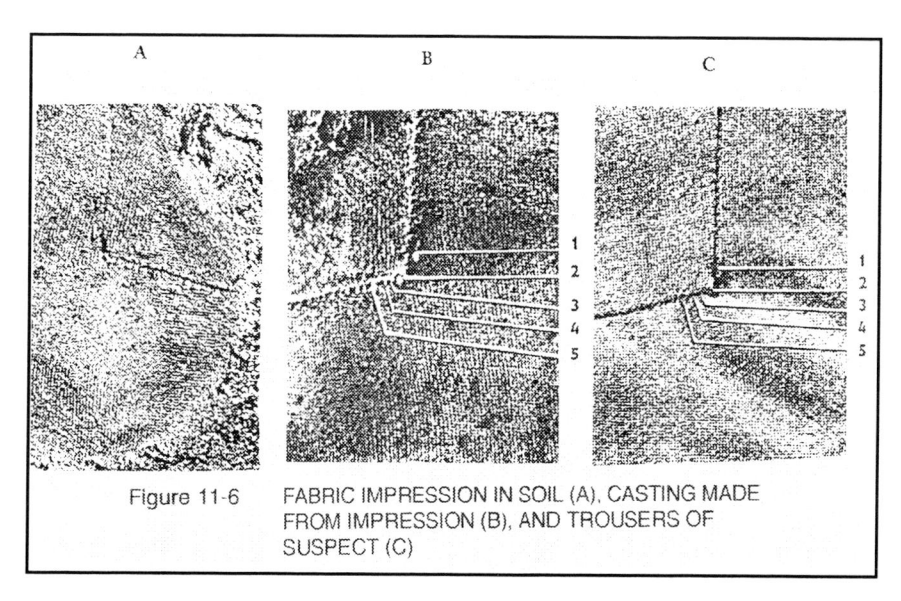

Impressions made by parts of the suspect's body (fingers, palms of hands, face, and body itself) in a plastic material such as clay can provide identifiable marks which may lead to the identify of the suspect. These type of impressions are also photographed from an overhead position. Casting may be required depending upon the severity of the crime and the condition of the impression.

Figure 11-6  FABRIC IMPRESSION IN SOIL (A), CASTING MADE FROM IMPRESSION (B), AND TROUSERS OF SUSPECT (C)

## TEETH MARKS

Both compression and scraping marks may be left from teeth marks in soft and pliable materials such as cheese, chocolate, and even gum. Bite marks may be found on the victim or on the suspect. These, when properly cast, may lead to the actual identification of a suspect.

Bite marks can be cast with various dental preparations. Bite marks on skin may change in appearance with time and require special handling. Plaster casts of the teeth are made from the cast impressions and compared with actual suspect dental casts (Figure 11-7). Many times, individual markings on teeth (positions of teeth, distance between the teeth, chipped teeth, location of a filling, missing filling, and ridges on the teeth) can provide an identity factor when matched to identical plaster casts taken from a suspect.

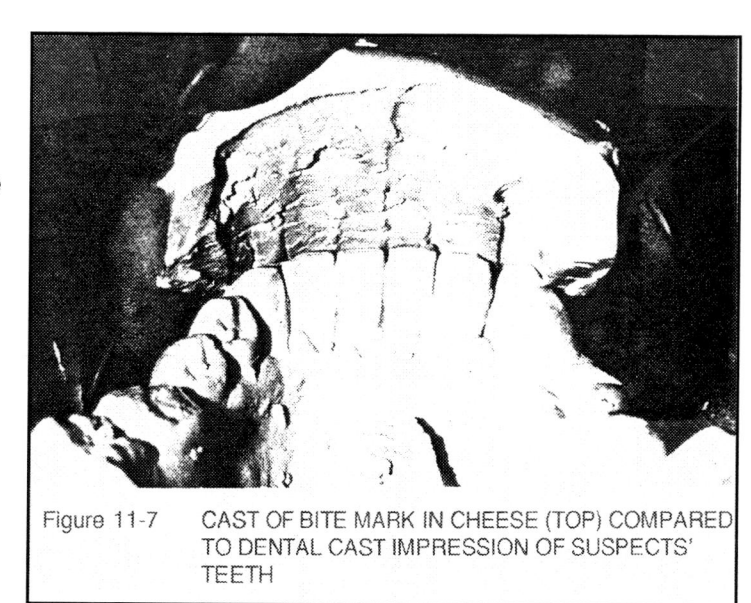

Figure 11-7  CAST OF BITE MARK IN CHEESE (TOP) COMPARED TO DENTAL CAST IMPRESSION OF SUSPECTS' TEETH

All photography should be completed as soon as possible in the event that the material bitten may decompose or melt and thereby distort the marks. Fruit which contain bite marks is preserved in 0.5% formalin solution which helps prevent dessication. If the fruit needs to be shipped for analysis, it should be wrapped after first soaking in formalin for two or three hours.

## CASTING MATERIALS

Plaster of Paris casts provide accurate detail which can be seen by the unaided eye. If, however, there is microscopic detail which is vital, a silicon based product should be used. Depending upon the environmental circumstances, the crime scene investigator should move quickly to preserve any impressions in dust or soft soils. A quick drying silicon spray can be used to 'set' the edges of these softer materials until the actual casting is completed. A non-water-soluble material should be sprayed on water-soluble materials (cheese and chocolate) to prevent the casting materials from altering the evidence. Regardless, all impressions should be thoroughly photographed (with a ruler in the picture to indicate the scale) before the collection of any residual prints. If there is a chance of rain, a box or other container should be placed over the prints and then covered with a piece of plastic to keep the area as dry as possible.

## PROCEDURE FOR PROCESSING RESIDUE PRINTS

Residue prints may be paints, ink, dust, blood, or some other foreign material on a surface. Any friction, as in the collection of latent fingerprints, may destroy residue prints. The detail left on a piece of paper by a shoe or a tire tread would constitute a residue print. There is not always a lot of detail in a residue print, but there can be sufficient individual characteristics revealed which would allow for positive identity to be established.

If possible, residue prints are lifted in a similar manner as latent fingerprints with tape. There are two types of residue prints. The first is made when an object such as a shoe or tire tread moves over an area and picks up dust or other material which then leaves the impression. The other type of residue print occurs when the shoe or tire tread leaves or deposits a foreign material on a surface (like a concrete driveway or a table top). In either case, tape is applied across the impression in a strip by strip manner (each strip overlapping the other by about 1/4 inch) until the entire impression has been covered. The impression is then lifted and applied to a transfer material which has a similar color to the impression material.

Attention should be given to any unusual markings, cuts, or brand marking. A class characteristic can be determined, but rarely is this sufficient to establish an individual identity. The shoes of suspects can be inked and 'printed' onto paper in a manner similar to fingerprinting. Elimination shoe and tire prints should also be taken of the crime scene area of all persons and vehicles known to have walked or driven on the crime scene. Tire treads can be inked and rolled over paper to produce impressions. All important information should be included with each impression.

## PROCEDURES FOR PROCESSING IMPRESSIONS

As soon as all the photography, sketching, measuring, recording, and protection of the impressions are completed, the crime scene investigator must decide which impressions to cast. When the twigs and leaves (or other materials) have been carefully removed, a silicon spray is applied to 'set' the soft edges of the impressions. This spray is dry in about 5 to 10 minutes. Care should be taken to not damage the edges of the impressions with the silicon spray by holding the spray can far enough away to insure that the propellant gases do not exert too much force. If the impression is in soil or other material which is capable of holding its shape, then the silicon spray is not necessary.

A casting frame is assembled to a size which is slightly larger than the impression to be cast (Figure 11-8). This casting frame is then set in place. Water is added to a rubber mixing bowl (the amount of water added would fill the impression). Plaster of Paris is added until the tip of a mound just breaks the surface. The mixture is stirred quickly. The mixing spoon is used as a baffle to break the fall of the mixture as the first pour is made continuously from one end of the impression to the other. There should be about 1/2 inch of plaster standing in the impression. Strips of wire or nylon mesh (depending upon the size of the impression) are added as reinforcement. The remainder of the mixture is added after re-stirring. Identifying information is then placed on the plaster cast using a hard instrument or sharp knife. This information should include the date, investigator's initials, and location of the cast. The material should be hard enough in about 30 minutes to remove and handle. If the cast is only 1/2 thick, an additional 30 minutes will be necessary to prevent the cast from breaking.

It should also be noted that there are a number of commercial preparations which are similar to plaster of Paris which exhibit less shrinkage. Figure 11-9 provides a view of a dental stone casting powder. The directions for each of these casting preparations will vary and should be followed accordingly.

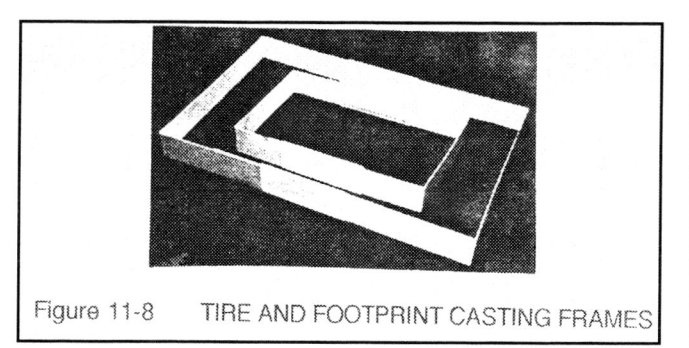

Figure 11-8  TIRE AND FOOTPRINT CASTING FRAMES

Tire treads may vary on the same vehicle. The investigator should sketch out the tread area and get a 'feel' for the direction of travel and then locate right and left. After initial photography and setting with the silicon spray. The same procedure will apply to tire treads as for shoe prints. Save the soil which may adhere to the bottom of the cast. It may be possible to match this soil with the soil found on a suspect to a particular crime scene.

**Physical properties:**
Consistency: 30 parts water to 100 parts powder by weight
Setting time: 7-10 minutes
Tensile strength 600 PSI
Maximum expansion: 0.13 to 1%

**DENTAL STONE CASTING POWDER**
Figure 11-9

PHOTOGRAPHY PROCEDURES USED TO PRESERVE PRINTS

Both tire tread marks and shoeprints are photographed from four angles using the oblique lighting technique to highlight special print features. Figure 11-10 illustrates a method to photograph a shoeprint in dirt. The camera is mounted on a tripod directly above the shoeprint in question. A portable flash is held at a low angle to the shoeprint from each of the four compass directions (north, south, east, and west). The resulting photograph (Figure 11-11), with oblique lighting from the north, shows shoe tread highlights with shadows to the south. Figures 11-12 and 11-13 show the same shoeprint with oblique lighting from the west. Specific detail missed with the north oblique lighting will be more pronounced with oblique lighting from another direction.

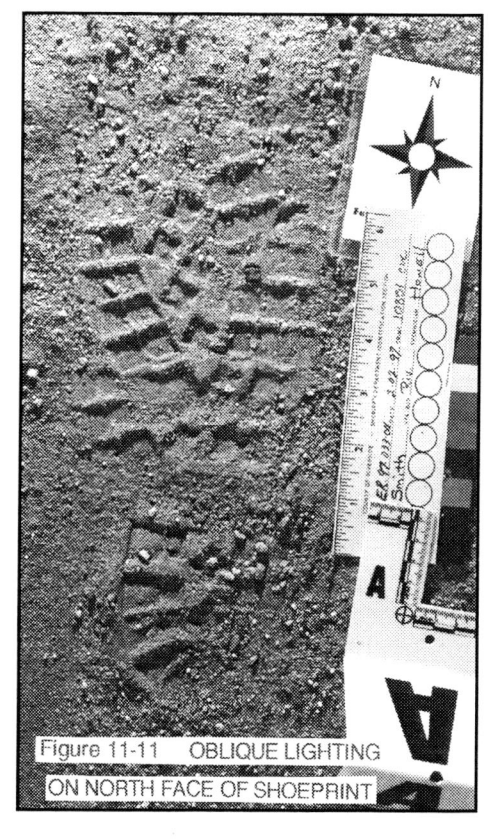

**CRIME SCENE SCENARIO-"ACCIDENT, SUICIDE, OR HOMICIDE?"**
-PART TEN: THE VICTIM'S GRANDMOTHER-

Additional test results arrived while Dodge and Summer were in their office. The footprint impressions photographed and cast in the soil near the back door of the garage were matched with the shoe impressions made from Steve Sorensen's shoes. Similar footprint impressions were recovered in the soil near the revolver in the

Figure 11-11  OBLIQUE LIGHTING ON NORTH FACE OF SHOEPRINT

Figure 11-10  OBLIQUE LIGHTING FROM NORTH ON SHOEPRINT

Figure 11-12  OBLIQUE LIGHTING FROM WEST ON SHOEPRINT

neighbor's back yard. The lifted shoeprints found in the blood at the rear garage door were matched to the left heal of Steve Sorenson's shoe. The lifted partial shoeprints found in the front of the garage were unable to be matched to the victim's shoes (found behind the weight bench), Sorenson's shoes, or Morganson's shoes.

The revolver's serial number had been filed down. The visible appearance was a number of file lines which completely masked over the actual serial number. As the filing of the stamped serial number was not very deep, it was possible to restore the number. Of the three processes available to the forensic technician (chemical etching, electrochemical etching, and heating), chemical etching was selected to restore the serial number. A chemical was selected which would react with the metal surrounding the edges of the formerly visible numbers. As the reaction proceeded, a faint outline appeared. This outline was dusted with fluorescent powder, amplified by shining a laser light source accross it, and then photographed. The photograph revealed the revolver's serial number: M13726J. The revolver's serial number was faxed to the State Handgun Registry division for identification of the owner.

Detectives Dodge and Summer arrived at 1457 Pocoima Ave. at 11:15 am on day three. They were greeted at the door by a middle-age woman who identified herself as Nora Mancini, a private nurse. After entering the residence, Nurse Mancini directed the detectives to the living room which was filled with medical supply items. She shared that Mrs. Adams had suffered a second stroke four days ago and was now unable to care for herself. When asked about a grandson, the nurse acknowledged that Mrs. Adam's grandson had been living with her for the past two months. She thought he was staying with friends when the second stroke occurred.

Figure 11-13  OBLIQUE LIGHTING ON WEST FACE OF SHOEPRINT

The nurse escorted the detectives into Mrs. Adam's bedroom. Mrs. Adams was awake and coherent. She was connected intravenously to a drip machine which was monitoring solutions of medication flowing into her blood. She was also connected to an oxygen supply. She asked her visitors if Wayne was in trouble again. She thought he was staying with friends since she went into the hospital four days ago. She had only been home a few hours.

Detective Summer asked if Mrs. Adams had a picture of Wayne. She pointed to a bureau at the side of her room. The nurse opened the top drawer and returned with a small, well-worn picture album. She, with the help of her nurse, turned to a particular page and she pointed to a picture of her grandson. Summer asked if she could borrow the picture of Wayne and only stated that they were working on a case that may possibly involve her grandson. Mrs. Adams said that Wayne had been living with his aunt, Mrs. Virginia Almstead, in another state. Mrs. Almstead was unable to handle Wayne due to health reasons. Wayne's father ran off when he was an infant and his mother died three years ago. Mrs. Adams said that she was the only living relative left to care for Wayne.

Upon leaving the Adam's residence, the detectives told Nurse Mancini that a young man's body had been discovered who may possibly be Mrs. Adam's grandson. They asked if she would wait until the identification was complete before Mrs. Adams was told. They also wanted to speak with Mrs. Adam's personal physician before sharing any possible negative news.

## SUGGESTED READINGS-

Abbott, J.R. *Footwear Evidence* . Germann, A.C., Editor. Springfield, Illinois: Charles C. Thomas, 1964.

Beckstead, J.W., et. al. "Review of Bite Mark Evidence." *Journal of the American Dental Association* . 99:69-74, 1979.

Bulbulian, A.H. "A Professional Look at Plaster Casts." *FBI Law Enforcement Bulletin* .34(9):2-7, 1965.

Cassidy, M.J. *Footwear Identification* . Ontario, Canada: Royal Canadian Mounted Police, 1980.

Dinkel, E.H., Jr. "The Use of Bite Mark Evidence as an Investigative Aid." *Journal of Forensic Science* . 19(3):535-547, 1974.

Ellen, D. M., et. al. "The Use of Electrostatic Imaging in the Detection of Indented Impressions." *Forensic Science International* . 15:53-60, 1980.

Fawcett, A.S. "The Role of the Footmark Examiner." *Journal of Forensic Science Society* . 10(4):227-244, 1970.

MacDonald, D.G. "Bite Mark Recognition and Interpretation." *Journal of Forensic Science Society* . 14(3):229-233, 1974.

Qamra, S., et. al. "Naked Foot Mark—A Preliminary Study of Identification Factors." *Forensic Science* . 16:145-152, 1980.

Sams, C. "The role of the Fingerprint Officer." *Journal of Forensic Science Society* . 10(4):219-225, 1970.

_____. "Tips on Making Casts of Shoes and Tire Prints." *FBI Law Enforcement Bulletin* . 32(10):18-22, 1963.

VanHoven, H. "A Correlation Between Shoeprint Measurements and Actual Sneaker Size." *Journal of Forensic Science* . 30(4):1233-1237, 1985.

# -CHAPTER TWELVE-
# PAINT AND GLASS

## INTRODUCTION

Crime scenes often involve the force of violent events. Hit-and-run, forced entry, and burglary can all involve damage and breakage to paint and glass. When objects (which are painted) are used to strike a person or another object, there are often small, tell-tale pieces of chipped paint left behind. Glass breakage may also leave behind small fragments of scattered glass. Many times the fragments are so small that they are handled as trace evidence and picked up as sweepings by the crime scene technicians. Tiny paint and glass fragments may also be embedded in the shoes and clothing of a suspect. When paint chips found on a suspect are large enough to be matched to their original site, the link between the suspect and crime scene is enhanced. Glass breakage may indicate the direction and velocity of a projectile and the crime scene.

## PAINT AND VARNISH AS EVIDENCE

The most common use for paint analysis involves the hit-and-run or an automobile murder. Other situations arise when a victim has been murdered and moved to another location (where paint from the actual murder scene has been carried on the victim to the new location) and when paint or varnish dust from the air adheres to the clothing of the suspect.

Paint is defined as a protective chemical coating which adheres to a substrate's surface area. The thickness of the coating ranges from less than a thousandth of an inch (fine lacquers) to many thousandths of an inch (latex and acrylic products). Most vehicles are painted with acrylic enamels and lacquers. This finish process requires many coats (in the lacquer finish) to a few coats (in the acrylic enamel finish) to provide the metal with protection from rust. Each of these layers of paint can be viewed in cross section with a light microscope. House paint ranges from oil-based enamels and lacquers to water-based latex and acrylic finishes. In general, wood requires an oil-based primer to properly adhere to the surface with subsequent finish coats of either enamel or latex/acrylic finishes. Masonary and interior drywall or plaster require a water-based primer to prepare the surface for the final finish coats of paint. Forensic technicians who specialize in paint analysis study solubility and chemical composition of paints. They, with help from the many paint manufacturers, are able to identify the type of paint, the pigmentation, and chemical fillers used by the paint companies.

Since there are so many types of primers and finish products available, each painted surface poses a unique combination of different chemical layers. When these layers can be matched with the layers from fragments of paint recovered from an object or a suspect's clothing, the object or suspect can be linked to the crime scene. In most cases, however, only class characteristics can be demonstrated (the paint fragment recovered from the suspect contains the same types of paint found at the crime scene).

The United States Bureau of Standards, working with the automobile manufacturers, maintains reference standards of paints used on all later model vehicles. Foreign vehicles and older American-made vehicles are not represented. The use of comparison is one form of analysis used where a sample is compared to a known standard collected at the crime scene. This comparison may be physical (where texture, coloring, stratification, and blemish or scratches are matched) and/or chemical analysis (to determine the type of pigment and filler used).

The area of evidence in question should be first photographed and sketched. When paint samples for comparison are collected, they should be chipped off rather than scraped. The layer structure of paint is altered when it is scraped which makes identification more difficult. Care should be taken to include any primer with the paint. They should be picked up carefully with a pair of tweezers or scooped up with a clean piece of paper. The paint chips should then be transferred to a clean plastic or glass vial with a screw-top lid. Paper envelopes may have tiny openings in their seams allowing the tiny paint fragments to fall out. The use of small plastic bags is not advisable since the static electricity of the plastic bag may prevent the technician from removing the tiny paint fragments. Two paint samples should be taken: one from the damaged area and one from the area which is adjacent to the damaged area. These two samples should be placed in separate clean containers. Care should be taken when the damaged area is a suspected tool mark. It that case, only paint from an adjacent area should be taken for analysis.

In hit-and-run cases, two paint samples should be collected from both vehicles (assuming the second vehicle has been located). One sample should include the damaged area and the other sample should be close to, but not include the damaged area. The damaged area should contain tiny fragments of paint from the other vehicle which can be used to compare with fragments of paint recovered at the crash site or actual paint recovered from the other vehicle.

## GLASS AS EVIDENCE

Glass, like paint, will only provide circumstantial evidence. Files of color, chemical composition, and physical characteristics are kept on all automobile headlight glass. Often, paint chips found with broken glass help to provide the clues which will link an object (such as a hit-and-run vehicle or an object used to commit murder) with the crime scene. Burglary may involve window glass breakage. Glass objects are sometimes used in assault and homicide cases. Broken glass is often present at the scene of a crime and its careful recovery and analysis can be a valuable tool to the crime scene investigator.

The direction of breakage is an important clue at a crime scene. Was the glass window broken from the outside or the inside of the residence? What object was used to break the glass? Answers to these and other questions provide the investigator with important pieces to the crime scene puzzle.

When glass is broken, conchoidal fracture lines appear along the broken edges (Figure 12-1). These fracture lines form as a series of curved lines. They begin as right angles to the breakage line (the side a force acted upon) and curve parallel to the plane of the glass (on the opposite side of the glass). These fracture lines help the investigator to determine which direction a force was applied to break the glass. When an object passes through a pane of glass, two types breakage patterns appear. The first pattern is the radial fracture which appears as fracture lines which radiate outward (like the spokes on a bicycle wheel) from the center of the break. The second pattern formed is the concentric fracture which are concentric circular cracks which occur from one radial fracture to another (Figure 12-2).

The direction of an object or projectile which causes radial and concentric fractures can be determined by examining the conchoidal fractures along the various pieces. A piece of glass with a radial fracture should display conchoidal fractures. The right angle lines of the conchoidal fracture indicate the side of the glass which was not acted upon by the force. The conchoidal fractures observed on the piece of glass with the concentric fracture should be at right angles to the surface of the glass which received the force of impact (Figure 12-3).

When the projectile is a bullet, there is a characteristic pattern of breakage similar to that described above. There is a hole produced with a crater formed at the back of the glass (Figure 12-4). The strength of a piece of glass lies in its surface. When the surface is damaged, the inner portion of the glass is easily fragmented. Glass is slightly flexible and will bend away from a point of impact. If the impact is caused by a non-penetrating object (such as a rock or a BB) a cone-shaped plug is ejected in a forward direction while tiny glass fragments from the impact are projected in a backward direction. When an object strikes a piece of glass with enough force to pass through (as with a bullet), there is a characteristic pattern of fracture (described above) which occurs. There will be some fragments of glass projected backward and a good portion of the fragments will be pushed in the direction of the force of the object. When a burglar uses a heavy object to break glass, tiny fragments of glass may fly back and land on the burglar's clothing. The majority of the broken glass will fall in the direction of the applied force (Figure 12-5). Tiny metal fragments (analyzed with a spectrophotometer) and GSR (gunshot residue) may be discovered on the glass fragments closest to the entry point of the bullet. Holes produced by small stones (thrown from a tire of a car, or propelled by a sling shot) produce very similar breakage patterns to those produced by bullets. The radial and concentric fractures are more geometric in shape than fractures produced by small stones.

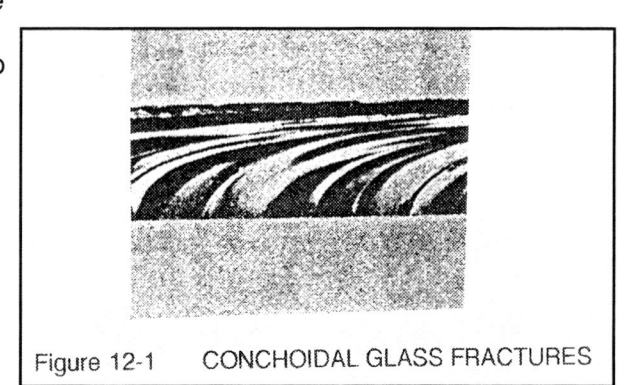

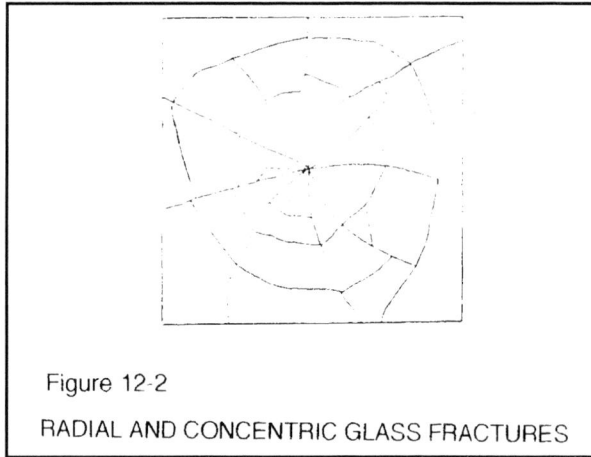

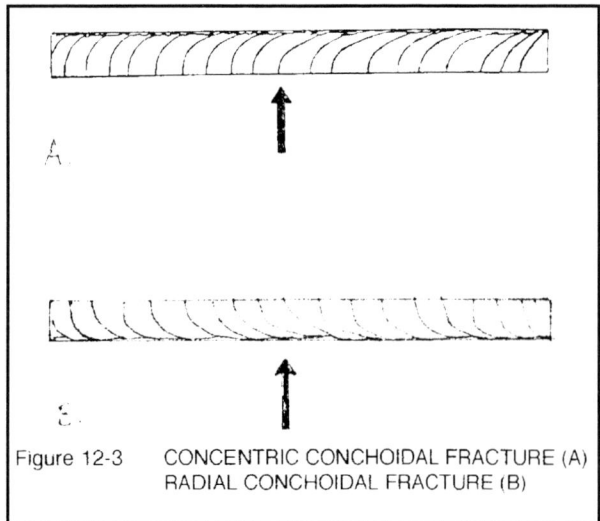

Figure 12-1   CONCHOIDAL GLASS FRACTURES

Figure 12-2
RADIAL AND CONCENTRIC GLASS FRACTURES

Figure 12-3   CONCENTRIC CONCHOIDAL FRACTURE (A)
RADIAL CONCHOIDAL FRACTURE (B)

Photographs and sketches should be accomplished at the beginning of the recovery of glass fragments. Glass analysis consists of shape and edge match of the fragment with the source. Smaller glass fragments are tested for density, color, thickness, chemical composition, refractive index, and light dispersion in order to identify the type of glass and, if possible, provide a comparative identification with its source at the crime scene. When glass is broken at a crime scene, the suspect and the suspect's clothing are thoroughly searched for fragments of glass. Glass is packaged in sheets of paper (to prevent breakage in transit) and packed in a box. Each piece should be carefully marked on its paper and on the crime scene sketch. This is very important when a large number of pieces of glass are collected and the investigator is asking the technician to reconstruct the original glass object.

Figure 12-4   BULLET HOLE PRODUCING CRATER IN GLASS- ARROW INDICATES DIRECTION OF FORCE

Figure 12-5   GLASS BREAKAGE WITH HEAVY OBJECT. DIRECTION OF FORCE CARRIES MOST FRAGMENTS. SOME TINY FRAGMENTS MAY FLY IN OPPOSITE DIRECTION.

## CRIME SCENE SCENARIO-"ACCIDENT, SUICIDE, OR HOMICIDE?"
-PART ELEVEN: MATT'S TESTIMONY-

At 1:15 pm of the third day since the shooting, Dodge and Summer had Matt Kenney called out of his class to the school's counseling office. A teacher had overheard conversation between two students regarding information that Matt Kenney had told them about Bill Morganson's involvement in a shooting. Since Matt had contact with Bill on the day of the shooting, the detectives questioned him regarding Bill's testimony on the previous day. Dodge and Summer told Matt that he could be charged with a felony for obstructing a criminal investigation by withholding vital evidence. Matt, after a short period of silence, said that Bill had told him that Joey had brought a handgun that morning and was upset about something in his family. Bill and Steve thought that Joey was joking and thought the gun was unloaded. Joey pointed the gun at his own chest and pulled the trigger. The gun fired and it flew up and away from Joey caused by the recoil force of the gun. Steve evidently caught the gun as Joey fell to the floor motionless. Bill panicked and ran out the front of the garage and down the street. When asked why this wasn't shared during the first interview, Matt said he was frightened and afraid he would be implicated in the shooting.

The paint discovered on the end of the barrel of the revolver was matched to the paint on the back door to the garage where the round barrel indentation was found. Analysis demonstrated an oil based, zinc pigmented white primer covered by a light brown coat of enamel, a dark green coat of exterior acrylic house paint, followed by a new top coat of dark blue exterior latex semi-gloss house paint on the door and the chip of paint taken from the barrel of the revolver.

Dodge and Summer returned to their office and reported to their superior officer in charge of homicide. It was decided to compile and list the known facts regarding the shooting of Wayne Joseph Adams. The facts were written on 4 by 6 inch index cards and pinned to a large cork board in the detective's office. The fact that Wayne Adams was shot with the recovered revolver was established. The fact that two other individuals (Bill Morganson and Steve Sorensen) were present at the shooting was also established. The remaining task was to determine who pulled the trigger and why. Was it an accident? Was it an intentional homicide? Was it a suicide? It was decided to pursue Bill Morganson's girlfriend, Andrea Coleman, for more information.

Dental records were requested from a dentist in the same town that Wayne's aunt, Mrs. Virginia Almstead, lived in. The information was supplied by Mrs. Almstead after she was told about the possible shooting of her nephew. She also supplied the medical clinic address where Wayne had been treated for viral pneumonia. These records would be supplied to the medical examiner and the forensic odontologist to make a positive identification of the body.

SELECTED READINGS-

Crown, D.A. *The Forensic Examination of Paints and Pigments*. Springfield, Illinois: Charles C. Thomas, 1968.

Fong, W. "Value of Glass as Evidence." *Journal of Forensic Science*. 18(4):398-404, 1973.

Ryland, S.G. and Kopec, R.J. "The Evidential Value of Automobile Paint Chips." *Journal of Forensic Science*. 24(1):140-147, 1979.

# -CHAPTER THIRTEEN-
# DOCUMENT ANALYSIS

INTRODUCTION

Document analysis becomes an important factor when there are written or typed papers found at the crime scene. There are some differences which exist between document specialists which have prevented this branch of forensic science from reaching its potential in crime solving. When documents are suspected of being forged or altered, the burden of proof lies on the technique of the lab technician as well as the expertise of the document specialist. Document forgery may include alterations to a person's will, contracts, birth certificates, checks, or other written documents. The forgery may involve a single letter or number alteration, a forged signature, or an entire altered document.

A FIRST LOOK AT THE DOCUMENT

Documents suspected of forgery must be handled carefully. The type of paper, identifying watermarks (placed on the paper by the manufacturer and changed periodically), and type of material used in the construction of the paper constitute the physical characteristics which must first be examined. Next, the chemical properties (type of inks or pencil used, handwriting, type of paper and its color and weight and its ability to fluoresce under ultraviolet light) are examined in order to establish where the paper was manufactured and sold and who, if possible, was the author and forger.

UPON FURTHER EXAMINATION

There are occasions when a forger will attempt to write over the document. This is called an alteration and is used when the forger is attempting to add to a number (changing a one to a seven, or adding more zeros to a numerical amount). At other times, a forger will intentionally destroy or obliterate a portion or all of an original document by writing over the document. If the same writing material is used for the forgery, recovery of the original writing can be very difficult. The use of a chemical erasure will render the original ink colorless, yet leave some ink residue which crime lab analysts can retrieve. If a mechanical eraser is used, the original ink as well as the fiber and physical structure of the paper is removed. Recovery of the original writing is sometimes impossible when this occurs.

AT THE CRIME SCENE

When written documents are discovered, they must be carefully handled to prevent damage and smudging. Improper handling of a document can limit its admissibility in court and ruin any latent fingerprints. If possible, the document should be preserved in the same condition and position that it was found. Plastic sheet protectors provide a protective covering which allows some examination without actually touching the document. Any latent fingerprints would also be protected. Documents which are discovered wet (from water or blood) should be allowed to air dry at room temperature, packaged in a cardboard box, and shipped to the crime lab for analysis.
When the crime scene investigator discovers a portion of a document which was torn or burned, every effort should be made to find the matching pieces.
Documents which have been completely burned will be brittle and need to be handled carefully. It is often possible to see a great amount of detail retained in paper ash. If the ash is found in a container (such as a wastepaper basket), then the entire container should be covered and brought into the lab for analysis. When the paper ash is found in a fireplace, a piece of paper should be inserted under a portion of the ash while the remainder is carefully pushed onto the paper. The paper with the ash should then be placed in a cardboard box for shipment to the lab. It is important that the charred document be preserved intact for laboratory analysis.
Documents should not be altered in any way. They should not be folded, stapled, written upon, hole-punched, labeled with stickers, or treated with any chemicals. The lab technologist will perform each test under controlled circumstances in a controlled laboratory environment. Treatment with various chemicals, special photographic methods, and illumination using ultra violet light are sometimes used to retrieve writing in charred documents.
The crime scene investigator should also be searching for indented writing left on a pad of paper when the top sheet is removed. Private eyes in the movies will usually rub the lead of a pencil at an oblique angle over

indented writing which leaves a shadow-like outline of the letters. One of the primary goals of the crime scene investigator is not only to collect evidence, but also to preserve the evidence. This type of writing can be read undisturbed by shining a light over the paper at a very low angle. The indentations show up as shadows (Figure 13-1). A photograph can be made of this type of writing to preserve the writing evidence. There are also commercial devices available which are designed to render and preserve indented writing.

## TYPEWRITERS AND OTHER PRINTING MACHINES

With the advent of word processors and computers, mechanical writing devices are becoming a thing of the past. There was a time when investigators were able to trace ransom notes to the actual typewriter. Typewriters have advanced to the point where it has become very difficult to trace written notes. The older typewriters had become worn from use and the type would become misaligned. Printers today have a more exact method of printing (dot matrix, ink jet, and laser ink) which does not vary with age. The crime scene investigator should be aware, however, that some criminals still use older machines to write their demands. Notes or letters written with these older typewriters may be traceable to the actual machines used.

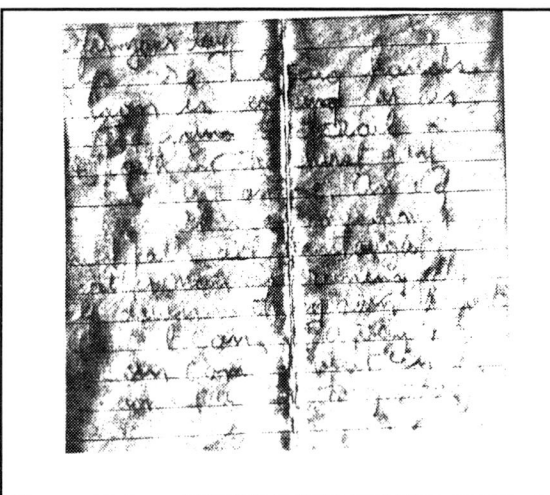

Figure 13-1    EXAMPLE OF INDENTED WRITING

## HANDWRITING

Handwriting identification is a science which tries to determine who wrote a certain document. This technique can also be used to eliminate a potential suspect by determining that a particular person did not write a certain document. Handwriting analysis attempts to uncover personality traits of the writer and is looked upon with caution by most handwriting identification professionals. There are two types of handwriting characteristics: style characteristics and personal characteristics. Almost all school children are taught to use cursive writing which forms the basis of style characteristics. Personal characteristics are developed by each individual and are deliberate (and sometimes unconscious) attempts to alter or change style characteristics learned as a child. Handwriting analysts study the personal characteristics of an individual in order to establish the identity.

The purpose of handwriting examination is to ascertain if a certain document is a forgery and to determine if two separate documents were made by the same person.

Some factors considered by handwriting experts include the slant of the letters, the shapes of the individual letters, the continuity of the letters (are they joined or separated), the use of large case (capital) letters and small case letters, spacing of letters, and steadiness of writing (known as quavering). There are a number of other factors involved in this type of analysis which are more nebulous to describe. Needless to say, years of experience are required before an individual is able to qualify as a handwriting expert in court.

After handwriting evidence has been recovered and properly handled, samples of writing need to be obtained from suspects and victims. These known samples are referred to as exemplar writings. Figure 13-2 is a table of handwriting sources which a crime scene investigator might use to

**SOURCES OF HANDWRITING SAMPLES**

| | | | |
|---|---|---|---|
| 1. | City Records | 11. | Military Documents |
| 2. | County Records | 12. | Motor Vehicle Departments |
| 3. | Department Store Records | 13. | On the Person |
| 4. | Pharmacy Records | 14. | Personal Documents |
| 5. | Education Documents | 15. | Police and Sheriff's Departments |
| 6. | Federal Records | 16. | Public Utility Records |
| 7. | Financial Documents | 17. | Real Estate Records |
| 8. | Hospital Records | 18. | Relatives |
| 9. | Library Records | 19. | Social and Fraternal Documents |
| 10. | Miscellaneous Documents | 20. | State Records |
| | 21. Vocational Documents | | |

Figure 13-2    HANDWRITING SOURCE TABLE

locate handwriting exemplars of the victim or suspect. Without exemplar writings, no connection can be made between the handwriting document evidence and the suspect or victim. The exemplar writings provide a known specimen of the individual's personal writing habits and style characteristics.

When samples of handwriting are obtained from suspects and victims, there are certain procedures which would help to eliminate the possibility of introducing variables which could alter the usual style of handwriting. First, if the suspect or the victim is upset, the handwriting may have a quaver which would provide an abnormal writing style. Second, unfamiliar writing materials (different pen or type of paper) may also promote altered handwriting. Third, an uncomfortable writing position, poor lighting, an irregular writing surface, or adverse conditions should be avoided. Fourth, the suspect or victim should be allowed to use their glasses (if they wear them). And fifth, it is important to have the victim or the suspect write several full pages and to specifically include the key words in question.

It is important that the investigator become familiar with the document in question. If large case printing or block lettering is used, then the requested exemplar should include large case printed or blocked letters. Whatever type or style of printing or cursive lettering used on the recovered document should be requested during the writing of the exemplar writing sample. A number of attempts may be required to obtain the necessary exemplar to be used to study the recovered handwriting document.

When a signature in question is compared with the known signature and there is an exact match, it can be assumed that the signature in question is a tracing. This type of forgery can be identified microscopically by the hesitations that would not be present in natural handwriting.

INKS AND DYES USED IN WRITING

Inks are colored liquids which are made of a variety of different chemicals. Each of the chemicals present in a given ink are represented by different molecular weights, polarities, and solubilities. It is possible to separate the different components of an ink by using paper chromatography with different solvents (Figure 13-3). Water, petroleum ether, ethyl alcohol, isopropyl alcohol, and n-butanol are among the many possible chromatography solvents available to the forensic technician to analyze the chemical composition of inks and dyes. The FBI maintains an Ink Standards Collection in Washington to aid investigators in the identity and age determination of ink.

Figure 13-3 PAPER CHROMATOGRAPHY REVEALING BLUE AND YELLOW PIGMENTS FROM A GREEN INK SAMPLE

**CRIME SCENE SCENARIO-"ACCIDENT, SUICIDE, OR HOMICIDE?"**
-PART TWELVE: BILL IS CROSSEXAMINED-

At 3:11 pm, on day three since the shooting, Bill Morganson was brought from the holding cell to an interview room. His parents, Mr. Knox (Bill's attorney), and Mr. Ortega (a juvenile authority) were present for the interview. Detective Summer turned on a tape recorder, gave the time and date, and identified each person in the interview room. Detective Summer read Bill's former statement (given on day two at 5:20 pm) regarding Joey shooting himself. Summer asked Bill if that statement was the truth.

Bill's only response was "That's what I said."

Detective Summer then read the statement given by Matt Kenney (given at 1:15 pm on day three) which stated that Joey intentionally fired the gun at his own chest and that he was upset over a family matter.

After a long silence, Bill said "Matt doesn't know what he's talking about. For crying-out-loud, he wasn't even there! Why would Joey want to shoot himself?"

"Matt mentioned that Joey was upset over a personal matter."

"I don't know anything about any 'personal' matter," retorted Bill, "All I know is that Steve shot Joey."

Detective Summer then read the statement given by Steve Sorensen earlier in the morning at 9:30 am. "Steve insisted that you intentionally shot Joey in what had started as a game of Russian roulette."

"That's a lie!" shouted Bill as he stood up. "Let him say that to my face!"

Detective Dodge, who had just entered the interview room and identified himself, warned Bill that the forensic investigation was compiling evidence which would soon identify the shooter. Bill gave no response to the investigator's warning and the interview was ended.

The identification that Steve Sorensen had first given to the police had been sent to a forgery specialist. The item in question was a state driver's license bearing the name of Eric Bendor. The license was determined to be a forgery of very high quality. The forger had included the holographic state seals and had utilized a driver's license from a recently deceased person (Eric Bendor).

Parent signature cards from Bill Morganson's high school as well as current parent signatures and samples of handwriting were compared with three notes submitted to the school attendance office by Bill for 12 absences during the past four weeks of school. The writing on the submitted excuse notes was jerky and irregular. The handwriting analyst determined the notes to be forged. Handwriting samples were obtained from Bill's teachers and compared with the submitted excuse notes. The handwriting analyst determined these to be written by the same person.

The gunshot residue (GSR) analysis on Bill Morganson was returned from the ballistics laboratory. Traces of GSR were detected around the fingernails and thumbnail of the right hand.

The trace on the revolver's restored serial number revealed the registered owner to be a Mr. Alfonso Zuccarelli whose address was 9453 Maple Street. Detectives Dodge and Summer drove to Mr. Zuccarelli's home at 4:20 pm on day three. Mr. Zuccarelli was a pleasant older gentleman who lived alone in a small one bedroom home. When told that his revolver had been discovered at a crime scene he seem confused. He walked over to a bureau in his living room, opened a drawer, and exclaimed that his revolver was missing. He said he was not aware of any break-in or burglary. He wore a hearing aid in each ear and claimed he took them out at night so he could sleep. He was unable to hear without his hearing aids. The detectives asked if their forensic crew could dust for fingerprints and were given immediate permission. Mr. Zuccarelli appeared very upset at the idea that someone had entered his home and stolen from him. After looking further, he declared that a box of .357 magnum cartridges for the revolver was also missing from the same bureau drawer.

The forensic crew arrived quickly and lifted a few good latent prints from the front of the bureau drawer. Mr. Zuccarelli also consented to provide his fingerprints as elimination prints. There was no sign of a forced entry into the Zuccarelli home.


SUGGESTED READINGS-

Brunelle, R.L., and Reed, R.W. *Forensic Examination of Ink and Paper*. Springfield, Illinois: Charles C. Thomas, 1984.

Harrison, W.R. *Suspect Documents: Their Scientific Examination*. New York: Frederick A. Praeger, 1958.

Hilton, O. "History of Questioned Documents Examination in the United States." *Journal of Forensic Science* 24(4):890, 1979.

Hilton, O. *Scientific Examination of Questioned Documents*. New York: Elsevier, 1981.

Leslie, A.G. "Identification of Single Element Typewriter and Type Elements, Part I." *Journal of the Canadian Society of Forensic Science*. 10(3):87-101, 1977.

Purtell, D.J. "Dating a Signature." *Forensic Science* 15:243-248, 1980.

_____. "Where to Find Handwriting Sample." *Law Enforcement Journal* October-November, 1972.

# -CHAPTER FOURTEEN-
# ARSON AND EXPLOSIVE DEVICES

## INTRODUCTION

Billions of dollars are lost each year in property losses due to arson. There is also a large loss of human life which is impossible to place a dollar value on. Arson is the deliberate burning of property. It is the malicious and intentional act of an individual to destroy property to defraud an insurance company, to conceal evidence of a crime, or to destroy human remains. Other motives for arson include revenge, juvenile mischief, sabotage, and pyromania. Arson is the most difficult felony to prove. Before fires are completely put out, the fire department has an arson team ready to investigate the cause of the fire. Once evidence of a crime is detected by the arson investigator, the appropriate police investigators are called in to assist in identification of the dead (if necessary) and apprehension of the arsonist.

The use of explosive devices is on the rise in our country. The World Trade Center bombing in New York City, the Federal Court House bombing in Oklahoma City, the Olympics bombing in Atlanta, and the Unibomber are all current examples of the terrorism criminals are using to 'pay back' individuals and society in general. The criminal who would use an explosive device is a coward who resorts to absentee and random murder. Explosive devices are not just limited to terrorists. Burglars and extortionists frequently rely on this method of destruction.

## ARSON INVESTIGATION

Hospital and fire department personnel (who are attempting to save the life of a victim or suspect and attempting to put out a fire) are not always able to preserve evidence at a crime scene. When a police investigator is called onto a fire scene it is extremely difficult to preserve the scene. Fire fighters, fire arson investigators, newspaper personnel, owners, and even the arsonist may have trampled and destroyed vital evidence by the time police investigators arrive. It may also be difficult to determine whether a fire was accidentally or intentionally set after a fire. These determinations may take days to analyze. Normally, human remains are quickly uncovered in a fire and it becomes the task of the investigator to determine the cause and time of death and whether the victim was murdered, committed suicide, or died accidentally.

Depending on the destructive force of the fire, the amount of usable evidence will vary considerably. Fire normally burns in an upward direction and if originated in one location will leave considerable evidence at the ground floor level. Fires originating in a number of locations (usually evidence of arson) can generate more destructive force and eliminate vital evidence.

Arson investigators are able to determine the origin of the fire by the location of hot spots, burn patterns on floors, walls, and ceilings, spalling (small chips and fragments of concrete are ejected resulting in a pitted and cleaned appearance in the surface), and the depth and extent of the burn on metals and glass. Every 30 seconds a fire will double in size. Fires begin in a vertical 'V' pattern. The fire spreads outward as it burns upward.

Fires are started by faulty electrical wiring, flammable materials, matches, igniters, and a host of other devices. Flammable fluids will leave a characteristic spalling pattern on concrete floors since they soak into the cracks and crevices and burn deeper than in areas not soaked by flammable liquids. The flammable liquids also burn only at the surface and edges of the liquid itself. As the liquid burns, the burn perimeter decreases in size leaving a particular pattern. Burning flammables are also very hard to extinguish since the vapor continues to rise from the cracks and crevices. Firefighters, through experience, know when they are fighting a fire fueled by flammable liquids. An area previously extinguished will suddenly burst back into flame when the vapors rekindle in the heat.

The arson and crime scene investigator should be aware of the on-lookers at the fire scene. Many times the arsonist will remain behind to watch the fire. Specially trained dogs are employed by local fire departments (K-9 fire teams) to search the fire scene for flammable liquids. They can smell in the parts per billion (humans can smell in the parts per million). They are usually trained to detect eight to ten different major flammable liquids (from gasoline to Coleman camp fuel). After ten minutes searching a hot fire scene, the fireman K-9 handler who handles the trained dog will bring the dog outside to rest and breathe fresh air. They will purposely lead the dog to the 'on-lookers' in an attempt to detect flammable liquid on their shoes and clothing. A number of arsonists have been arrested in this manner right at the fire scene. Trained K-9 dogs (many of which are Labrador Retrievers), upon discovery of a flammable odor, will stop and point with their nose and paw at the spot in question. They wear specially constructed "booties" which help protect the bottoms of their paws. They are trained not to destroy the evidence they discover. Since the cost of each discovered sample is so high, the handler will take each recovered sample (placed in a sealed metal container to prevent evaporation) away from the fire site and have the dog retest them. Only those that pass the test the second time are sent to the lab for analysis.

Labs need less than a drop of the liquid using a gas spectrophotometry apparatus to determine chemical identity. Flammables are sometimes referred to as accelerants and include gasoline, kerosene, paint thinners, turpentine, camp stove and lantern fuels, coal oil, and charcoal lighter fluid. Most fire, police and sheriff departments send these samples to private companies who specialize in this type of analysis using sophisticated and expensive equipment.

The presence of flammable liquids and containers (especially out of the normal storage places for these items), multiple points of origin, and forced entry are all indicators of arson. All the standard crime scene procedures apply to the fire scene. Of special interest is the igniter or device to delay the start of an arson set fire. Usually these devices are not totally destroyed and often provide identity evidence of the arsonists fingerprints. A thorough search of the suspect and suspect residence may provide samples of flammables or incendiary igniters and devices. The suspect's clothing (even when it has been washed a number of times) will still provide a positive test for flammable odors.

When a body is discovered at a fire scene, it is important for the medical examiner or pathologist to determine the cause of death. The victim may have been murdered and brought to the fire scene before the fire was set. If it was determined that there was smoke inhalation damage to the lungs, the victim most likely died in the fire. If there is no damage to the lungs, the victim died before the fire was set.

## EXPLOSIVE DEVICES

Chemicals which cause explosions and bombs are mentioned in Chapter 10 on Chemicals. There seems to be a good and a bad side with every discovery and invention. Man, in his search to solve everyday problems, discovers and invents amazing and powerful tools. Many times the discovery of tools that were meant to benefit mankind and society are turned into destructive and dangerous weapons. One such invention is the explosive.

Explosives are chemical compounds or mixtures that undergo rapid burning with the generation of large amounts of gas, heat, and the consequent production of sudden pressure effects. Mostly used for blasting and quarrying, explosives are used in a variety of commercial applications. They are also used as propellants for projectiles (such as bullets) and rockets, bombs, and mines.

Gunpowder (also called black powder) was invented by the Chinese in the 9th or 10th century and used in firecrackers. By the 13th century, the formula for making gunpowder had reached England. It was the only explosive known for over five hundred years. A use was quickly found for gun powder: propelling projectiles. Powder manufacturing plants were built in England and Germany during the 14th century. Regulations regarding the manufacture and use of gunpowder were placed into effect by the government in England in the early 1600's. Nitrocellulose and nitroglycerin were both discovered in 1847 and were the first modern explosives.

Explosives are grouped into two main classes: low explosives and high explosives. Low explosives (such as black powder) burn rather than explode. High explosives are detonated by shock and possess very high detonation velocities.

## LOW EXPLOSIVES

Damage produced by low explosives is caused by the forces exerted by the rapid expansion of gases as the explosive burns. Black powder (or gun powder) is a mixture of potassium or sodium nitrate, charcoal, and sulfur. It is extremely sensitive to heat, sparks, friction, and impact. It needs to be confined in order to detonate. A commercial use of black powder is in the safety fuse which is used to ignite explosives without using electrical current. Safety fuse is composed of black powder jacketed by cotton or jute, layered over with asphalt (providing water resistance). The asphalt is then covered by a plastic covering. Rate of burning (from 30 to 40 seconds per foot) will vary in safety fuse depending on the humidity, altitude, and age of the fuse.

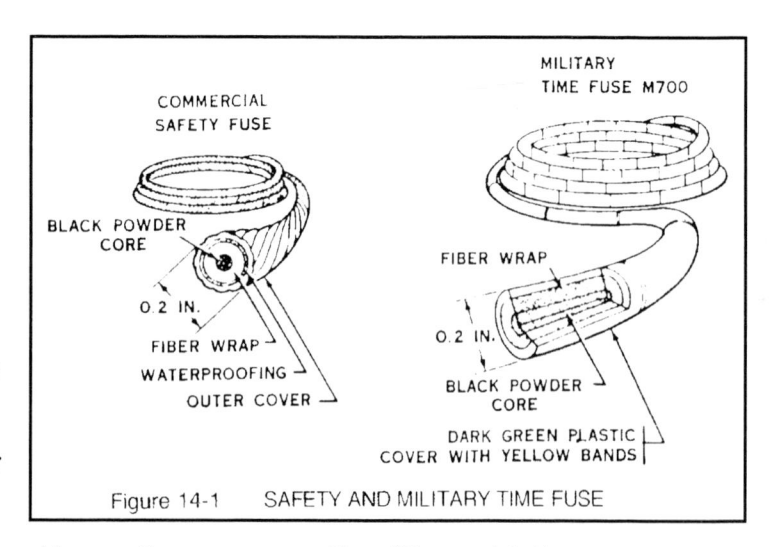

Figure 14-1    SAFETY AND MILITARY TIME FUSE

Smokeless powder is made of nitrocellulose and is used in small arms ammunition (Figure 14-1).

## HIGH EXPLOSIVES

High explosives can be classified into two groups: primary explosives and secondary explosives. Primary explosives are used as initiators of high explosives and detonate when subjected to impact or heat. Blasting caps and firearm primers on cartridge casings are types of primary explosives. Secondary explosives are detonated by primary explosives and are used to destroy an object. Detonating cord, which is similar to safety fuse with the replacement of black powder with RDX (cyclonite) or PETN (pentaerythritol tetranitrate), is used to detonate high explosives.

Nitroglycerin (developed in 1847 and highly unstable) was desensitized by the addition of diatomaceous earth and packaged in cylindrical form by Alfred Nobel in 1867. He called his discovery dynamite. Dynamite is detonated by a booster (capable of producing an electric shock) connected by a detonating cord to a blasting cap which is connected to a stick of dynamite (Figure 14-2).

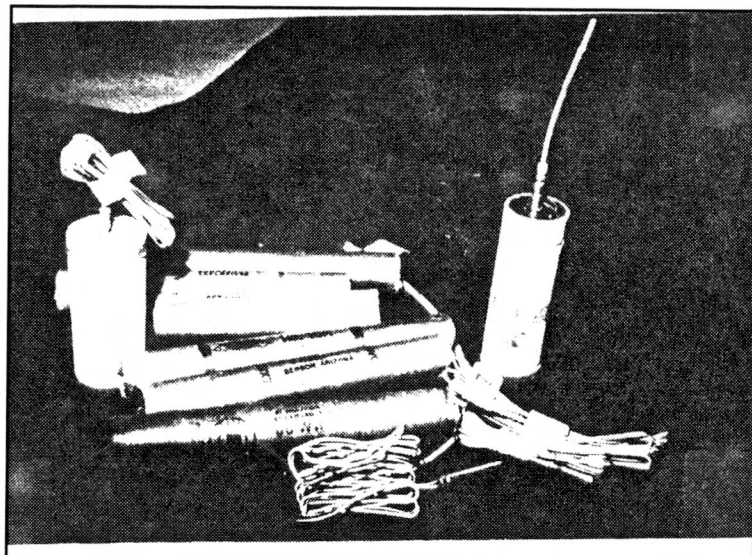

Figure 14-2    DYNAMITE, DETONATING CORD, AND BOOSTERS

Blasting agents consist mainly of nitrocarbonitrate (NCN) and ammonium nitrate. ANFO is a blasting agent which is composed mostly of ammonium nitrate and a small amount of fuel oil.

Military explosives are TNT (trinitrotoluene) and plastic explosives (C-3 and C-4 containing varying amounts of the high explosive RDX) which are labeled with a C for composition. The plastic explosives are able to be molded like clay to fit the contour of the object targeted for destruction.

EXPLOSIVE DEVICES USED ILLEGALLY

Experimentation with a large number of chemicals can produce explosive devices. The illegal amateur is capable of producing extremely destructive explosive devices. Blasting caps, flashbulbs, and ammunition primers are all capable of igniting heat-sensitive explosives. Investigators should be aware of certain chemicals (such as nitrates, chlorates, nitric acid, magnesium, sodium, sulfur, charcoal, sulfuric acid, and sugar) discovered at locations under investigation. These may indicate homemade bomb construction.

When a bomb is involved in an investigation there are a number of questions which should be addressed by the crime scene investigator. These are:

1. Who made the bomb?
2. Where was the bomb assembled?
3. What materials were involved in the bomb's construction?
4. Where were the bomb materials purchased?
5. Where was the bomb located?
6. How was the bomb detonated?
7. Who or what was the bomb's intended target?

When an unexploded bomb is discovered, the investigator should clear the area of all persons. Most larger police departments have a bomb squad who are capable of defusing the device. Photographs should be taken of the bomb as it was originally placed before it is disarmed and possibly altered. The entire location should be searched for all forms of evidence (fingerprints, footprints, tool marks, and any trace evidence) which may help to identify the bomber.

When an explosive device has been detonated, there are a number of factors added to the normal crime scene search. The investigator will need to determine if the structure is safe to inhabit after the impact of explosives by consulting with local building inspectors. A search will have to be conducted to determine if there are other explosive devices in the area. There are usually a large number of individuals who arrive at a bomb scene. Fire department, rescue workers, utility company workers, on-lookers, and newspaper people all add to the confusion of an already chaotic situation. After the injured people have been attended to, the scene will have to be secured and all unofficial individuals asked to leave. Witnesses and victims should be interviewed as soon as possible. The investigator will need a large variety of tools to sift through the debris in search of evidence. Protective eye goggles, gloves, hard hats, coveralls, and heavy boots are required to protect the forensic workers. If other agencies are involved, there should be a command center to gather and process evidence gathered. The bomb scene damage should be assessed establishing a focal point (seat) where the bomb was detonated and the perimeter of the blast (Figure 14-3). A buffer area should be added to the perimeter and included in the search.

The search for evidence should include items which would lead to the identity of the bomber. Of prime importance are pieces of the bomb, a timer (if used), wire, fuses, blasting caps, batteries, or any other items which might provide useful information. Trace materials should be gathered which would provide information as to the type of explosive used. If a suspect has been found, a full search of his skin and clothing for explosive residue should be conducted. The search should include the suspect's vehicle, residence, and place of business. An evidence log needs to be kept in detail recording location of all collected evidence.

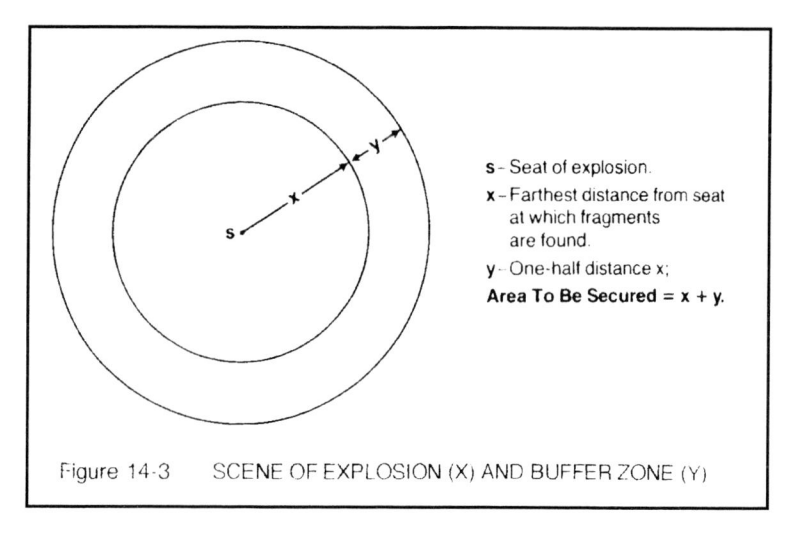

**s** - Seat of explosion.
**x** - Farthest distance from seat at which fragments are found.
**y** - One-half distance x;
**Area To Be Secured = x + y.**

Figure 14-3   SCENE OF EXPLOSION (X) AND BUFFER ZONE (Y)

## -CRIME SCENE SCENARIO-"ACCIDENT, SUICIDE, OR HOMICIDE?"
### -PART THIRTEEN: ANDREA'S STORY-

Detectives Dodge and Summer, at 9:20 am on the morning of the 4th day since the shooting, visited Bill Morganson's high school at the request of a school counselor, Ms. Ragotti. Ms. Ragotti related this story. On the day prior to this, the discipline office referred a student named Andrea Coleman to my office for counseling. Andrea had been misbehaving in several of her classes for the past two days. She was sent to OCS (on campus suspension) and given two one-hour detentions. She is normally a bright, well-adjusted student who has never been sent to the discipline office. While in my office this morning, she broke down and began to cry, almost hysterically. After ten minutes she began to share what was bothering her. Three days ago, when Andrea returned home after school, her boyfriend (Bill Morganson) was waiting outside her house by her bedroom window. She opened her window and Bill climbed into her bedroom. He was visibly upset. He told Andrea that there had been an accident at his home earlier that day. Joey had been shot in the chest and was probably dead. He told her that they were foolishly playing a dangerous game of Russian roulette with a revolver. She helped Bill wash up and gave him her father's old shoes, jeans, a shirt, and a coat. He told Andrea that he was going over to Matt Kenney's house to get some things and figure out a place to hide until he could think more clearly. When she heard that Bill had been arrested, she hadn't slept for the last two nights. She couldn't decide what to do. She was doing and saying terrible things to her teachers and friends.

Andrea was called out of her class and interviewed by the detectives in Ms. Ragotti's office. When asked if Bill told her who had shot Joey, she answered that she didn't know. She had thrown Bill's clothing and shoes into a trash dumpster located down the street from her house where a new home was being built.

A patrol car was dispatched to the location described by Andrea Coleman. A pair of tennis shoes, jeans, and a t-shirt were recovered from the construction site trash dumpster buried under some insulation and pieces of sheet rock. These items were sent to the crime lab for analysis. A search warrant was obtained and the Coleman residence was searched for evidence related to the shooting. Fingerprints were lifted from Andrea's bedroom window sill and jambs which matched those of Bill Morganson. The bathroom sink, trap, faucet, and floor were examined and two samples were collected from the lip of the drain edge using paper chromatography. These were placed in a clean test tube, labeled, sealed, and sent to the lab for analysis. Elimination prints were taken from Andrea and her parents.

Blood splatter analysis on the garage floor place the victim, Wayne Joseph Adams, sitting on the weight bench facing the front door of the garage. The blood was type O positive. The drops of blood had serrated edges with tiny outward-extending spikes from each serration indicating a vertical fall from approximately 60 to 80 centimeters from the floor. The drops of blood further out from the weight bench toward the front door of the garage had the characteristic bowling pin shape. The head of these marks was toward the front door which supported the idea that the victim was facing the front door of the garage when he was shot. The path of the bullet was determined to have originated from the center of the front of the garage in a line which crosses the end of the weight bench. The tiny droplets of blood were scattered in a 'v' shaped pattern originating at the end of the weight bench and ending in a 100 centimeter long arc approximately 142 centimeters from the origin.

Copies of the developed shoe print lifts from the front of the garage were matched with the shoe prints taken from the tennis shoes recovered from the trash dumpster near Andrea Coleman's house. One particular print included the label from a tennis shoe with missing portion of one of the letters in the label. The recovered tennis shoe also had a missing portion out of one of the letters in its label. There was a perfect match.

When Dodge and Summer returned to their office at 10:45 am, there was a phone message from Mrs. Green earlier in the morning. Detective Summer called Mrs. Green and made an appointment to talk to Laura Green after lunch.

SUGGESTED READINGS-

Beveridge, A.D., et al. "Systematic Analysis of Explosive Residues." *Journal of Forensic Science* 20(3):431-454, 1975.

Boudreau, J.F., et. al. *Arson and Arson Investigation Survey and Assessment* . National Institute of Law Enforcement and Criminal Justice, Law Enforcement Assistance Administration, U.S. Department of Justice. U.S. Government Printing Office, 1977.

Brodie, T.G. and Gleason, A.W. *Bombs and Bombings: A Handbook to Detection. Disposal and Investigation for Police and Fire Departments* . Springfield, Illinois: Charles C. Thomas, 1973.

Carroll, J.R. *Physical and Technical Aspects of Fire and Arson Investigation* .Springfield, Illinois: Charles C. Thomas, 1979.

Fisco, W. "A Portable Explosives Identification Kit for Field Use." *Journal of Forensic Science* 20(1):141-148, 1975.

Hoffman, C.M. and Byall, E.B. "Identification of Explosive Residues in Bomb Scene Investigations." *Journal of Forensic Science* 19(1):54-63, 1974.

Kempe, C.R. and Tannert, W.T. "Detection of Dynamite Residues on the Hands of Bombing Suspects." *Journal of Forensic Science* 17(2):323-324, 1972.

Lenz, R.R. *Explosives and Bomb Disposal Guide* . Springfield, Illinois: Charles C. Thomas, 1965.

Stone, I.C., et al. "Accelerant Detection in Fire Residues." *Journal of Forensic Science* 23(1):78-83,1978.
Townshend, D.G. "Identification of Electric Blasting Caps by Manufacture." *Journal of Forensic Science* 18(4):405-409, 1973.

Twibell, J.D., et al. "Transfer of Nitroglycerin to Hands During Contact with Commercial Explosives." *Journal of Forensic Science* 27(4):783-791, 1984.

Yallop, H.J. "Breaking Offenses with Explosives—The Techniques of the Criminal and the Scientist." *Journal of Forensic Science Society* 14(2):99-102, 1974.

Yallop, H. J. *Explosion Investigation* . Harrogate, England: Forensic Science Society Press, 1980.

# -CHAPTER FIFTEEN-
# DETERMINING HUMAN IDENTITY

## INTRODUCTION

Death by violence has been highly popularized in movies and books. We can all visualize the scene where there is a neatly dressed victim lying on the floor as if calmly sleeping. The room is nicely decorated and everything appears in perfect order. The suave detective, of course, will notice the one or two items out of place in a room otherwise untouched by a violent crime. The family and next of kin are standing in the room of the deceased emotionally unattached to this scene of violence: each one knowing that they are a potential suspect.

In real life, the murdered victim is not a pretty sight. The entire room is in disarray with over-turned chairs and tables, pieces of broken articles and papers strewn everywhere, blood splattered against walls, floors, furniture, draperies, and even on the ceiling. Arms, legs, and even heads can be missing from the body. The body may have been burned or partially burned to mask identity. Fingers and entire hands can be cut off to delay identification. If discovered outside, animals may have eaten and ravaged portions of the body. There is usually an unbelievably foul odor. Flies, maggots, and other insects are usually present after a certain amount of time. There is really no way to prepare a new investigator for this type of work. Identity determination can be a long and arduous task. The difficulty increases when possible next of kin are brought to the morgue to identify the body. What had been a cognitive and scientific endeavor becomes personalized and wrought with emotion. Most investigators will agree that working with the bodies of children is the hardest and most emotionally draining part of their work.

Occasionally, a victim is discovered who is not easily identified. When this occurs, it takes the best investigative powers possible by the crime scene investigator, the coroner or medical examiner, and the lab technicians to make a positive identification. The same crime scene procedures are followed that were outlined in chapter two. There are a number of specific procedures and tests which can be accomplished to enhance the investigator's chances of determining the identity of the victim. These include: an autopsy including the time and cause of death, blood type determination and hospital records, dental records, hospital or clinic wound charts, identification markings, physical data gathered from family, neighbors, or fellow workers, clothing or other personal items, and fingerprints.

## HOMICIDE INVESTIGATION

The crime scene involving the death of a victim or victims requires a concerted effort of a number of professional groups. The police investigators will have to coordinate and collect information from a number of these groups. These include forensic technicians who collect the evidence, the lab technicians who process and analyze the evidence, medical examiners and pathologists who examine the body or bodies, speciality laboratories who process and analyze evidence which the local forensic lab is not equipped to handle, other law enforcement agencies who provide assistance, and the interview process from witnesses, suspects, and victims who are still alive. Only through this interdisciplinary approach and focus on detail can a crime scene investigator successfully reconstruct the crime scene and solve the crime mystery.

When the investigator arrives at the crime scene where a dead body has been found, a determination needs to be made concerning the identity of the body and the time and cause of death. The crime scene search and procedures and techniques have been covered in previous chapters.

There have been cases where the criminal has murdered an individual and tried to make it look like an accident or a suicide. According to police investigators, it is advisable to assume a homicide (willful killing) has been committed with the discovery of a victim unless specific evidence is found to indicate otherwise. Not only is the cause of death a vital beginning question, but were the injuries inflicted on the victim capable of being self-inflicted? Was there a struggle? Was a weapon found?

## THE BODY WHERE IT WAS FOUND

The crime scene investigator must make sure that the body is not moved from the position in which it was found until two criteria are met. First, is the victim actually dead? If not, paramedic personnel need to be summoned immediately. Second, photographs need to be taken of the victim and the surrounding environment before any essential piece of evidence is moved and not recorded properly. Once these criteria are met, the crime scene investigator should conduct a victim search including the clothing (color, size, labels, laundry markings, presence of buttons, and trace materials), and any personal effects on the victim.

When a victim is badly decomposed, burned, or missing body parts, it is necessary to gather as much evidence and information as possible to aid in the identification process. Blood samples are taken, hair and fiber samples are collected, and fingernail parings and scrapings are gathered. Dental examinations are usually reserved for the autopsy. The skin is meticulously taped to remove any trace materials (such as hair, fibers, fragments of metals, powders, or any soil). Weapons embedded in the victim are only removed once they have been sketched, photographed, and recorded. See Figures 15-1 and 15-2 for victim and suspect evidence kits which are prepared specifically for sexual assault kits. The victim is placed in a body bag and sealed to prevent the loss of any additional evidence until the autopsy can be performed.

**Victim Evidence Collection Kit**

The kit is organized in a step-by-step manner, and the instruction sheet explains in detail each step of the collection procedure. Components needed for each step are provided in separate, numbered envelopes.

Step 1. Authorization for collection and release of evidence and information form.
Step 2. Medical history and assault information form
Step 3. One 20" x 30" white paper sheet, tow outer clothing bags and one panties bag.
Step 4. Debris collection for nail scraping.
Step 5. Towel and comb for pubic hair combing.
Step 6. Envelope for pulled pubic hairs.
Step 7. Slides, swabs and boxes for vaginal swabs and smear.
Step 8. Slide, swabs and boxes for rectal swabs and smear.
Step 9. Slide, swabs and boxes for oral swabs and smear.
Step 10. Envelope for pulled head hairs.
Step 11. Paper disk and envelope for saliva sample.
Step 12. Two blood vials for known blood sample collection.
Step 13. Anatomical drawings chart.

**Figure 15-1 VICTIM EVIDENCE COLLECTION KIT (FEMALES)**

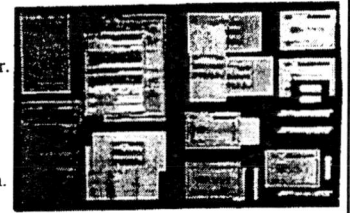

## TIME OF DEATH

The crime scene investigator may place a preliminary apparent cause of death on the victim, but the real or actual cause of death will be given by the forensic pathologist or medical examiner. The investigator should have a good working knowledge of the anatomy and physiology of the human body in order to make conclusions regarding the extent of various types of wounds. Postmortem lividity, rigor mortis, core body temperature, and the presence of insects can all be used to approximate the time of death.

**Suspect Evidence Collection Kit**

The Suspect Evidence Collection Kit is different from the above kit is that the types of evidence collected are specific for males. Each sealed box comes with an instruction sheet explaining all of the steps of the kit.

Step 1. Two outer clothing bags and one underwear bag.
Step 2. Debris collection for nail scraping
Step 3. Towel and comb for pubic hair combing.
Step 4. Envelope for pulled pubic hairs.
Step 5. Envelope for pulled head hairs.
Step 6. Paper disk and envelope for saliva sample.
Step 7. Two blood vials for known blood sample collection.
Step 8. Anatomical drawings chart.

**Figure 15 – 2 VICTIM EVIDENCE COLLECTION KIT (MALES)**

## LIVIDITY

The body (referred to as the corpse or cadaver) will begin to decompose almost immediately upon death. When the blood ceases to flow in the arteries and veins, it will pool in the lower portions of the body causing a deep reddish-purple color. This is know as postmortem lividity. This coloration may begin to show as early as twenty minutes to four hours after death. It may not be complete until twelve hours after death. Once postmortem lividity forms, it will not change. This fact can be used to show that a body has been moved after death and the onset of postmortem lividity.

## RIGOR MORTIS

Rigor mortis begins to set in within two to six hours after death. The muscle tissue begins to solidify in a rigid manner starting in the face and jaw muscles, proceeding to the neck and trunk muscles, and finally, to the extremities. It is complete in two to six hours after the onset. More healthy and muscular victims take a longer time for rigor mortis to set in. Rigor mortis will last from twenty-four to forty-eight hours after the process is complete. This means that the body will become more supple after the effects of rigor mortis have left the muscles. This entire process is sped by increased temperature and is delayed by colder temperatures.

# CORE BODY TEMPERATURE

Another method to determine the time of death is the core body temperature. The core body temperature can be determined by the use of an anal thermometer for the victim and a room thermometer to determine the ambient air temperature. There are a number of factors which will affect the body temperature after death and these will all need to be taken into account. Generally speaking, there can be a drop of one degree Fahrenheit for each hour after death in the core body temperature. Normal body temperature is 98.6 degree Fahrenheit. This rule is not considered entirely reliable due to a variety of complicating factors such as sunlight position, room or air temperature, time of day, and type of death. Some medical examiners will make a tiny incision in the victim's abdomen and insert a thermometer to prevent disturbing the crime scene by using an anal thermometer.

# PRESENCE OF INSECTS

Flies are the first insects to invade a body. They lay their eggs in the wounds and any mucous membrane areas (eyes, mouth, and nose). The eggs are white, laid in groups, and about 1-2 millimeters in length. The most common are the houseflies (*Musca domestica*) which are commonly found in victims who have died indoors. If a body is discovered outside and common housefly larvae are present, it can be assumed that the victim was killed indoors and moved outside at a later time. Flies which lay their eggs on bodies in the outdoors are the sheep maggot flies (*Lucilia sericata*), and the common bluebottle flies (*Calliphora erythrocephala*) and any known species which a local entomologist will be able to identify. The fly larvae hatch after 1 or 2 days and feed off the victim's tissues. The larvae change into pupae after 10 to 14 days. After 12 to 14 days in the pupae stage, adult flies are hatched and the life cycle begins again. Burial and carrion beetles, ants, and worms may also aid in the decomposition of a body. If a body is buried before any flies can lay their larvae, the presence of worms can verify burial soon after death.

Clocks and wrist watches which have been stopped due to violence at the crime scene are not always a reliable source of the victim's time of death. They can be useful, however, in approximating time of death and as a source to eliminate alibis.

# THE AUTOPSY AND CAUSE OF DEATH

The purpose of the autopsy or postmortem examination is to determine the cause of death. The interaction and codependence between the pathologist and the crime scene investigator provide vital information which may help to reconstruct the crime scene moments just before, during, and after the crime was committed.

Many hospitals have an area which is designated as the morgue. There are examination tables which resemble shallow trays equipped with drains to contain body fluids released during the autopsy. There is usually a microphone hanging directly over the examination tables through which the pathologist will describe the autopsy in specific detail. Beside the regular medical tools, a camera with flash and close-range lens is available to photograph wounds and physical markings. There are also refrigerated drawers which house the bodies until claimed by the mortuary for embalmment or cremation. The coroner may also have these facilities. In some states, a local pathologist (a medical doctor who specializes in identification of disease and cause of death) may also perform this task. It is interesting to note that some coroners are attorneys and have had limited training in medical pathology.

The pathologist and crime scene investigator (or a designated representative) are usually present. The body is photographed fully clothed (or with the clothing found on the body at the crime scene) and then fully unclothed. The victim should be fully examined before the removal of the clothing to add any items of evidence or trace evidence missed at the crime scene. Color close-up photographs which include a measurement scale should be taken of the face, wounds, bruises, tattoos, and physical markings. The clothing should be removed without cutting or tearing, if possible. If cutting is necessary, care should be taken to avoid disturbing any weapon tears or stain marks. If the clothing is damp, it should be air dried before it is packaged separately in clean sheets of paper and placed in paper bags (plastic may cause any body fluids to putrefy or decompose). Samples of blood from blood stains can be collected by swabbing with a cotton swab dipped in a saline solution (a dilute solution of sodium chloride in distilled water) and placed in a sealed glass vial. Dried blood can be scrapped off and place in a saline solution in a sealed glass vial. This procedure prevents the red blood cells from lysing (tearing apart) as they dehydrate.

The body should be fingerprinted and thoroughly searched for any sign of visible or latent fingerprints. Fingernail samples and scrapings are collected as well as a blood sample. The entire body is then washed and cleaned up and identity photographs are taken of the face. The entire body (including wound areas) is rephotographed. If the victim died from a bullet wound or a deep knife wound, x-rays should be taken to record the undisturbed pathways taken by the bullet or knife.

There are occasions to call in a forensic dentist. Most of the time this will be a regular dentist who has an interest in forensic dentistry and has offered his/her services to the police department. Dental records are kept by all dentists. They may use slightly different graphic charts, but the end result is similar enough to provide vital clues to identify an unknown victim. Records are kept of all prior dental work and usually planned treatment work. Dental casts are made and used in comparison studies (Figure15-3). The dental pattern is not as foolproof as the fingerprint. However, when compared to the known dental record, a match with the unknown victim can leave little doubt as to identity. Problems arise when teeth are missing or whole portions of the upper and lower jaw are missing. Scurvy (a dietary condition caused by the lack of vitamin C) is common among the homeless and drug abusers who commonly have missing teeth. Loss of teeth after death is much more common among these groups of people. It is important to screen the soil where these bodies are found to retrieve any lost teeth to aid in identification.

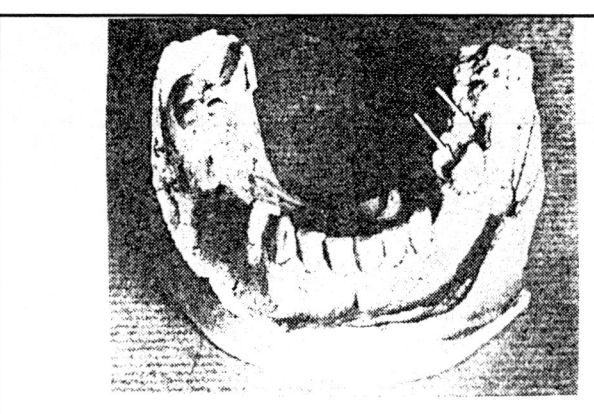

Figure 15-3   DENTAL CAST OF LOWER JAW-ARROWS POINT TO DECAYED TEETH

Once the physical autopsy is complete, samples of tissue from the victim (brain, heart, liver, spleen, muscle, lung, and any other tissue in question) are sent to the lab for analysis and interpretation by a pathologist. Even though the cause of death may be determined, identity is still largely a function of a number of variable factors. This is why the crime scene investigator must work in concert with the coroner or medical examiner and other lab technicians to make a positive identification.

RECORDS

The crime scene investigator will have to request medical and dental records of the deceased when and if the identify is unknown. The pathologist will create a medical chart during the autopsy which can be used to compare with records of various individuals reported missing by family and relatives. Hospital and doctor's records will provide a large source of information. There are instances when a missing person's medical records are compared to an unknown victim and a positive match is made. X-rays, wound charts, and other pictorial records help to pin-point identity. It is possible, with our present computer technology, to reconstruct the victim's face with only a portion of the skull. A Russian anthropologist, I.A. Gerasimov, pioneered a procedure for facial reconstruction. He based his work on the muscle structure and attachment to the skull. William Krogman, of the FBI, was another individual who helped to perfect the facial reconstruction technique.

**-CRIME SCENE SCENARIO-"ACCIDENT, SUICIDE, OR HOMICIDE?"**
-PART FOURTEEN: IDENTITY OF THE VICTIM-

Portions of this crime scenario (included in each of the preceding chapters) were designed to accompany this chapter to provide the experience of the process involved in identification of the unknown dead and provide the reader with the challenge of working with crime scene evidence and clues to reconstruct the crime scene and solve the mystery. Evidence from the crime scene was provided in those chapters which specialized in that type of evidence. Hopefully, this provided a more graphic picture of how evidence is handled.

In our on-going scenario ("**ACCIDENT, SUICIDE, OR HOMICIDE?**") there are a number of questions which need to be addressed. Was Wayne Joseph Adams killed by accident? Did he plan and commit suicide? Was he intentionally murdered? If he was shot by accident, then who shot him? If he was murdered, then who shot him? Evidence and analysis of that evidence has been presented to the reader in a manner in which a crime scene investigator might receive information. When there are numerous facts, the task of crime scene analysis is almost overwhelming Chapter 16, THE CRIME SCENE SCENARIO, presents a format which the reader might find useful to gather, organize, analyze, and synthesize the evidence presented in order to solve the mystery. The following is a continuation of "**ACCIDENT, SUICIDE, OR HOMICIDE?**"

After speaking with Mrs Adams personal physician (grandmother to Wayne Adams), Detectives Dodge and

Summer decided to ask Mrs. Virginia Almstead (Wayne's aunt) to come and identify the body. Since Mrs. Adams has had two strokes and has a weak heart, the physician thought the shock of seeing her grandson lying dead in the morgue would precipitate further physical complications. Arrangements were made to fly Mrs. Almstead to the detective's city, identify the body, and accompany the body to her city for burial.

Wayne Adams dental records were compared to the dental impressions and charts prepared by the forensic dentist. Although there was a perfect match, identification by next of kin is a state requirement for identity of the unknown dead. There was no fingerprint match available. Wayne Adams had no previous juvenile or police record nor had he received a driver's license (where a thumbprint is a state requirement).

The blood recovered from the clothing tossed into the construction dumpster by Andrea Coleman was type O positive. The blood recovered by paper chromatography from the bathroom sink in the Coleman's bathroom was also type O positive. Medical records indicated that Andrea and her parents were all type AB positive blood.

The fingerprints recovered from Andrea Coleman's bedroom window sill were matched with Bill Morganson's fingerprints. The fingerprints recovered from Mr. Zuccarelli's bureau drawer were matched to the victim's fingerprints. A small metal file was found in Wayne Adam's bedroom in a dresser drawer. The rasps on the metal file matched the striation patterns on the revolver where the serial number had been filed off.

At 12:21 pm on the afternoon of the 4th day since the shooting, Mrs. Almstead identified the body of the victim as Wayne Joseph Adams. After a brief visit with Mrs. Adams, Mrs. Almstead returned to the County morgue and took possession of Wayne's body.

Detectives Dodge and Summer presented a portfolio of evidence to the district attorney who has been preparing a prosecution case against Steve Sorensen and Bill Morganson for the murder of Wayne Joseph Adams. Steve Sorensen would be tried as an adult and the prosecutor is requesting that Bill Morganson (although 17 and a minor) also be tried as an adult in a court of law. If premeditated murder can be proved, the prosecutor would ask for the death penalty for the shooter and life imprisonment for the accomplice. If manslaughter is shown due to accidental death, a lessor prison sentence will be requested for the shooter and accomplice. If suicide is shown, then lessor sentences will be requested for obstruction of justice and tampering with crime scene evidence.

Although primarily a defense attorneys' task, the detectives must satisfy their own conscience by a thorough review of all the evidence in an objective manner. A poorly done job is not an excuse to provide the evidence to convict an individual of a capital crime. A missed clue, an overlooked item, a piece of evidence which is out of place, a preconceived bias, or a comment given by a witness or a suspect, all might provide the investigator with another point of reference to view the crime scene.

Detective Dodge had been troubled by the interview with Laura Green which occurred on day one of the shooting. He had gone over that interview again and again in his mind. There was something about the mailman regular schedule. The detectives were on their way to Mrs. Green's home to reinterview Laura Green.

DESCRIPTION OF ADDITIONAL CRIME SCENE SCENARIOS

The **CRIME SCENE SCENARIOS** (available with the lab manual which accompanies this text) are written in a two-step format to provide a hands-on laboratory experience.

The first step (which is the emphasis in this chapter) is **"Mix Up At The County Morgue"** where a victim's body has been accidentally mixed up with three other bodies. **"Mix Up At The County Morgue"** provides blood type, dental records, hospital wound charts, morgue identification markings, physical data, and fingerprints of four unidentified bodies accidentally mixed up at the morgue. By analyzing this evidence through laboratory analysis, it is possible to identify the unknown victim as well as the other three bodies.

The second step is **"Two Are Charged, One Is Guilty"** where evidence gathered from a crime scene is analyzed to provide clues which will verify the guilt or innocence of an Intruder and a Suspect. Below is a list of the **CRIME SCENE SCENARIOS** available with the lab manual. Each one includes **"Mix Up at the County Morgue"** and **"Two Are Charged, One Is Guilty"** written with different characters and evidence. These provide the opportunity for a teacher to work with up to 9 lab groups who must rely on their own crime scene scenario to solve the mystery.

The **CRIME SCENE SCENARIOS** are:

1. **WRIGHTWOOD WAS THE WRONG HOUSE**
2. **REVENGE AT PILGRIM HOUSE**
3. **THE CASE OF AN EYE FOR AN EYE**
4. **MYSTERY AT BULLET HILL HOUSE**
5. **THE CASE OF THE VENGEFUL GANG MEMBER**
6. **THREE'S A CROWD AT BANKERS-CREST MANSION**
7. **HIGH SCHOOL SWEETHEARTS**
8. **MYSTERY AT STONECUTTER MANSION**
9. **MURDER AT PORTER PLACE**

SUGGESTED READINGS-

Burnharn, J.T., et al. "The State of the Art of Bone Identification by Chemical and Microscopic Methods." *Journal of Forensic Science* 21(2):340-342, 1976.

Emson, H.E. "Problems in the Identification of Burn victims." *Journal of Canadian Society of Forensic Science* 11(3):229-236, 1978.

Gustafson, G. *Forensic Odontology* . New York: Elsevier, 1966.

Luntz, L.L. and Luntz, P. "Dental Identification of Disaster Victims by a Dental Disaster Squad." *Journal of Forensic Science* 17(1):63-69, 1972.

Noble, H.W. "The Estimation of Age from Dentition." *Journal of Forensic Science Society* 14(3):215-221, 1974.

Rodriquez, W.C. and Bass, W.M. "Insect Activity and Its Relationship to Decay Rates of Human Cadavers in East Tennessee." *Journal of Forensic Science* 28(2):423-432, 1983.

Smyth, F. *Cause of Death: the Story of Forensic Science* . New York: Van Nostrand Reinhold Company, 1980.

Stewart, T.D. *Essentials of Forensic Anthropology* . Springfield, Illinois: Charles C. Thomas, 1979.

Sundick, R.I. "Age and Sex Determination of Subadult Skeletons." *Journal of Forensic Science* 22(1):141-144, 1977.

Usher, A. "The Role of the Pathologist at the Scene of the Crime." *Journal of Forensic Science Society* 10(4):213-218, 1970.

Watanabe, T. *Atlas of Legal Medicine* . 2nd ed. Philadelphia, Pennsylvania: J.B. Lippincott, 1972.

Wilson, K. *Cause of Death: A Writer's Guide to Death, Murder and Forensic Medicine.* Cincinnati: Writer's Digest Books, 1992.

# -CHAPTER SIXTEEN-
# THE CRIME SCENE SCENARIO

## CAUSE OF DEATH

Since murderers have purposely altered a crime scene to give the appearance of accident or suicide, the crime scene investigator should approach every suspicious death as a homicide. As much detail as possible should be gathered in the event that accident and suicide are ruled out. The crime scene becomes altered as soon as the evidence collection process begins. The timely collection of evidence, then, is of primary importance.

The cause of death should be determined as soon as possible. The autopsy will reveal the actual cause of death, but the investigator should make a preliminary assumption which would be referred to as the apparent cause of death. The investigator must have a good working knowledge of the human anatomy and physiology in order to make this determination. Wounds can be deceiving. Knife wounds are mistaken for gunshot wounds. This erroneous observation could lead the entire forensics crew the wrong direction: instead of seeking a gun, everyone will be on the alert for a sharp object.

## SUICIDE OR HOMICIDE?

The next issue involves the elimination of a possible suicide. The investigator must determine if the victim was capable (physically and mentally) of committing suicide. Some of the common mechanisms of suicide are poisoning and overdosing on drugs, stabbing, slicing arteries, drowning, hanging, jumping from tall places, strangulation, and shooting. Men are capable of all of the above while women tend to select less physically damaging methods such as overdose and cutting arteries. Is the weapon or poison used close to the victim? Position of the wounds may indicate suicide as a physical impossibility. Wound patterns, gunshot tattoos, hesitation markings from repeated attempts, blood stain patterns on the victims hands would all be considered in an attempted suicide. Any defense wounds (the arms raised to protect the head or body) would not support a suicide theory. Are any suicide notes left by the victim? (Handwriting samples should be collected and used by a handwriting expert to compare with the suicide note). Is the victim in a room which was locked from inside the room? Are any relatives able to verify any suicidal tendencies shown in the past by the victim?

Are there any signs of a fight or struggle? Are there overturned chairs and tables, splatters of blood in different places, broken items around the room, signs of trace evidence in various places. In the event of murder, bloodstains are probably the most reliable source of evidence to reconstruct the crime scene. Victims who are not killed immediately will place their hands on their wounds. The blood from their hands will then leave marks and fingerprints that provide vital clues as to their position during a struggle. Footprints in blood are also an excellent source of information. It is possible to determine the locations of the victim and suspect during a fight or a struggle. Overturned tables and chairs are a good indicator of which direction the victim was fleeing from the suspect.

Finally, the search for a weapon must be conducted as soon as the apparent cause of death is determined. The absence of a weapon at the crime scene is a good indication of a homicide. If a weapon is found at the crime scene, its position relative to the victim is important in determining evidence for suicide. The weapon could have been placed in the victim's hand and very close to the victim's body in an attempt to cover a homicide. The distance from the body and its position should be considered before ruling out a suicide.

Once a homicide is determined, the crime scene investigation should proceed as quickly as possible. The crime scene evidence will deteriorate with the passage of time and so will the investigator's ability to reconstruct the events that led up to, included, and followed the act of violence.

## CRIME SCENE SCENARIO-"ACCIDENT, SUICIDE, OR HOMICIDE?"
### -PART FIFTEEN: LAURA'S STORY-

The latent fingerprint lifted from the single cartridge casing discovered in the revolver came back negative from state and federal fingerprint agencies. The same lifted fingerprint matched Wayne Adams right thumb print.

Detectives Dodge and Summer arrived at the Green residence at 1:30 pm on the fourth day since the shooting. Mrs. Green had a worried expression on her face as she greeted the detectives. Laura Green was playing with her dolls on the living room floor.

"I'm glad you could make it, detectives," began Mrs. Green. "Laura has not quite been herself. She's been having nightmares."

"Do you know what is troubling her, Mrs. Green?" asked Detective Dodge.

"Laura told me she was afraid of the boys next door."

Summer asked Mrs. Green "Do you mind if I ask your daughter a few questions?"

Mrs. Green noded yes. Detective Summer walked over where Laura Green was sitting and sat down on a chair next to her. "Laura, is there more that you can tell us about the other day?" asked Summer. "un-huh."

"Why don't you start with the arrival of the mailman," prompted Summer.

Laura looked up at her mom who gave her a nod of approval. She looked down at her dolls as she spoke. "I went out to say hello to our mailman, Bert, and get the mail. He came right on time at 11:15. He gave me the mail and asked why I was home from school. I told him I was sick. He told me to get well and drove on to the next mailbox. I was looking at the letters when I heard the boys next door yelling. Our mailbox is next to a big tree so I hid behind the tree. The boys were yelling louder and louder. I was scared. I thought they would see me behind the tree. I wanted to go into our house, mother, but they would have seen me."

Laura was crying and obviously frightened. Detective Summer put her arm around Laura to help her calm down. "Could you see into the garage?" asked Summer.

"Only when I would peek out from behind the tree."

"What did you see?"

"I saw a boy sitting on a weight bench and two boys were standing."

"Was one boy standing near the front of the garage?"

"Yes, he was wearing a green shirt. He's the boy who lives next door."

"Were you still behind the tree when you heard the loud bang?"

"Yes." Laura was more calm now. She appeared relieved that she was finally able to share what she had seen. "I couldn't help but look. The boy on the weight bench fell over. I thought the boy in the green shirt had pushed him over."

"Was the boy on the weight bench facing the boy in the green shirt when you heard the loud noise?"

"I think so," said Laura, "will he be okay?"

The detectives knew that Laura would need some personal counseling to help her through this traumatic time. They were both searching for an answer to Laura's question when her mother spoke. "Honey, the boy who you saw fall off the weight bench was shot."

Laura held back tears. "He's dead, isn't he?"

"Yes." Summer was also holding back the tears. "Did you see the boy in the green shirt holding a gun?"

"The other boy in the back of the garage handed him something shiny. He did something to it because I could hear a clicking sound."

"How many clicks did you hear, Laura?"

"A lot of clicks at first and then they slowed down. There was a loud bang and that boy fell off the weight bench." Laura was crying again.

The detectives thanked Laura and Mrs. Green for their testimony. They handed Mrs. Green a card giving the name and phone number of a child counselor who worked for the County and had experience in child trauma cases.

Dodge and Summer returned to their office and placed each discovered fact and event in a chronological order. They listed the evidence gathered from the crime scene, for the victim, for Steve Sorenson, and for Bill Morganson. From this evidence they needed to determine if Wayne Joseph Adams committed suicide, was accidentally shot, or was intentionally shot. Was Steve Sorenson or Bill Morganson a murderer, an accomplice to murder, or guilty of an accidental homicide?

ANALYSIS OF EVIDENCE AND RECONSTRUCTION OF THE CRIME SCENE

Use the **CRIME SCENE EVIDENCE LOG** (Appendix A) to list each fact or evidence discovered in the scenario. Use the **CRIME SCENE CHRONOLOG** (Appendix B) to include all important facts and events according to the time they occurred. Use the **CRIME SCENE WITNESS LOG** (Appendix C) to record important testimony from ten people in the scenario. This will also help you to organize important data and keep tract of witness and suspect testimony. Use the **CRIME SCENE OPINION** organizer (Appendix D) to map out your solution to the crime. You should also cite the evidence and testimony which supports your thinking. Once you have gathered and organized the evidence on the above organizers, you should be able to formulate conclusions to determine the following:

1. Did Wayne Joseph Adams commit suicide?
2. If not, who shot Wayne Adams?
3. Did someone shoot Wayne Adams by accident?
4. Did someone shoot Wayne Adams on purpose?

## IN SUMMARY: A FURTHER LOOK

The crime scene investigator will receive many hours of training: some from books, and some from real life, on-the-job experience. As educators and theoreticians look at the learning experience, they believe that theory (based on content material) as well as the real life experiences (based on the hands-on process) are both necessary for effective learning to occur. It is with this two-fold premise that the **CRIME SCENE SCENARIOS** were written. It is the purpose of this chapter to provide a framework upon which to gather evidence, analyze the evidence, reconstruct the crime scene, and formulate the conclusions which will support the guilt or innocence of the individuals involved. The reader has been following a specific **CRIME SCENE SCENARIO** entitled **"ACCIDENT, SUICIDE, OR HOMICIDE?"** in each chapter of this text. Each portion of the scenario presents various evidence discovered and collected from the crime scene. Occasionally, the analysis of specific evidence is presented along with statements from suspects and witnesses.

This text has included fifteen chapters which have described the science of criminal forensics. The major categories of crime scene evidence (the crime scene, proof of identity, fingerprints, body fluids, trace materials, tool marks, firearms and ballistics, illegal and legal drugs, chemicals, casting and residual prints, paint and glass, document analysis, arson and explosive devices, and determining human identity) have been presented in a descriptive format. These are meant to provide a beginning approach to forensic concept and technique and are, therefore, a starting point for the novice. Laboratory application plays an important part in the process of studying criminal forensics and should be included in each chapter of study. A lab manual has been prepared which is designed to follow this text with specific lessons and lab kits prepared for each chapter by the Kemtec Educational Corporation (T&S).

Chapter 16 presents the methodology to utilize each of the prepared labs in one final **CRIME SCENE SCENARIO**. Nine other **CRIME SCENE SCENARIOS** have been written and are available as a supplement to the lab manual. Basically, what students have learned in their study and laboratory experience can now be applied in an analysis of evidence and search for the truth concerning an unidentified body at the morgue and two individuals charged with murder.

## DESCRIPTION OF THE SCENARIOS

The **CRIME SCENE SCENARIO** is a fictional story involving a victim, an intruder to the victim's home, and a suspect who is known by the victim. The Scenario is written to include the story from the investigator's viewpoint with supportive evidence from the hospital, a neighbor, the morgue and medical examiner, a forensic dentist, and various independent laboratories.

The actual **CRIME SCENE SCENARIO** involves two steps. The first is **"Mix Up At The County Morgue"** which is described in chapter fourteen. The second is **"Two Are Charged, One Is Guilty"** which involves the actual process of working with and analyzing gathered evidence from the crime scene in order to logically establish the guilt or innocence of the persons involved.

Both of these steps involve a number of laboratory procedures and techniques which, hopefully, have been practiced and learned through the use of the labs and lab kits. The following is a listing of the nine **CRIME SCENE SCENARIOS**:

## LIST OF THE SCENARIOS

1. WRIGHTWOOD WAS THE WRONG HOUSE
2. REVENGE AT PILGRIM HOUSE
3. THE CASE OF AN EYE FOR AN EYE
4. MYSTERY AT BULLET HILL HOUSE
5. THE CASE OF THE VENGEFUL GANG MEMBER
6. THREE'S A CROWD AT BANKERS-CREST MANSION
7. HIGH SCHOOL SWEETHEARTS
8. MYSTERY AT STONECUTTER MANSION
9. MURDER AT PORTER PLACE

SUGGESTED READINGS-

Adelson, L. *The Pathology of Homicide* . Springfield, Illinois: Charles C. Thomas, 1974.

Blanke, R.V. "Role of Toxicology in Suicide Evaluation." *Journal of Forensic Science* 19(2):284-291, 1974.

Eisele, J.W., et al. "Sites of Suicidal Gunshot Wounds." *Journal of Forensic Science* 26(3):480-485, 1981.

Gerdin, B. "A Case of Disguised Suicide." *Forensic Science* 16:29-34, 1980.

Hirsch, C.S. and Adelson, L. "A Suicidal Gunshot Wound of the Back." *Journal of Forensic Science* 21(3):659-666, 1976.

Kurland, M. *How to Solve a Murder: the Forensic Handbook* . New York: Macmillan, 1995. Marriner, B. *On Death's Bloody Trail: Murder and the Art of Forensic Science* . New York: St. Martin's Press, 1993.

Snyder, L.M. *Homicide Investigation* . 3rd ed. Springfield, Illinois: Charles C. Thomas, 1977.

# FORENSICS-THE SEARCH FOR CLUES
## BY
## JAMES VERNE SUTTON

## ILLUSTRATION LISTING FROM EACH SOURCE

1. Sutton, James. Classroom Photography and Sketches Taken at Poly High School, 1997.

    Figures 1-7 to 1-14 .........Permission given by James Sutton.
    Figures 2-5 to 2-9 .........Permission given by James Sutton.
    Figures 5-1 to 5-7 .........Permission given by James Sutton.
    Figures 5-9 to 5-11 .......Permission given by James Sutton.
    Figures 13-2 to 13-3 .......Permission given by James Sutton.

2. . Fisher, Barry, et al. *Techniques of Crime Scene Investigation* New York: Elsevier Science Publishing Co., Inc., 1987.

    Figure 1-16 ............... page 264, Figure 10.15
    Figure 1-17 ............... page 265, Figure 10.16
    Figure 3-1 ............... page 152, Figure 7.8
    Figure 3-2 ............... page 257, Figure 10.8
    Figure 3-3 ............... page 12, Figure1.7
    Figure 4-4 ............... page 112, Figure 6.22
    Figure 5-8 ............... page 192, Figure 8.6
    Figure 6-7 ............... page 180, Figure 7.30
    Figure 6-8 ............... page 181, Figure 7.31
    Figure 6-9 ............... page 150, Figure 7.5
    Figure 6-10 ............... page 152, Figure 7.7
    Figure 6-11 ............... page 151, Figure 7.6
    Figure 7-3 ............... page 243, Figure 9.25
    Figure 7-4 ............... page 183, Figure 7.33
    Figure 8-1 ............... page 254, figure 10.3
    Figure 8-2 ............... page 253, Figure 10.2
    Figure 8-3 ............... page 255, Figure 10.4
    Figure 8-4 ............... page 281, figure 10.24
    Figure 8-5 ............... page 280, Figure 10.23
    Figure 8-6 ............... page 275, Figure 10.21
    Figure 8-7 ............... page 262, Figure 10.12
    Figure 8-8 ............... page 262, Figure 10.13
    Figure 8-11 ............... page 263, Figure 10.14
    Figure 8-12 ............... page 268, Figure 10.18
    Figure 8-13 ............... page 266, Figure 10.17A
    Figure 8-14 ............... page 267, Figure 10.17B
    Figure 8-17 ............... page 255, Figure 10.5
    Figure 8-18 ............... page 290, figure 10.35
    Figure 9-1 ............... page 329, Figure 12.6
    Figure 9-2 ............... page 335, Figure 12.11
    Figure 9-3 ............... page 337, figure 12.14
    Figure 11-1 ............... page 215, figure 9.6
    Figure 11-2 ............... page 224, Figure 9.11B
    Figure 11-3 ............... page 224, Figure 9.11A
    Figure 11-4 ............... page 228, figure 9.14
    Figure 11-6 ............... page 229, figure 9.15
    Figure 11-7 ............... page 42, Figure 3.3
    Figure 12-1 ............... page 167, Figure 7.18
    Figure 12-2 ............... page 168, Figure 7.19
    Figure 12-3 ............... page 168, Figure 7.20
    Figure 12-4 ............... page 169, figure 7.21
    Figure 12-5 ............... page 172, Figure 7.24

Figure 13-1 . . . . . . . . . . . . . . . page 103, Figure 6.18
Figure 14-1 . . . . . . . . . . . . . . . page 306, Figure 11.8
Figure 14-2 . . . . . . . . . . . . . . . page 310, Figure 11.12
Figure 14-3 . . . . . . . . . . . . . . . page 317, Figure 11.14
Figure 15-3 . . . . . . . . . . . . . . . page 213, Figure 9.5

3. Dox, Ida G., et al. Eds. *The Harper Collins Illustrated Medical Dictionary*. New York: Harper Perennial, Harper Collins Books, p. 385, 1993.

Figure 4-3 . . . . . . . . . . . . . . . page 385

4. Forensics Laboratory Manuals: Forensics Science and Chemistry and Crime Solving Kits. West Chester, Ohio: Kemtec Educational Corporation, 1980 to present.

Figure 4-2 . . . . . . . . . . . . . . . .Permission given by Kemtec Educational Corp.
Figure 4-3 . . . . . . . . . . . . . . . .Permission given by Kemtec Educational Corp.
Figure 4-10 . . . . . . . . . . . . . . . .Permission given by Kemtec Educational Corp.
Figure 4-12 . . . . . . . . . . . . . . . .Permission given by Kemtec Educational Corp.
Figures 6-1 to 6-6 . . . . . . . . . .Permission given by Kemtec Educational Corp.

5. Forensics Products Catalog. Salem, Oregon: Lightning Powder Company, Inc., 1996.

Figure 1-1 . . . . . . . . . . . . . . . .page 4, section 3
Figure 1-2 . . . . . . . . . . . . . . . .page 6, section 3
Figure 1-3 . . . . . . . . . . . . . . . .page 7, section 3
Figure 1-4 . . . . . . . . . . . . . . . .page 4, section 3
Figure 1-5 . . . . . . . . . . . . . . . .page 8, section 6
Figure 1-6 . . . . . . . . . . . . . . . .page 3, 8, section 6
Figure 1-15 . . . . . . . . . . . . . . . .page 28, section 1
Figure 4-4 . . . . . . . . . . . . . . . .page 1, section 1
Figure 4-5 . . . . . . . . . . . . . . . .page 3, section 1
Figure 4-6 . . . . . . . . . . . . . . . .page 9, section 1
Figure 4-7 . . . . . . . . . . . . . . . .page 14, section 1
Figure 4-8 . . . . . . . . . . . . . . . .page 25, section 1
Figure 4-9 . . . . . . . . . . . . . . . .page 31, section 1
Figure 4-15 . . . . . . . . . . . . . . . .page 2, section 1
Figure 4-16 . . . . . . . . . . . . . . . .page 16, section 2
Figure 4-17 . . . . . . . . . . . . . . . .page 4, section 2
Figure 4-18 . . . . . . . . . . . . . . . .page 4, section 2
Figure 4-19 . . . . . . . . . . . . . . . .page 10, section 9
Figure 4-20 . . . . . . . . . . . . . . . .page 5, section 9
Figure 7-1 . . . . . . . . . . . . . . . .page 1, section 4
Figure 7-2 . . . . . . . . . . . . . . . .page 2, section 4
Figure 8-9 . . . . . . . . . . . . . . . .Page 16, section 4
Figure 8-10 . . . . . . . . . . . . . . . .page 16, section 4
Figure 8-15 . . . . . . . . . . . . . . . .page 27, section 1
Figure 8-16 . . . . . . . . . . . . . . . .page 25, section 4
Figure 9-4 . . . . . . . . . . . . . . . .page 10, section 7
Figure 9-5 . . . . . . . . . . . . . . . .page 3, section 7
Figure 9-6 . . . . . . . . . . . . . . . .page 2, section 7
Figure 11-5 . . . . . . . . . . . . . . . .page 5, section 4
Figure 11-8 . . . . . . . . . . . . . . . .page 5, section 4
Figure 11-9 . . . . . . . . . . . . . . . .page 5, section 4
Figure 15-1 . . . . . . . . . . . . . . . .page 17, section 4
Figure 15-2 . . . . . . . . . . . . . . . .page 17, section 4

6. Marshall, Evan. "A Lawman Looks At Stopping Power." *Guns And Ammo Handgun Manual*.Page 51, 1985.

   Figure 8-19 . . . . . . . . . . . . . .    page 51

7. Administration of Justice Materials from Riverside City College, Riverside, California, 1996.

   Figures 2-1 to 2-4              Administration of Justice Search Patterns

8. Williams, Peter. Photography by the Senior Forensics Technician at Riverside County Sheriff's Department, Riverside, California, 1997.

   Figure 1-18 . . . . . . . . . . .Permission given by Peter Williams to publish (prepared with this text in mind).
   Figure 4-21 . . . . . . . . . . .Permission given by Peter Williams to publish (prepared with this text in mind).
   Figures 5-12 to 5-18 . . . .Permission given by Peter Williams to publish (prepared with this text in mind).
   Figures 6-12 to 6-16 . . . .Permission given by Peter Williams to publish (prepared with this text in mind).
   Figures 11-10 to 11-13 . .Permission given by Peter Williams to publish (prepared with this text in mind).

9. Fingerprint Instructinal Materials from the United States Marshall's Office, Los Angeles, California.

   Figure 4-11 . . . . . . . . . . . . . . . . . . . . Loop Ridge Counts
   Figure 4-13 . . . . . . . . . . . . . . . . . . . . NCIC Fingerprint Classification System

10. Yankee, R.L. *CAL-ID and Presentation of Fingerprint Evidence at Trial*. Riverside, California: Riverside Country Sheriff's Department. January, 1988.

    Figures 4-22 to 4-25 . . . . . . . .Permission given by Peter Williams to publish.

# APPENDIX A

**DIRECTIONS**

*Record physical evidence for **Victim, Suspect 1 and Suspect 2** by placing a check mark in the appropriate column.*

| TYPE OF EVIDENCE | VICTIM | SUSPECT 1 | SUSPECT 2 |
|---|---|---|---|
| **NAMES** | | | |
| **AGE** | | | |
| **GENDER** | | | |
| **RACE** | | | |
| **HEIGHT** | | | |
| **WEIGHT** | | | |
| **HAIR COLOR** | | | |
| **EYE COLOR** | | | |
| **PHYSICAL MARKINGS** | | | |
| **BLOOD TYPE** | | | |
| **BLOOD ALCOHOL LEVEL** | | | |
| **CLOTHING-SHIRTS/COATS** | | | |
| **CLOTHING-PANTS** | | | |
| **CLOTHING-SHOES** | | | |

# APPENDIX A *(CONTINUED)*

**DIRECTIONS**

*Record crime scene evidence for **Victim, Suspect 1 and Suspect 2** by placing a check mark in the appropriate column.*

| TYPE OF EVIDENCE | CRIME SCENE | VICTIM | SUSPECT 1 | SUSPECT 2 |
|---|---|---|---|---|
| **SHOEPRINTS-BACK OF GARAGE** | | | | |
| **FIBERS-EXT. REAR GARAGE WINDOW** | | | | |
| **BLOOD-ON FLOOR NEAR BACK GARAGE DOOR** | | | | |
| **SHOEPRINT IN BLOOD NEAR REAR GARAGE DOOR** | | | | |
| **BLOOD-NEAR WEIGHT BENCH** | | | | |
| **BLOOD-"V" SHAPED SPLATTER** | | | | |
| **FINGERPRINTS-ON WEIGHT BENCH** | | | | |
| **FINGERPRINTS-ON REAR GARAGE DOOR** | | | | |
| **FINGERPRINTS-ON EXT. REAR GARAGE WINDOW** | | | | |
| **HAIR-ON VICTIM'S CLOTHING** | | | | |
| **FIBERS-ON VICTIM'S SHIRT** | | | | |
| **FIBERS-ON VICTIM'S JEANS** | | | | |
| **FABRIC-ON BACK FENCE** | | | | |
| **FLUID-ON BLUE DENIM FABRIC** | | | | |
| **FINGERPRINT-ON REVOLVER** | | | | |
| **FINGERPRINT-ON CARTRIDGE CASING** | | | | |
| **GUNSHOT RESIDUE** | | | | |
| **BLUE PAINT** | | | | |
| **TOOL MARK ON INT. REAR GARAGE DOOR** | | | | |
| **WHITE POWDER** | | | | |
| **BALLISTICS** | | | | |
| **REVOLVER SERIAL NUMBER** | | | | |

# APPENDIX B

**DIRECTIONS** - *Record events at times listed below.*

## DAY ONE - EVIDENCE AND / OR TESTIMONY

*11:15 AM* _____

*11:28 AM* _____

*11:30 AM* _____

*11:32 AM* _____

*11:37 AM* _____

*11:42 AM* _____

*11:52 AM* _____

*12:05 PM* _____

*12:10 PM* _____

*12:18 PM* _____

*12:23 PM* _____

*1:15 PM* _____

*1:17 PM* _____

*1:21 PM* _____

*1:36 PM* _____

*1:40 PM* _____

*2:20 PM* _____

*3:10 PM* _____

*4:05 PM*

## APPENDIX B  *( CONTINUED)*

**DIRECTIONS** - *Record events at times listed below.*

### DAY TWO - EVIDENCE AND / OR TESTIMONY

*2:30 PM* _____

*13:30 PM* _____

*4:04 PM* _____

*5:20 PM* _____

### DAY THREE - EVIDENCE AND /OR TESTIMONY

*9:30 AM* _____

*10:06 AM* _____

*11:15 AM* _____

*3:11 PM* _____

*4:20 PM* _____

### DAY FOUR - EVIDENCE AND /OR TESTIMONY

*9:20 AM* _____

*10:45 AM* _____

*12:21 PM* _____

*1:30 PM* _____

## APPENDIX C

**DIRECTIONS** - *Record individual testimonies from the crime scene scenarios.*

## CRIME SCENE WITNESS LOG   "ACCIDENT, SUICIDE, OR HOMICIDE?"

WITNESS #1        MR. RODRIQUEZ

WITNESS #2        MRS. BLAKE

WITNESS #3        DR. ISSAC KRAMER

WITNESS #4        BILL MORGANSON

WITNESS #5        STEVE SORENSON

WITNESS #6        MRS. ADAMS

WITNESS #7        MATT KENNEY

WITNESS #8        ALFONSO ZUCCARELLI

WITNESS #9        ANDREA COLEMAN

WITNESS #10       LAURA GREEN

**APPENDIX D**

**DIRECTIONS** - *Use arrows to indicate your choices. Cite specific evidence to support your choice.*

**CRIME SCENE OPINION** *"ACCIDENT, SUICIDE, OR HOMICIDE?"*

VICTIM

DEATH BY

| ACCIDENTAL HOMICIDE | SUICIDE | INTENTIONAL HOMICIDE |
|---|---|---|
| BY | | BY |
| SHOOTER    ACCOMPLICE | | SHOOTER    ACCOMPLICE |
| ECIDENCE    EVIDENCE | | EVIDENCE    EVIDENCE |

*Kemtec Kit available for most of these procedures.*
*For information, call 1-877-536-8321.*